Marriage Material

Marriage Material

How an Enduring Institution Is Changing Same-Sex Relationships

ABIGAIL OCOBOCK

The University of Chicago Press
Chicago and London

The University of Chicago Press, Chicago 60637
The University of Chicago Press, Ltd., London
© 2024 by The University of Chicago
All rights reserved. No part of this book may be used or reproduced in any manner whatsoever without written permission, except in the case of brief quotations in critical articles and reviews. For more information, contact the University of Chicago Press, 1427 E. 60th St., Chicago, IL 60637.
Published 2024
Printed in the United States of America

33 32 31 30 29 28 27 26 25 24   1 2 3 4 5

ISBN-13: 978-0-226-83624-9 (cloth)
ISBN-13: 978-0-226-83626-3 (paper)
ISBN-13: 978-0-226-83625-6 (e-book)
DOI: https://doi.org/10.7208/chicago/9780226836256.001.0001

Library of Congress Cataloging-in-Publication Data

Names: Ocobock, Abigail, author.
Title: Marriage material : how an enduring institution is changing same-sex relationships / Abigail Ocobock.
Description: Chicago : The University of Chicago Press, 2024. | Includes bibliographical references and index
Identifiers: LCCN 2024011412 | ISBN 9780226836249 (cloth) | ISBN 9780226836263 (paperback) | ISBN 9780226836256 (ebook)
Subjects: LCSH: Same-sex marriage—United States. | Marriage—United States.
Classification: LCC HQ1034.U5 O363 2024 | DDC 306.84/80973—dc23/eng/20240320
LC record available at https://lccn.loc.gov/2024011412

♾ This paper meets the requirements of ANSI/NISO Z39.48-1992 (Permanence of Paper).

Contents

Introduction: Rethinking Marriage ... 1

PART I. Gaining Marriage

1. Marriage Embracers: The Power of Marriage, Old and New ... 27
2. Marriage Rejecters: Navigating the Pulls of Marriage ... 51
3. Marriage Assumers: It's Just What You Do ... 82

PART II. Doing Marriage

4. Proposal Pressures ... 111
5. Fights and Finances ... 136
6. Marital (Non)Monogamy ... 163

Conclusion ... 189

Acknowledgments 203
Methods Appendix 207
Notes 217
References 241
Index 259

Introduction

Rethinking Marriage

Keith first started having sex with other men in the mid-1980s, during the middle of the AIDS crisis. He quipped that instead of "coming of age," he had "come of AIDS." In his young adulthood, being gay was "incredibly stigmatized," and all his relationships were "secretive." During college, he attended gay rights rallies, but as an "ally," not as someone who identified as gay. By the early 2000s, Keith had a "vibrant gay life" in private but was still "closeted" professionally and with his family. When same-sex marriage became legal in his home state of Massachusetts in 2004, he was just beginning to live a more openly gay life. He started dating his now-husband four years after same-sex marriage became legal, in his late thirties.

Keith felt deeply conflicted over same-sex marriage, something that he was still actively wrestling with during his two-hour interview with me. He had never felt "entitled" to marriage, nor "aspired" to it. He said, "There was never a time in my life as an out gay man that I ever thought I was going to get married. It never seemed relevant to me." Part of this, he thought, was probably the result of "internalized homophobia," of feeling "less than," like he "didn't deserve" marriage, or "wasn't capable" of having the kind of "amazing egalitarian" marriages he saw role models have. But another part was also a rejection of the institution of marriage. Keith was deeply committed to social justice work and thought about marriage through that lens. He described himself as having "been really radicalized by college and graduate school" and deeply involved in a range of progressive politics and movements, from the women's movement to anti-racism and anti-war campaigns. He was frustrated by the narrow focus of the marriage equality movement and the way it "marginalized other voices and concerns." Having been "a feminist much longer than a homosexual," Keith also thought about marriage "as this completely confining normative, traditional institution" that he "wanted no part of." "Who the fuck wants to imprison yourself like that?" he asked me.

Keith and his partner were at a political rally when they "spontaneously decided to get married." As Keith explained it, "It wasn't planned, there was no vacation, no beach proposal, nothing like that. It was impulsive, and strange." His partner had always been more interested in marrying than he was, and their differing interest levels in marriage "caused some tensions in the buildup to the wedding," but ultimately Keith thinks he made the right decision. Trying to explain why he agreed to marry, Keith drew on both love and politics as rationales: "I wanted to get married because I love him and I want to be with him forever. That's the principal reason. Also, I'm political, and I want to be married and show people who think gay marriage is wrong, and a sin, and an abomination, downfall of civilization, I want to tell them to go fuck themselves."

Keith confided that he has been "surprised" by how much being married has changed their relationship, including how they fight, how they socialize with others, how they interact with their extended families, how they have sex, and their desire to open up their relationship sexually. A couple of years into being legally married, he was still trying to come to terms with what it meant both for them as a couple and him as an individual. "One big tension" he was working through was whether he was "a hypocrite or a role model" by getting married. Could he criticize and change the institution of marriage from within it? Or had he "sold out" to the institution? Ultimately, he concluded, "There are days when I'm like, 'Why the fuck am I married?' But I never think, 'Why am I married to [my spouse]?' I'm a radical queer who got gay married. It's a lot of stuff to work out, but at the end of the day, I think it works."

Keith is just one of the 116 lesbian, gay, bisexual, and queer (LGBQ) people living in Massachusetts that I interviewed for this book. Some, like Keith, were disinterested in marriage or even very critical of it as an institution. Others were strong embracers of marriage. Still others gave it little thought, simply assuming that getting married was just what you did. Some were in committed relationships that had already lasted decades before the legalization of marriage. Others were young enough to have come of age with it already legal. There is no single same-sex marriage story. LGBQ people are a diverse group, and these differences matter for how they experience marriage. Nevertheless, they all felt pulled into the institution of marriage. And all those who married experienced transformative shifts in the way they felt about their partners and relationships.

This is a book about same-sex marriage and the ways that LGBQ individuals experience gaining access to legal marriage. But it is also a book about marriage in the United States more broadly. I use the case of same-sex marriage to advance our understanding of the changing and enduring meaning of marriage as an institution. Several broad sociological questions about the institution of marriage motivate the research in this book: How, and how much, does marriage govern individual relationship choices and behaviors? How does marriage endure as an institution in the midst of historic changes to its meaning and practice? What role do individual marriage actors play in contributing to broader processes of institutional change in marriage?

The scholarly fields that one might expect to have already addressed these questions offer few answers. Family scholars refer to marriage as an institution but have only rarely attempted to theorize or empirically study exactly what this means. Institutional scholars have focused primarily on formal organizations, such as corporations and bureaucracies, and typically mention marriage only in passing as an example of an institution. Sexualities scholars interested in the effects of same-sex marriage have engaged in the topic mostly from the perspective of heteronormativity and have not addressed questions of institutional processes or change. More than a decade after it first became legal in the United States, there remains surprisingly scant empirical work on same-sex marriage.[1] Connecting these disparate fields of study, I offer new analysis of the character and strength of contemporary marriage as an institution, providing family scholars a more comprehensive and nuanced examination of marriage, institutional scholars a new case study for thinking through institutional processes, and sexualities scholars much-needed empirical data on contemporary LGBQ relationships in a rapidly changing legal and social landscape.

I use the case of same-sex marriage to make several interrelated arguments. First, I use the case of same-sex marriage to challenge the prevailing narrative in family sociology that marriage has fundamentally weakened as an institution. Although marriage has undergone numerous and continuing changes, it remains a powerful institution that shapes our individual choices and behaviors in profound ways. It remains strong enough to make LGBQ people embrace its meanings, rituals, and practices even without legal access to it; to convince the staunchest queer critics of marriage to get married; and to decide the fate of new same-sex relationships. It shapes behaviors as mundane as how same-sex couples manage their money and as exciting as how many people they have sex with. Second, I draw on over a hundred same-sex marriage accounts to illuminate the institutional mechanisms through which marriage continues to govern individual choices and behaviors. Marriage continues to operate through a variety of institutional mechanisms that work independently and in tandem for different marriage actors. But I argue that marriage works most powerfully through taken-for-granted cultural scripts about the distinctive relationship between marriage and commitment. Third, I contend that gaining access to the institution of marriage has had a transformative power on same-sex relationships—one that is much stronger than the power of LGBQ individuals to change the meaning and practice of marriage. The changes occur both across the lifespan of relationships, as couples who did not have access to marriage gain access to it, and across cohorts of LGBQ individuals, as new groups of LGBQ individuals with access to marriage understand and enact their relationships in ways that are fundamentally different from those who maintained them without it. The institution of marriage has changed same-sex relationships for both better and worse. It offers same-sex couples new forms of joy, belonging, and security, but also creates qualitatively new forms of work, anxiety, and conflict.

Taken together, the findings from this research help to interrogate what is colloquially referred to as marriage material. Who is marriage material? Are same-sex couples marriage material, easily assimilated into the institution as it already is, or do they transform it in important ways? Which kinds of LGBQ people are most susceptible to the pull of marriage? And what material is marriage made up of today? What are the institutional mechanisms through which it operates and endures? Are the materials that make up marriage today weaker than in the past, or just as strong?

Is Marriage a Weakening Institution?

Family scholarship provides a wealth of data with which to evaluate the contemporary status of marriage in the United States. The available data typically leads to an overview that goes something like this. Fewer adults are marrying.[2] A record-high share of forty-year-olds in the United States have never been married. And as the share of adults currently married has declined, the share living with an unmarried partner has risen.[3] Although the share of adults who are *currently* cohabiting still remains far smaller than the share who are married, the share of adults who have *ever* lived with an unmarried partner has surpassed those who have ever been married, as premarital cohabitation has become the norm.[4] Childbearing outside of marriage has also become much more common.[5] However, changes to family life are being driven mostly by Americans without a college degree, who have lower lifetime rates of marriage, and are much more likely to have children outside of marriage and to divorce than the college-educated.[6] As such, family scholars now describe a "two-tier family system" or "diverging destinies,"[7] in which college-educated Americans still center their lives around marriage, while non-college-educated Americans rely more on alternatives to marriage.

Despite these changes, overall there has been no decline in the importance young people attach to marriage, with young adults expecting that marriage will be more important to their lives than parenting, careers, or leisure activities.[8] Over two-thirds of unmarried eighteen- to twenty-nine-year-olds report wanting to get married.[9] Most Americans also still expect to marry.[10] And once coupled, most Americans do eventually get married.[11] Nearly 90 percent of different-sex couples are married according to the most recent nationally representative data.[12] It is clear that marriage continues to matter to people. Americans might be waiting longer to marry, cohabiting first, and even having children outside of marriage, but they are not rejecting marriage.

A wealth of research also shows that contemporary marriage is still associated with a range of social, psychological, and economic advantages. Those who marry experience better individual and relationship outcomes than those who do not. Married people have better health, both mental and physical, than unmarried people, especially those who are divorced or widowed.[13] Even after controlling for demographic differences (such as gender, age, race, religion, and educational attainment), married adults are significantly more likely than those who are cohabiting to express a great deal of trust in their partners and higher levels of satisfaction with their relationship.[14] Married individuals enjoy higher average outcomes across multiple positive dimensions of relationship quality (happiness, support, and commitment) than those in unmarried relationships.[15] Taken together, the empirical data points to the continuing importance and distinctiveness of marriage even amid notable social and cultural changes to relationships.

However, these statistics tell us little about marriage as an institution. Family scholars do not typically define what institutions are, but they describe the institution of marriage broadly as a governing structure with weakening power and influence over individual lives and relationships.[16] Marriage is generally understood as having transitioned from an "institutional to companionate" model of marriage in the early to mid-twentieth century, and then from a "companionate to individualized" model in the late twentieth century.[17] Prior to the first transition, an institutional model of marriage meant that the stability of the family took precedence over the needs of individual family members. Although many marriages involved strong ties of affection, practical considerations figured more prominently than love. Legal restrictions and community norms made divorce difficult. By the beginning of the twentieth century, marriage gradually became less about social and religious obligations and more focused on ideas about love, companionship, and compatibility. Nonetheless, marriage remained the only socially acceptable way to have a sexual relationship and raise children, and it was still strongly bound by religious ideals and community norms.

Beginning in the 1960s, as unmarried cohabitation became much more acceptable (both before or instead of marrying) and childbearing outside marriage less stigmatized,[18] marriage appeared to have less of an institutional hold over people's relationships and lives. A wider array of alternative relationship choices emerged, and marriage was no longer necessary to access all the legal and social benefits it once had monopolized.[19] Moreover, as alternatives to marriage grew, marriage itself became a qualitatively different kind of relationship. Under this new "individualized" model of marriage, there has been a shift in emphasis "from role to self" and a growing focus on individual fulfillment and satisfaction as the basis of contemporary marriage.[20] Love has become absolutely essential to marriage, and marriages are successful only to the extent that they fulfill each partner's innermost psychological needs. Relationships are increasingly expected to be based on equality, choice, discussion, and negotiation.[21]

Much scholarship on marriage presumes that the increasing individualization of marriage has occurred in parallel with a decline in its institutional basis. Rather than coexisting, individualization and institutionalization are assumed to be mutually exclusive. Two theories about the declining power of marriage as an institution dominate the sociology of marriage: de-traditionalization and deinstitutionalization. In 1992, Anthony Giddens proposed the "de-traditionalization" thesis in *The Transformation of Intimacy*, now one of the most widely cited works on changing relationship forms in the West. Giddens argues that the "pure relationship" has taken the place of relationships once built primarily for procreation and economic and social stability.[22] Pure relationships, premised only on individual satisfaction and needs, represent a shift away from marriage defined by law, tradition, and necessity, giving individuals much greater freedom from institutional power and influence.

More than a decade later, the deinstitutionalization thesis emerged from an article by Andrew Cherlin, now one of the most highly cited articles in family sociology.[23] Cherlin argues that there has been a weakening of the social norms that define people's behavior in marriage. Instead of adhering to taken-for-granted social norms, roles, and traditions relating to getting and being married, individuals now have much greater personal choice about whether or not to marry and for their behaviors once married. Marriage no longer governs our relationship behaviors because there are fewer shared understandings of what marriage means or should entail. Marriage, he claims, has declined in power as a social institution, but remains important to individuals on a symbolic level, as a choice-based personal achievement. As such, people will continue marrying in high numbers despite its declining significance as an institution.

Statements about the weakening institutional basis of marriage have been ubiquitous throughout family scholarship. Family demographers went so far as to claim that "the declining centrality of marriage in defining and guiding human behavior and relationships is one of the most important stories of the past several centuries of Western history."[24] Recently, theories about the weakening institutional basis of marriage have begun to be challenged and revised in important ways.[25] Yet this has not translated into empirical research. Because most sociological research on marriage today treats it as a greatly weakened institution, the way it operates to shape individual's choices and behaviors remains poorly understood. We know very little about how people actually experience marriage as an institution.

And where does one of the biggest changes to the institution of marriage—its expansion to include same-sex couples—fit into these broader historical shifts and scholarly debates? Initially, same-sex marriage was heralded as an obvious example of deinstitutionalization. It was assumed that, with no clear social norms or rules governing their marriages, same-sex couples would be free to fashion them in highly individualized ways.[26] Later though, as the legalization of same-sex marriage progressed, it seemed like a better example of institutional expansion: marriage was expanding to govern a large number of couples previously beyond its scope. Widespread interest in marriage served as an endorsement of its continuing salience as an institution.[27] But scholars have not moved beyond theoretical speculation to empirically examine same-sex marriage in relation to the institutional character and strength of marriage more broadly.

The findings in this book serve as a counterpoint to dominant ideas within family scholarship about the declining institutional power of marriage. By drawing on what we know from institutional sociology about the way institutions work, and empirically studying the newest entrants into marriage (those individuals most attuned to how marriage shapes choices and behaviors), I present a very different perspective on marriage as an institution. Far from deinstitutionalized, I contend that marriage remains firmly institutionalized. The marriage accounts in this book help to illuminate how and why it remains strong as an institution despite ongoing changes.

Turning to Institutional Scholarship

In one of the only empirical studies of same-sex marriage to date, sociologist Katrina Kimport concluded that "marriage is only an institution; it cannot do anything. People *do* things. How they do things and what they say about their actions—how they make meaning of them—are where change is encouraged or blocked."[28] Kimport ascribed individual marriage actors much agency and power within institutions, drawing attention to the importance of their motivations and intentions for the possibility of institutional change. But arguments like these—and about the weakening institutional power of marriage more generally—are typically made without reference to sociological knowledge about the way institutions work. Without attending to basic insights from institutional scholarship, family scholars cannot get very far in answering questions about the character and strength of contemporary marriage as an institution. We know that institutions can *do* something because a substantial body of institutional scholarship exists to show us how institutions govern individual action. This work also pushes us to conceptualize institutions as more than just the sum of individual interests and actions.

Institutions are structures and practices that are widely adopted and taken for granted, providing stability and meaning for social behavior. Institutional analysis is fundamentally concerned with how individual choices and behaviors are shaped, mediated, and channeled by institutional arrangements. Institutions do not provide individuals with a guidebook for social action, nor do they govern their behavior in any simple or unitary way. Instead, they shape action through multiple mechanisms, which can work differently for different people at different times and across varying contexts. There is no doubt that the magnitude of institutional scholarship is theoretically complex and, with its usual focus on organizations, can seem far removed from the realities of a very personal institution like marriage. This might be why most marriage scholars have avoided it. But I review some basics here because it offers useful theoretical models for thinking about different kinds of mechanisms through which marriage shapes individual choices and behaviors today.

According to Richard Scott, institutions are supported by three "pillars"— "regulative, normative, and cultural-cognitive"—and these are useful for thinking about the way marriage works.[29] The regulative pillar focuses on the way institutions govern action through formal rules that constrain and enable behavior.[30] Formal rules might be developed at the level of the state but can also be found in the bureaucratic rules of organizations. We can see coercive institutional mechanisms that shape individual choices and behaviors toward participation in marriage in the policies of state and federal governments in the United States. These policies provide married couples access to rights denied to the nonmarried, and at the organizational level, where benefits, such as healthcare coverage for dependents, are also usually provided based on marital status. Formal laws and policies at the state and federal level around who is allowed to marry or not demarcate clear boundaries of inclusion and exclusion in the institution of marriage and shape the relationship choices that individuals are able to make as well as their aspirations and behaviors.

The normative pillar of institutions consists of informal norms, expectations, and values that shape individual action. These tend to develop slowly outside of formal organizations, as actors develop a shared sense of what behaviors are expected and appropriate. Other members of social groups then enforce these rules and norms by applying varying levels of social pressure. With regard to marriage, informal norms and expectations around marriage might operate to make individuals feel they should marry as a means of creating stability before having children, or that they should be monogamous and adhere to certain gendered norms for behavior once married.[31] In these ways, individuals act out of a sense of duty, or at least an awareness of what one is supposed to do. But often cultural norms become so internalized that they shape individual behavior without any awareness on an individual's part. It was the weakening power of norms for behavior that formed the basis for the deinstitutionalization of marriage thesis, as social norms for marital behavior weakened. But even if ideas about what one *should* do have weakened, institutions still shape social behavior in other ways.

One of the most central contributions of neo-institutional theory has been to raise awareness of a third pillar of institutional influence—the cultural-cognitive pillar.[32] This "cognitive turn" has changed the way social scientists think about human motivation and behavior, placing emphasis on the more purely cognitive aspects of routine social behavior. Instead of acting under rules or because of obligation, individuals also act because of the things they are able to imagine. They make certain choices because they cannot conceive of any alternative. In this way, institutions are built on shared cognitions that define what has meaning and what actions are possible.[33] They are the context within which our interests are developed. Institutions do not just constrain options; they establish the very criteria by which people discover their preferences.[34] If an individual cannot imagine alternatives because shared meanings have constrained what options they perceive, then what people intend or do has already been fundamentally shaped by the institution itself.

These are not mutually exclusive perspectives on the way institutions govern behavior. Many of the marriage stories in this book illuminate the way marriage operates through multiple institutional mechanisms at once.

Nonetheless, the approaches that predominate in sociology conceive of institutions as providing models, schemas, or scripts for behavior rather than rules or norms. As the institutional scholars Walter Powell and Paul DiMaggio put it in their foundational book on neo-institutionalism, "not norms and values but taken-for-granted scripts, rules, and classifications are the stuff of which institutions are made."[35] The stories in this book make clear that even if rule- and norm-based institutional mechanisms have weakened, shared cognitive understandings about marriage have not.

CULTURAL SCRIPTS AND MARRIAGE

I have already alluded to a tension in theories about the weakened institutional basis of marriage: individuals will continue to place a high value on marriage and marry in high numbers because of its symbolic value. Marriage is considered symbolically important *in spite* of its declining institutional foundation. Yet institutional sociology makes clear that symbolic components of marriage are channeled through shared cultural scripts—the cultural-cognitive pillar of the institution. The symbolic value of marriage does not exist outside its institutional basis, some vestige left over after the institution has declined; rather it represents its continuing institutional power. The same-sex marriage stories in this book demonstrate that the symbolic value of marriage persists through shared cultural scripts in several different forms as a unique means of obtaining social status, legitimacy, and love and commitment. Ann Swidler famously argued that "culture" is best thought of as a "tool kit" from which people select both institutionalized ends and the strategies for their pursuit.[36] Through the rich and nuanced stories they share, we see LGBQ individuals draw upon cultural scripts in tandem and separately to shape a range of relationship choices and behaviors.

Importantly, we do not know from a marital outcome alone what shared cultural scripts have shaped the individual actions that led there. For example, the high take-up rate of marriage by same-sex couples has been regarded as evidence that "marriage is a meaningful marker of a successful personal life for many LGBTQ+ Americans."[37] But we do not know from these take-up rates which cultural scripts are being utilized by individuals when forming their marital motivations and plans. In fact, achievement and social status based cultural scripts were seldom drawn upon by the LGBQ individuals in this book.

One prominent cultural script utilized by LGBQ individuals centers on the idea of marriage as a means of obtaining social legitimacy. LGBQ individuals in this study took for granted that they would gain social legitimacy through legal marriage and believed that marriage had the power to automatically grant them and their relationships legitimacy in the eyes of others, even in the absence of full societal support for same-sex marriage. Drawing on this shared cultural script about marriage as a means to legitimacy, LGBQ individuals altered the way they behaved in everyday interactions with strangers and acquaintances to demand more respect and rights.[38]

The most dominant and widely shared cultural script the LGBQ individuals in this study drew upon concerns marriage's distinctive relationship to love and commitment: that marriage represents a unique form of love and commitment and is its ideal and highest iteration of it. Marriage, as the epitome of love and commitment, permeates popular culture. Love and commitment were also the basis on which the movement for marriage equality won heterosexual support for same-sex marriage in a remarkably short span of time.[39] They were scripts that heterosexuals could understand and get behind when a rights-based framework for marriage equality failed. They were also one of the primary bases on which the US Supreme Court made same-sex marriage legal. Justice Kennedy argued, "The right to marry is fundamental because it supports a two-person union unlike any other in its importance to the committed individuals."[40] He concluded, "No union is more profound than marriage, for it embodies the highest ideals of love, fidelity, devotion, sacrifice, and family. In forming a marital union, two people become something greater than once they were ... marriage embodies a love that may endure even past death." After it became legal, almost every major news source contextualized the victory as about love. The *New York Times* opinion headline read "Love Has Won,"[41] while the *USA Today* headline declared, "Ohio Man 'Fought for His Love,' Won Gay-Marriage Case."[42] When President Obama tweeted his reaction to same-sex marriage becoming legal, he used the hashtag "Love Wins!"[43]

In her interview study of middle-class heterosexual Americans, the cultural sociologist Ann Swidler identified two very consistently used yet different cultural scripts about love and marriage that shape individual decisions and behaviors: conceptualizations of love as "prosaic" and as "mythic."[44] Prosaic scripts include ideas that love requires continuing hard work, compromise, and change, and it grows slowly. By contrast, mythic scripts include ideas about love as a decisive choice involving a unique other, overcoming obstacles, and lasting forever. Although they might sound contradictory, individuals access both in different contexts. When thinking about the choice of whether to marry or stay married, people turn to cultural scripts about love in mythic terms. Mythic scripts endure, despite the fact that prosaic scripts are much more in line with people's everyday experiences of relationships, because the institution of marriage upholds romantic love myths and keeps them culturally relevant. As Swidler puts it, "It is the structure of marriage as an institution that makes the love myth plausible."[45] Without marriage as an institutional framework, it would be almost impossible for people to enact the core features of the mythic love script: to make a decisive choice about who to be with, to publicly state that they have a unique love for one person, to prove that obstacles to love can be overcome, and to make a commitment that is meant to last forever. The institution of marriage keeps these cultural scripts alive.

The accounts in this book mostly direct attention away from the formal rules and informal norms that once governed marriage to the far more pervasive and powerful cultural scripts that lie at the heart of the institution today. These scripts feature both prosaic and mythic ideas about love, but center more firmly on mythic beliefs. The narratives in this book also illuminate other, centrally important, scripts that uphold the institution of marriage and help explain its endurance amid substantial change. In particular, cultural scripts about the distinctive relationship between marriage and commitment continue to drive many individual relationship choices and behaviors. Moreover, the longer LGBQ individuals have access to marriage, the more taken-for-granted and internalized cultural scripts pertaining to it appear to be, and the more they operate to guide new same-sex relationship choices and behaviors.

INSTITUTIONAL ENDURANCE AND CHANGE

Most early institutional scholars focused on how institutions came to achieve stability, typically in two ways. First, shared cognitive scripts or models become "taken for granted" through repeated use in interactions.[46] Second, these shared cognitive models are endorsed by some authoritative or powerful individual or organization and therefore come to be regarded as legitimate.[47] As shared scripts or models for action get reinforced through repeated interaction and legitimation, eventually alternative scripts become meaningless, even "unimaginable."[48] When this occurs, we can think of a structure or behavior as having become fully institutionalized.[49] Institutionalization is a gradual process akin to sedimentation—an incremental layering, settling, and solidifying of expectations as they eventually become accepted as fact and other possibilities become inconceivable.[50] When this happens, no collective mobilization or authoritative social control is necessary to get individuals to adhere to them.

Marriage can be thought of as institutionalized to the extent that it provides taken-for-granted models or scripts for action, which are also widely endorsed by powerful organizations, including local and federal bodies and religious organizations. It is routinely practiced by individuals without the need for collective mobilization or authoritative social control, though a robust system of social incentives connected to marriage does play a role in upholding it. Government agencies and organizations, fearful of the decline of marriage among particular populations, do promote marriage.[51] Yet these actions do not explain why so many people continue to marry or grant marriage so much importance in their lives.

Once a practice, such as marriage, is institutionalized, how does it withstand changes and endure as an institution? Which changes incrementally alter the shape of an institution without undermining its institutional basis, and which fundamentally undermine or weaken the institution itself? Smaller scale "developmental changes" can occur in institutions without leading to any weakening of the institutional basis of the institution. With developmental change, a majority of the original practices and beliefs of the institution are retained, but new ones appear alongside them.[52] By contrast, "transformational changes" to institutions entail more radical restructuring, and the practices and beliefs of an institution fundamentally change.[53] Marital beliefs and behaviors that used to be practiced unthinkingly by the majority of a population would now only be adhered to by a minority. Cultural scripts that were once taken for granted would now be widely challenged and contested. To date, there is little empirical evidence of that kind of transformational change within marriage, at least among heterosexuals.[54] One example of a developmental change that has occurred is that there have been some important shifts toward more egalitarian sharing of both paid and domestic work in heterosexual marriage.[55] This has changed the practice and experience of marriage for those within it. However, these shifts have not, thus far, undermined deeply internalized beliefs with regard to the gendered differences or inequalities that structure marriage. The conscious and "ongoing effort required to change gendered roles within marriage is testament to the continuing institutionalization of marriage."[56] And other cultural norms pertaining to marital behaviors have changed little, including around assumptions of lifelong commitment,[57] financial pooling,[58] monogamy,[59] and raising children,[60] with the vast majority of heterosexuals adhering to similar beliefs and practices.

Of course, those who believe marriage is fundamentally heterosexual might perceive same-sex marriage to have already radically transformed the institution. But if same-sex couples apply the same marital meanings and engage in the same marital practices as heterosexuals, it is questionable how much their marriages can be thought of as a transformational change to the institution. Institutional theory predicts that individual LGBQ actors will do little to fundamentally challenge the beliefs and practices associated with marriage, even when given opportunities to do so. That is because individuals tend to fall back on what is known, even when change is possible. Because change is risky, more individual choice does not necessarily lead to creativity in choices or behaviors. People tend to either fall back on what they know or engage in mimetic processes, imitating others, choosing to reduce uncertainty, and following tried and tested practices rather than forging their own uncharted paths.[61] The significance of same-sex marriage to broad processes of institutional change in marriage has not been empirically examined.

Because early institutionalist scholars regarded institutions as stable, unquestioned arrangements, individuals were by extension presented in a passive role. Most human behavior was presented as routine and unreflective.[62] Newer institutional scholarship has made a more concerted attempt to understand the role of individuals in affecting and transforming institutions, giving them more of an agentic role. But it focuses on organizational leaders and elites, those with the most interest in enacting change, and occupying the positions and with the resources to achieve it.[63] These highly skilled, resourced, and strategic "institutional entrepreneurs" might include policy makers who draft and pass legislation, political action groups who lobby for regulatory change, or managers who use their technical or market leadership to try to influence change in their institutional contexts.[64] Individuals have largely been presented as one of two extremes: traditionally they were viewed as unreflective cultural dopes, while more recently they are heroic and savvy change agents.[65]

When I conducted the research for this book, same-sex marriage had been debated and legally introduced and legitimized at the state level. But it was far from fully institutionalized. It had not yet been widely adopted across states, nor become broadly approved of or understood within them, and certainly not taken for granted as a natural arrangement. We might think of marriage equality movement organizations and activists as institutional entrepreneurs. They achieved momentous legal change by challenging the institutional logic of marriage as heterosexual.[66] But, as I have shown elsewhere, as beneficiaries of the initial legal change, average LGBQ individuals still had much work to do on the ground.[67] They were not just passive recipients of a change that had already been fully achieved. They were trailblazers, the first to enact legal same-sex marriage in their own relationships and lives. They had to figure out what it meant to them, how to do it, and explain it to others, all with the eyes of the nation on them.

In some areas of married life, LGBQ individuals appear to do little to challenge the institution of marriage, applying the same meanings to it—especially pertaining to marriage as about commitment, security, and raising children. They also enact many of the same marital practices, for example around financial pooling and in meticulously following rituals for getting engaged and married. But in other areas they are challenging fundamental ideas and practices, especially in rejecting and resisting existing areas of married life that center on gender inequality and sexual ownership, such as expectations about who should propose and for sexual monogamy. They are able to challenge some of these fundamental premises of marriage because they have a fuller cultural toolbox than most heterosexuals. Strongly held and widely shared beliefs emanating from the LGBTQ+ community concerning gender equality and sexual freedom provide them with a wider array of scripts for shaping their choices and behaviors. Nonetheless, these alternative cultural scripts interact and mesh with more dominant marital scripts, resulting in a rather messy mix of resistance and conformism. Attempts to do marriage differently butt up against the dominance of taken-for-granted ideas about the meaning of marriage that seep into their beliefs and practices even as they attempt to resist institutionalized ways of doing things.

Throughout this book, I illuminate the ways in which LGBQ individuals carve out space for change within the institution of marriage as well as the difficulties of doing so. Overall though, it is not individual same-sex relationships that are remade by marriage. Instead, by examining changes across same-sex relationships, I reveal a much more transformative impact. Transformative changes in same-sex relationships have occurred across cohorts of LGBQ individuals, as new groups with access to marriage understand and enact their relationships in ways that are fundamentally different from those who maintained relationships without it.

The Study

The findings in this study are drawn from in-depth interview and survey data collected from 116 individuals in married and unmarried same-sex relationships in Massachusetts in 2012 and 2013. Because the few existing studies of same-sex marriage had taken place before or immediately after legalization, I knew I wanted to try and gain a longer-term perspective on the impact of marriage on same-sex relationships. At the time of data collection, Massachusetts offered the best possible research site; Massachusetts had provided access to legal marriage for much longer than other states. In 2003, the Massachusetts Supreme Judicial Court made history by becoming the first state in the United States to legalize same-sex marriage. It ruled it unconstitutional to deny same-sex couples the right to marry and specified that anything less than full and equal marriage would be unconstitutional.[68] It took four more years for another state to legalize same-sex marriage.[69] Massachusetts also made the most sense as the research site for this study because it had already overcome attempts to introduce constitutional amendments banning same-sex marriage,[70] whereas other states were still grappling with ongoing efforts to halt it. In fact, in the years immediately following same-sex marriage legalization in Massachusetts, the marriage equality movement experienced mostly losses.[71] I wanted access to marriage to feel as secure as possible to the LGBQ individuals in this study, so that I could adequately examine its impact on their relationships. Massachusetts was well ahead of its time.

As soon as same-sex couples could get married in Massachusetts, on May 17, 2004, large numbers rushed to take advantage of the opportunity. In the first week it was legal, 2,468 same-sex couples applied for marriage licenses.[72] By 2010, 68 percent of all resident same-sex couples in Massachusetts had legally married.[73] Same-sex couples in Massachusetts were nearly three-quarters of the way to the same cumulative take-up rate for marriage as different-sex couples in Massachusetts after just six years.[74] These high rates occurred despite the fact that same-sex couples did not yet have access to federal marriage benefits and protections. I was actually just finishing up data collection for this book in June 2013 when the Supreme Court struck down part of the federal Defense of Marriage Act,[75] requiring the federal government to recognize same-sex marriages from the states where they are legal. By then, same-sex couples in Massachusetts had had access to legal same-sex marriage for nine years, and a total of nine other states had made same-sex marriage legal.

Same-sex marriage would not become legal nationwide for another two years after I finished data collection, when, on June 26, 2015, the US Supreme Court ruled in *Obergefell v. Hodges* that all state bans on same-sex marriage were unconstitutional,[76] granting same-sex couples in all fifty states the right to full, equal recognition under the law. By the time of that ruling, same-sex couples could already legally marry in thirty-seven states, and nearly 72 percent of the US population lived in a state issuing marriage licenses to same-sex couples.[77] To give a sense of the pace of change, just four years before, only 4 percent of the population lived in states where same-sex marriage was legal.[78] This fast-changing legal landscape represents the backdrop to the lived experiences of the LGBQ individuals in this book.[79]

This book captures a unique historic moment that social scientists will not have the opportunity to study again, analyzing the experiences of the first groups of LGBQ individuals to gain access to legal marriage. These groups were both experiencing and contributing to institutional change in motion.

I made specific efforts to include some groups of individuals I felt had been excluded from prior research. Whereas other research on same-sex marriage had only examined the experiences of LGBQ individuals who married, I knew that including both married and unmarried individuals was crucial. We know that institutions can shape individual behavior both before and without formally participating in them, and so to capture its full effects, I needed to explore how having access to legal marriage impacted unmarried individuals too. I also made it clear in my recruitment materials that it did not matter what their views on marriage were or whether they had any interest in marrying. The only criteria I imposed was that they needed to have been cohabiting with a same-sex partner for at least a year. I wanted marriage to feel as if it could be a real possibility for them and their relationships, rather than as only an abstract or imagined future. Being in relationships positioned participants to reflect on and describe in depth how marriage impacted them. However, this means that the book does not speak to the experiences of single LGBQ people, or to those who are not in dyadic relationships, although they too are likely impacted by gaining access to legal marriage.

Other aspects of the sample I ended up with further limit the generalizability of the findings. I examine the characteristics and limitations of my sample in further depth in the Methods Appendix, but two characteristics are especially important to note here. First, as none of my participants identified as transgender, I cannot speak to their experiences. I therefore refer to "LGBQ people" throughout the book unless I am presenting direct quotes from participants in which they refer to something different, for example, "LGBT" people. When relevant, and I am not describing the people who took part in this book, I refer to the "LGBTQ+ community" more broadly. Second, the sample is highly educated. A wealth of family scholarship demonstrates that there are major dividing lines in family experiences by education. Rising expectations that couples be economically settled prior to marrying puts marriage increasingly out of reach for those without college degrees.[80] A larger percentage of college-educated women and men marry during their lifetimes than do those with less education.[81] Trends in divorce also show strong differences by education. During the society-wide increase in divorce in the 1960s and 1970s, the rates rose for all education groups and peaked around 1980, but since then divorce rates have declined much further among the college-educated than among those with less education.[82] As a result of their higher levels of marriage and lower levels of divorce, the percentage of adults who are currently married is higher for the college-educated.[83] This is a change from the 1970s, when adults with a high school diploma were as likely as college graduates to be married.[84] The college-educated are also much more likely to wait until marriage to have children.

Among women without college degrees and aged under forty, a majority of all births occur outside of marriage. Among women with college degrees, only 12 percent of births do.[85] Taken together, family scholars now identify something close to two different subsystems, one primarily involving individuals with college degrees and the other primarily involving those without.[86] Given this, the data in this book offer insights about those Americans who are most likely to marry and center their lives around it.

Nonetheless, the economic bar for marriage could be lower for same-sex than for different-sex couples because high levels of discrimination and stigma may make the legal protections offered by marriage critically important for same-sex couples. In fact, the available research shows that socioeconomic differences are less prominent among same-sex couples than among different-sex couples.[87] That said, it is still important to keep in mind that the experiences of this sample—highly educated and cisgender—do not necessarily speak to the experiences of all LGBQ people.

Some of the people in this study already lived in Massachusetts before same-sex marriage became legal there, while others moved to Massachusetts only afterward. Their relationship histories and current relationship situations varied greatly, but what they all have in common was that they had gone from a position of not having access to legal marriage to now having access to it. Half of them started their relationships before marriage had become legal, while the other half entered their relationships only after. This proved very important, allowing me to consider how the timing of legal marriage in one's relationship matters such that I could examine shifts over time by comparing newer relationships to older ones. Participants ranged in age from twenty-three to sixty-nine and had been with their partners anywhere from one to thirty-two years. Only a few had been actively involved in the marriage equality movement. Their experiences therefore reflect those of very ordinary, rank-and-file LGBQ people.

You will notice that throughout the book, I draw on both survey and interview data. All participants first completed an online survey and then took part in an in-depth face-to-face interview with me. As a primarily qualitative researcher, I rely most heavily on the interview data, which was essential for understanding the mechanisms through which marriage shapes relationship experiences and for exploring meaning-making—how LGBQ people assigned meaning to their experiences and the way they drew on cultural scripts as they did so. Yet having mixed methods data proved very useful for identifying major cleavages and differences in marital experiences. I knew from the outset that I wanted to pay close attention to variation and not ignore important differences within LGBQ marital experiences. Examining both data sources together enabled me to do this more rigorously. Throughout the book, I pay attention to a range of important differences when they are relevant to the analysis, including those based on gender, cohort, relationship duration and timing, and parenthood status. I also organize the book around three marriage archetypes that I came to feel best captured the major cleavages in marriage experiences among LGBQ individuals that I observed in the data.

Embracers, Rejecters, and Assumers

The three marriage archetypes in this book—Marriage Embracers, Rejecters, and Assumers—have very different feelings about legal marriage. They gained access to it at different life and relationship stages and use it in different ways. They are not intended to be overly simplistic caricatures of LGBQ people, nor to encapsulate all axes of possible difference. Nevertheless, each group captures a fundamentally different bundle of marriage experiences and illuminates the workings of marriage as an institution in a different way. Of the 116 participants in this study, 31 were Marriage Embracers, 28 were Marriage Rejecters, and 41 were Marriage Assumers. Sixteen participants did not fit neatly into any of these categories, exhibiting characteristics of more than one; I refer to these as In-Betweeners and include them when relevant for the analysis, noting their status in the endnotes.

Marriage Embracers had already formed committed relationships before legal marriage was a possibility and did not expect to gain access to legal marriage in their lifetimes. Yet they all embraced the value and importance of marriage, and the different marriage-like experiences and statuses available to them in the years before full same-sex marriage became legal. They aspired to be part of an institution that they believed would always exclude them and found creative ways to do so. They attributed to marriage a wide range of distinct cultural meanings and social capabilities but were also acutely aware of the distinctiveness of legal marriage. Both before and after marriage became legal, Marriage Embracers used the institution of marriage for what it could provide them and were mindful of its immense cultural, social, and legal power. Yet once married, they felt remarkably free from any pressure to conform to marital scripts that they felt did not apply to them. They had always used the institution of marriage creatively to get what they needed out of it, and they continued to do the same after they got married. Marriage was, and always had been (legal or not), theirs for the taking, and they made of it whatever felt right to them.

Marriage Rejecters, like Keith introduced at the start of this book, were a more varied group in terms of age and the timing of their relationship formation than Embracers. But they were united in their rejection of marriage. It was unnecessary, undesirable, or even inappropriate for their relationships. Some simply rejected marriage for their own personal relationships, insisting that they did not need marriage, while others rejected marriage as an undesirable institution for all same-sex couples. Historic exclusion from the institution and exposure to varying forms of radical queer politics translated into a lack of interest in, or resistance to, the institution of marriage. Yet there was frequently a disconnect between the feelings and beliefs Rejecters expressed about marriage and the decisions they ultimately made to do it. Disinterest in, even apathy toward, marriage proved no match for its institutional power, as Marriage Rejecters found themselves being pulled into marriage through a range of legal, social, and relational mechanisms. Once married, Rejecters frequently struggled with what it meant to reject an institution from within and adhering to marital scripts for behavior they had once challenged.

Marriage Assumers were predominantly young (typically in their twenties and thirties) and had entered serious same-sex relationships only after same-sex marriage had already become legal. They had come out and formed committed relationships in a world in which legal same-sex marriage was already possible. They took marriage for granted as "just what you do" when you love someone, are committed to them, and want to have children with them, and they understood marriage as part of the "natural progression" of a relationship. They found it difficult to envisage long-term committed relationships in the absence of marriage, saw little point in investing time or energy in relationships that were not "marriage material," and were unforgiving of a partner's hesitancy about marriage. On the one hand, they gave marriage little thought. Marriage was so taken for granted and internalized as the relationship gold standard that they found it hard to articulate what it meant to them. And they were unaware of the degree to which marriage was shaping their choices and behaviors. Just as it was for heterosexuals, marriage was mostly an unexamined institutional backdrop in their lives.[88] On the other hand, they spent vast amounts of time thinking about marriage because they cared deeply about doing it "the right way." In getting and being married, they invested much time and emotional energy in attempting to follow marital scripts for behavior.

In organizing the book around these three archetypes, the point is not to tease apart exactly why individuals fall into one group or another—why, for instance, some embrace the cultural power of marriage, while others reject it. Instead, comparing across the groups helps to illuminate important features of the institutional character and power of marriage. First, it shows that rather than having uniform institutional effects, the institution of marriage transforms individuals' relationships in varying ways, depending on their position vis-à-vis the institution. How LGBQ individuals experienced the impact of marriage on their relationships depended on where they were in their relationships and lives when they gained access to it and the meanings they already attached to the institution. Given that Embracers considered themselves already married in a variety of ways, that Rejecters rejected the need for marriage, and that Assumers simply took marriage for granted, one should not expect the institution of marriage to shape their relationships in the same way. For Embracers, access to legal marriage transformed abstract marital beliefs and practices into concrete realities with clearer social meaning and significance for their relationships. For Rejecters, access to legal marriage transformed the way they felt about marriage as an institution and their willingness to participate in it. For Marriage Assumers, access to legal marriage transformed their relationships even before they started, defining its very meaning and purpose.

Second, comparing across the three groups allows us to better recognize the diverse mechanisms through which the institution still pulls individuals into it and shapes their relationships. Instead of finding that some institutional mechanisms have lost their power while others remain strong, as deinstitutionalization theorists might predict, I find that the regulative, normative, and cognitive pillars of the institution all continue to exert power, but in different ways for different people. Embracers are pulled into the institution of marriage by a complex mixture of regulative, normative, and cultural-cognitive forces. Rejecters are pulled into it mostly through regulative mechanisms. Assumers are pulled almost exclusively through the cognitive-cultural arm of the institution. The institution of marriage does not depend on one institutional mechanism alone but has the power to pull individuals into it through a system of mechanisms that work both together and independently as necessary.

Lastly, comparing across the groups makes clear how much access to legal marriage has transformed the meaning and practice of same-sex relationships. In this sense, the book pays attention to changes both within and across relationships. Looking within each group we can identify the varying ways gaining access to marriage transforms individual relationships across the life course. But by looking across the groups we can see how much gaining access to marriage has changed the meaning and experience of same-sex relationships more generally. Throughout the book, the experiences of Marriage Assumers appear fundamentally different from those in the other two groups, making clear just how much having access to legal marriage has redefined same-sex relationships. Within only a decade of legal marriage, a new cohort of LGBQ people has come to take marriage for granted and to internalize dominant scripts about it in ways that their counterparts in the Marriage Embracer and Rejecter groups could not even fathom. Now that every new same-sex relationship starts with access to legal marriage, these differences and the ways in which marriage impacts relationships have become harder to observe.

A Road Map to *Marriage Material*

This sociological story of same-sex marriage unfolds in two interrelated parts. Part I of *Marriage Material* examines what gaining the right to legally marry means to the three different archetypes of LGBQ people and the varying institutional pulls toward and into marriage they experience. Each chapter introduces a different archetypal group of LGBQ people—Embracers, Rejecters, and Assumers—and examines how they experience gaining access to legal marriage, and how access transforms their relationships. Chapter 1 focuses on Marriage Embracers. Their marriage stories show that marriage has the power to shape same-sex relationships even when LGBQ individuals are excluded from the institution. Their accounts also help to bring into sharp relief the different institutional dimensions of marriage and show how they operated independently prior to legalization and then more strongly and interdependently after it. Chapter 2 homes in on the experiences of Marriage Rejecters. Their stories illuminate the power of marriage over individuals who resist it and the ways in which they make sense of their choices and behaviors within an institution they had previously rejected. Chapter 3 presents the experiences of Marriage Assumers. Their marriage experiences offer the strongest indicator of the institutionalization of marriage among LGBQ people. They show that gaining access to legal marriage has fundamentally changed LGBQ people's relationships and the meanings and expectations they attach to them.

Part II of *Marriage Material* shifts attention away from the impact of marital *access* toward the impact of marital *status*—the impact that getting and being married has on same-sex relationships. It focuses on how same-sex couples actually do marriage, paying particular attention to agency and constraint in their marital practices. Each chapter explores a different marriage practice for which there remain strong social norms governing behavior in heterosexual marriage. Chapter 4 focuses on how LGBQ individuals get engaged to be married, as getting engaged and marriage proposals remain one of the most socially prescribed marital moments for heterosexuals. It illuminates the additional work, anxiety, and stress caused by entering marriage.

Chapter 5 examines how married LGBQ individuals manage their finances, as research continues to show a strong connection between marriage and financial pooling for heterosexuals. The chapter highlights the ways in which being married creates heightened feelings of trust, security, and commitment among same-sex couples, enabling them to combine financial assets in new ways. The final empirical chapter, chapter 6, examines how LGBQ individuals manage monogamy, as heterosexual marriages remain premised on an assumption of sexual monogamy. Here we see LGBQ individuals most clearly challenging expected marital behaviors. Nonetheless, marriage impacts their relationships through normative pressures to publicly conform and through adherence to cultural scripts that seep into their beliefs and practices even as they attempt to resist existing ways of doing things. In the concluding chapter, I review what we have learned about the regulative, normative, and cultural marriage materials that shape individual choices and behaviors today, summarize how having access to legal marriage has transformed same-sex relationships, and outline how and when LGBQ people have the potential to also help remake the institution of marriage.

PART 1

Gaining Marriage

1

Marriage Embracers

The Power of Marriage, Old and New

Ann, a fifty-four-year-old woman, had been legally married to her wife for two years when I met her. But she was still struggling to wrap her head around it. It was as if talking to me about marriage made her aware once again how extraordinary it was. No matter how many times she said the words "wife" and "married," somehow she still felt as if the words could not be true. She explained:

> I came of age in the '70s. The possibility of being able to say "I'm married" and have it have legal meaning was just mind boggling. "I have a wife." Like, oh my god, I have a wife! It feels like I'm lying. Like this is technically impossible. I came of age when it was not even conceivable. Even when I came out through the '80s, it's just not something you could have imagined happening. It just felt like it couldn't be true.

You might be surprised to learn that Ann never let the unimaginableness of legal same-sex marriage quash her marital aspirations. Nor did it stop her acting on them. With the exception of a short-lived "rebellious phase" in college, Ann had always wanted to get married. By the time same-sex marriage became legal, Ann had already had a commitment ceremony, a "big honeymoon," and a civil union with a previous same-sex partner.

Ann belongs to a group of LGBQ people in this study whom I call Marriage Embracers. Of the 116 participants in this study, 31 were Marriage Embracers. Marriage Embracers were both a cohesive and heterogeneous group. They had all already formed committed relationships before legal marriage was a possibility and did not expect to gain access to legal same-sex marriage in their lifetimes. Yet this did not stop them from embracing the value and importance of marriage. To differing degrees, they also embraced varying marriage-like experiences and statuses available to them in the years before it became legal. But they differed in the ways they embraced it and the reasons for which they did so. Some participated in whatever form of marriage was available, doing everything marriage-like they could; others embraced marriage more selectively, participating in some kinds of marital experiences and statuses but not others; still others wholeheartedly embraced the idea of marriage but chose not to participate in anything marriage-like until it was legal.

Why did Marriage Embracers, like Ann, aspire to be part of an institution they believed would always exclude them? In what ways did they understand themselves as already married before legal marriage became possible? Why did so many of them still rush to get legally married as soon as they could? What exactly did they gain from legal marriage? What was new and distinct about it?

To answer these questions, one must begin by understanding that same-sex marriage did not burst into existence the day it became legal. When Massachusetts became the first state to legalize same-sex marriage, it was common to encounter statements implying that same-sex couples could marry for the first time or that same-sex marriage was a totally new thing. The Boston Globe, for example, declared that same-sex couples were now "Free to Marry!" while the national marriage equality organization Freedom to Marry states that same-sex couples in Massachusetts "began marrying on May 17, 2004."[1] Although legal marriage was a new option for LGBQ people, marriage was not. This is more than mere semantics. Marriage already existed—as a *cultural* ideal, aspiration, and ritual. And it also already existed in the form of alternative *legal* marriage-like statuses that were nonetheless very clearly not legal marriage. Like all institutions, marriage consists of several independent and interdependent parts. Some of these parts are cultural and social in nature, others are legal. Some aspects of marriage exist and exert power without the law; others are dependent on it. Having lived through multiple marital options, Marriage Embracers were acutely aware of these differing dimensions of marriage, and their experiences help bring them into sharp relief. They offer a kind of "outsider within" perspective on the institution of marriage.[2]

To understand how the institution of marriage works, it is helpful to tease apart which aspects of marriage stem from (1) its cultural and social status, (2) its legality, and (3) the coming together of both. For some Marriage Embracers, the appeal and power of marriage emanated from its rituals and traditions—the ability to publicly participate in ceremonial, symbolic practices that they believed everyone could easily understand as signs of love and commitment. For others, they saw marriage as a distinct cultural means of gaining recognition as a family unit and inclusion from other family members. Some embraced marriage mostly for the specific, tangible rights and protections they could get from it, gains that varied enormously across the differing legal marital statuses available to them, including domestic partnerships, civil unions, and then legal marriage. Others saw it more as a kind of insurance policy, a legal protection for their families just in case they ever needed it. Still others embraced marriage for the external validation it granted and the significance of having a legal authority figure declare them to be an official couple. These different meanings were not mutually exclusive; Marriage Embracers combined them in varying ways when they thought about and engaged in marriage, both before and after it was legal.

Though this book centers on the ways legal marriage has transformed same-sex relationships, it's important to start by recognizing that the institution of marriage already shaped them. The fact that many LGBQ people embraced marriage before it was legal shows how much the power of marriage extends beyond its legal status. Marriage Embracers certainly did not need marriage to be legal to see value in it and find ways to participate in it, but they also saw legal marriage as distinctive. At a simple level, legal marriage brought all the cultural, social, and legal dimensions together, offering them the package deal. But, in more complex ways, legal marriage also changed the meaning and significance of marriage. Legal marriage was greater than just the sum of its many parts. For example, it was not only that legal marriage offered social recognition *and* tangible legal rights and benefits; it was that its legal status bolstered claims to recognition as a married couple and made social legitimacy more easily achievable. It was not only that legal marriage offered a way to demonstrate love *and* gain external, legal validation as a couple. It was that external legal validation made the declaration of love feel stronger and more binding. All the cultural and social dimensions of marriage—rituals and traditions, love and commitment, and familial and social recognition—felt more real and meaningful with the weight of the law behind them. The experiences of Marriage Embracers show both that marriage is much more than just a legal status and that its legal status fundamentally transforms the cultural and social significance of marriage.

"We Were Already Married"

Regardless of its legal status, marriage exists as a cultural idea and ideal that is available to any socialized member of society. Most LGBQ people have been raised and, at least partly, socialized in heterosexual families and communities. Even if LGBQ people spent most of their time in nonheterosexual communities, our nation's obsession with marriage and weddings is hard to escape. Much like heterosexuals, LGBQ people have always been surrounded by a culture of marriage—reading about it in magazines and books, watching it on TV and in films, and attending engagement parties and weddings. They have been exposed to the same cultural messages about the importance and status of marriage as heterosexuals. It should not then be all that surprising that marriage did not need to be a legal possibility for LGBQ people to imagine and aspire to it.

Perhaps more surprising is that it also did not need to be legal for them to get married. The cultural rituals associated with weddings can be enacted and performed by anyone wishing to evoke the meanings marriage has come to symbolize. For decades before same-sex marriage became legal, some LGBQ people sought ways to create marriage-like unions through commitment ceremonies.[3] Some were big, public weddings, involving families and friends. Others were small, private affairs between the couple. Enacting the ceremonial aspects of marriage was a way for couples to symbolize their commitment—to others and to themselves—over and above simply being together. Twelve of the 116 LGBQ people in this study had already had commitment ceremonies prior to marriage becoming legal.[4] Though the government did not recognize these cultural events as marriages, the couples involved usually considered themselves to be married and hoped the ceremony would help them gain recognition from family and friends as a married couple. Most attributed the same broad cultural meanings to the practice as people do to legal marriage, describing the ceremonies as public, outward displays of their commitment to their partners. Having a ceremony meant being willing to publicly declare love and commitment to their partner and have the people attending witness it.

When I asked Ann, the woman introduced at the start of this chapter, why she had wanted a commitment ceremony, she told me that her partner had wanted them both to wear rings, but Ann had refused unless her partner was also willing to have a public ceremony. For her, there was something crucial about the public nature of marriage, of having other people be involved in and supportive of it. She thought about her parents' divorce and attributed it in part to how "isolated" and "private" they had been. Trying to explain, she said, "I cannot even really tell you why, but I just needed it. Something in me needed a public ceremony. The legal recognition never meant as much to me as it does to some people. It was the social part that mattered." Remembering her commitment ceremony, she recalled, "It made my head spin how powerful that was, having my family witness that. It was transformative for us both. It changed our families' feelings about us, really, and changed our sense of ourselves as a couple."

Family recognition and inclusion figured heavily in people's descriptions of their commitment ceremonies. Theresa, a sixty-eight-year-old woman who had a commitment ceremony with her partner in the mid-1990s, described it as "a big church wedding, with one hundred or so people there" and a "long ceremony with hymns and rituals." She saw it as an opportunity to declare, publicly and symbolically, commitment and gain recognition from family. She and her partner took champagne over to her father to "announce" that they were "going to get married." Theresa told me that after the ceremony she felt as if "there was another level of acceptance" from family: "It made me a member of the family in a different way." As evidence that everyone saw them as "married" after the commitment ceremony, Theresa told me that when they told their families they were getting *legally* married over a decade later, her brother said, "I don't understand; I thought you got married years ago?!"

Similarly, Beth, a fifty-eight-year-old woman, had a "Holy Union wedding" in the mid-1990s, a year after she and her partner got together.[5] To her, "it [was] meant to say that we're going to stick together in this. I want to make my life with you." She understood that, at the time, a commitment ceremony was "still a very new thing" and knew that "some people were a little uncomfortable with it," but she ultimately believed that other people recognized it as a wedding and treated them as married afterward. She laughed as she told me, "At the end of the day a lot of straight friends came and the women from the church decorated for the reception, and we had a gay old time!" She also described the ceremony as having a profound impact on her sense of family belonging, explaining, "For vows, we chose to use Ruth 1:14. So, wherever you go, I will go. . . . Your people will be my people. . . . And when I said those vows, I felt like something in the universe, like a giant spiritual Rubik's cube had shifted and locked into place. I was connected to her and connected to her family, and she to mine."

On the one hand, people described their commitment ceremonies as "just like any other wedding" and described the traditional wedding rituals they embraced. On the other hand, some also recognized that there was something radical and political about the act. For example, Caroline, a thirty-five-year-old who had gotten together with her partner in the mid-1990s, had a Holy Union ceremony in 2000—four years before it was an option to marry legally. She described it in very traditional terms and thought it "meant what marriage would to anybody": a public celebration of love and commitment.

> It was a chance for our community, our friends, and our family to come together in a way that anybody comes together for any wedding—to celebrate love and to celebrate hopefully a lifetime of two people making a commitment

together. . . . You know, like you go to your cousins' weddings, your friends' weddings. It was just like that. There are bubbles, you blow them. You sing the songs. Somebody dings on the glass and you kiss. There's a registry. My aunt sent us a jar of her pickles. She's like, "Oh, she's getting married, she needs my pickles." So everybody knows what it means.

At the same time, however, she recognized that enacting marriage without the law was nontraditional, even radical: "It was a radical move to take this institution that's so traditional and to truly make it our own, to embrace the words and to embrace the traditions." Taking the cultural rituals of marriage and enacting them in the context of legal exclusion was, in some ways, an act of defiance—a statement that marriage belonged to them, and that they could claim it for themselves.

"WE WOULD HAVE DONE IT ANYWAY"

Although relatively few LGBQ people in this study actually enacted marriages by having a commitment ceremony, several more insisted that they would have gotten married through a commitment ceremony had the option to marry legally not become available to them. The only difference was timing. These tended to be somewhat younger LGBQ people. For example, Erin, a thirty-six-year-old woman, and her partner got together the year before same-sex marriage became legal and had started talking about weddings before they knew they would have the opportunity to ever do it legally.[6] She said:

> We never needed this to be legal to know we were going to do this. Our intention was to be married and have some kind of ceremony, and the legality was secondary. Whether you call it a wedding or a commitment ceremony, or whatever, we always knew we were going to do that.

Similarly, Maddy, a thirty-two-year-old, got engaged to her girlfriend the year before marriage became legal and emphasized that they had never regarded being able to do so legally as a necessary condition for getting married.

> I was always one that thought if you found the right person, whether it was legal or not, I'm going to somehow have some kind of a ceremony or something because it's something I wanted to do. I wanted everybody to share that love with me, just like they do for straight people. . . . It was about the ceremony and the sharing of the love with your family and friends, more so than just some priest or justice of the peace saying "You're married."

Maddy did not need an authority figure, religious or legal, to deem her married. She felt able to claim the rituals of marriage for herself and use them to celebrate her love and gain recognition from the people who mattered to her.[7]

A few participants expressed annoyance or dismay toward other LGBQ people who were only able to conceptualize marriage in the context of legality. Erin told me that it "bugs her" that now it was legal people only talk about marriage in those terms: "When I talk to people in other states, and they're like, 'Oh, so you got married because you can do that there,' I'm like, 'Actually, you can do that anywhere. It may not be recognized, but you can do it.'"

These Marriage Embracers who had, or would have had, a commitment ceremony assigned marriage varying cultural and social meanings, none of which depended on the law. As the cultural sociologist Kathleen Hull explains, same-sex couples believed they could use "rituals to fulfill some of the functions normally performed by legal recognition," thereby making "culture do the work that law would otherwise (supposedly) do."[8] Nevertheless, it is important to note that this group constituted only a small minority of the Marriage Embracers. A far greater number chose not to have a commitment ceremony, and, as I discuss later, this was in part because they did not believe that enacting the cultural rituals of marriage without legal support would help them achieve the kind of family and social status they desired.

The Closest Thing to Legal Marriage

Before full legal marriage, some states and local municipalities offered other legal, marriage-like statuses to same-sex couples. Some same-sex couples in Massachusetts could register as domestic partners as a means of gaining access to benefits typically reserved for married couples. Massachusetts did not recognize domestic partnerships at a state level, but, starting in 1992, several cities and towns offered them to residents.[9] They provided group health insurance benefits for domestic partners of municipal employees and their dependents at the municipalities' expense. Those who worked for employers that recognized domestic partnerships also stood to gain benefits, such as being able to add a partner onto health insurance plans, access sick and bereavement leave policies to care for partners, and claim accident and life insurance policies in the case of a partner's death.

Additionally, nearby Vermont became the first state to offer civil unions to same-sex couples in 2000, which allowed partners to declare one another as "reciprocal beneficiaries" and claim some limited state-level benefits typically reserved for married couples, such as rights to hospital visitation or to make medical decisions on their partner's behalf. Due to Vermont's close proximity to Massachusetts, some same-sex couples traveled there to take advantage of this right in the years before same-sex marriage became legal, though they stood to gain no tangible benefit from it, as civil unions were never recognized under Massachusetts state law.

Twenty-two people in this study had already entered into a domestic partnership or civil union with a same-sex partner prior to marriage becoming legal.[10] The longer a couple had been together, the more likely they were to have entered one of these marriage-like statuses.[11] No one younger than age thirty had had one.[12] The meanings Marriage Embracers attached to them and the ways they experienced them differed in important ways from commitment ceremonies. Most treated domestic partnerships and civil unions as private agreements between partners rather than wedding-like celebrations and did not invite others to attend.[13] They occupied a kind of intermediate status—neither clear cultural events like weddings nor clear legal statuses, offering only very limited benefits and recognition. Yet, because most Marriage Embracers did not expect legal marriage to occur, they thought of them as the closest approximation to the real thing they were likely to get.

Domestic partnerships were typically entered into simply to gain access to a specific benefit or protection that was otherwise denied to LGBQ couples. For example, Beth (quoted earlier, who had also had a commitment ceremony) simply said, "The first thing we did after moving here was get a domestic partnership in Cambridge, because that got me on her insurance." But, beyond the specific thing they were using the domestic partnership for, it usually had little meaning or significance for the couple's relationship. This helps explain why Patrick, a fifty-year-old who was with his partner fifteen years before marriage, could not remember or fathom why he and his partner had had one! He explained: "We did file a domestic partnership at the municipal level, which had almost no legal bearing. I'm trying to remember if there actually was some reason that we had done it. It's not like one of was trying to get on the other's insurance or something. I can't remember exactly what the point of that was. But there must have been some kind of benefit we gained. The domestic partnership was such a lightweight thing to do that it kind of slipped my mind that we'd even done it!" Like Patrick, most said that they would not have bothered unless they also actually stood to gain some tangible benefit from it.

The legal gains from domestic partnerships were so limited that sometimes they were not even immediate or fully tangible. Rather, they offered same-sex couples a more ambiguous sense that, because they were akin to marriage, they *might* help protect them and their families if they ever really needed it. Theresa, another participant who had a commitment ceremony, told me that she and her partner registered as domestic partners as a kind of insurance policy. She hoped that "it would've meant that if something happened to my son at school, [my partner] could get him or, god forbid, I thought that it would perhaps get me into a hospital if I had to." She wasn't sure if it would really help protect her and thankfully never needed to find out, but she had clung to the feeling of added security it offered. She confided that she still carries around with her the domestic partnership card they were given even though they are now legally married, just in case, suggesting the card came to symbolize a form of protection that she was reluctant to abandon even after she no longer needed it.

Civil unions were another kind of approximation of full legal marriage, the best legal status LGBQ people thought they could get at the time. However, these unions held even less clear meaning. Whereas commitment ceremonies were clearly understood as weddings and domestic partnerships as efforts to gain a legal benefit or protection, civil unions occupied a messier and more ambiguous space between the two. They offered fewer guaranteed legal gains than a domestic partnership because they were not recognized under Massachusetts state law. Yet civil unions also represented more of a commitment because they were harder to dissolve than a domestic partnership—though this fact was not always fully understood at the time of getting one.[14] Those that had civil unions simultaneously told me that they meant something *and* that they didn't mean that much.

Most often, civil unions were explained with reference to external validation and recognition. Unlike getting a domestic partnership, which required only a trip to a city clerk's office and completing some paperwork, civil unions needed to be officiated by a justice of the peace. Marriage Embracers understood that there was something powerful about having someone in authority deem them officially, legally, a committed couple. At the same time, they felt that seeking this kind of validation was a less legitimate or worthy reason for marriage than love or even gaining some tangible benefit. It was for this reason that Evan, a forty-seven-year-old man, recalled his civil union with a previous partner with some regret:

> When Vermont passed civil unions [my ex] and I went up and had a civil union.
> *What did that mean to you?*
> [*sighs*] I think at the time it was about wanting what everybody else [heterosexuals] could have and validating me, that my choices were as valid as everybody else's, which was kind of a shame because I didn't do it because we were madly in love and so I think we did it for the wrong reasons. It was really about the "I'm valid" and to say that I matter here and my choice in relationships matters.

Unfortunately, those who had civil unions often found them hard to explain to friends and family as well. They got validation in the moment from a justice of the peace but not necessarily afterward from anyone else. This resulted in the unfortunate reality that civil unions were entered into for the external validation but interactionally experienced as not validated by others.

Caroline's story encapsulates the kind of mixed feelings that accompanied civil unions. Although Caroline and her partner had already had a Holy Union wedding ceremony, they also decided to go to Vermont to get a civil union in 2001. They did not invite anyone else, but they saw it as an opportunity to get formally recognized and validated as a couple:

> We were like, "Civil unions? Ugh. It's not a true marriage." You know, you grow up and you dream about a wedding. You don't dream about your civil union in Vermont that's only good in one state. But on the other hand, it was the closest thing we had. And so at the time, even though we were Massachusetts citizens, we really wanted to go to Vermont and kind of, like, get counted, just, kind of legally to get our names out there. It was just a way that we could publicly declare our relationship, even just to each other. And we hung a copy of the civil union license up in our apartment.

She described the moment an authority figure recognized them as emotional and powerful:

> I cried so hard during the ceremony. I mean, to hear somebody say—even though it wasn't marriage, it was still the first time I had ever heard somebody say, "By the power vested in me by the state of Vermont, I pronounce you civilly unioned," or whatever; I don't even remember the exact words but it was still so powerful.

Nonetheless, Caroline felt ambivalence toward her civil union because she knew that it lacked both social and legal significance. On the social side, she explained that although they had told people they had done it, no one understood: "People don't know what the word[s] 'joined in civil union' mean, you know?" On the legal side, she said, "It wasn't worth the paper it was printed on, really," referring to the fact that "for it to be valid we would have had to live in Vermont."

This ambiguity and ambivalence surrounding the meaning of civil unions could also leave LGBQ people feeling unsure about how to enact one and socially awkward about the event. There were no clear cultural scripts guiding behavior in a civil union, as compared to a commitment ceremony (understood as a wedding) or a domestic partnership (understood as an administrative appointment). For example, Nora, a forty-two-year-old woman who had a civil union in Connecticut, where she lived at the time, described how her and her partner's attempts to include cultural symbols of marriage in the event, like rings, had felt awkward. "It wasn't a pleasant memory, actually. . . . I think in the parking lot of like the registry of deeds or whatever it is, [my partner] had given me [*laughs*] a ring [*laughs*], which was like the most unromantic thing ever. It was lovely, but it was unromantic." She explained that they had not known whether to do things like exchange rings or invite others to celebrate with them. And, in the midst of this uncertainty, she felt they made rash decisions, like exchanging rings in a parking lot, and inviting a random group of people to celebrate with them because they already happened to be coming over. Looking back, Nora concludes, "The whole thing was fine, but awful. I mean [*laughs*], like—it just didn't mean much."

Marriage Embracers who had participated in commitment ceremonies, domestic partnerships, and civil unions understood them as each offering access to different aspects of marriage, including public declarations of love and commitment, family recognition and inclusion, limited but important rights and benefits, and external, formal validation as a couple. At the time, they considered them the best means of accessing these marital benefits. But they were unable to obtain from any one of these alternative marriage options *all* the social and legal benefits marriage stands to offer. And having engaged in these alternative forms of marriage did not weaken their desire to legally marry once it became available. Below, I discuss why most Marriage Embracers still "rushed" to legally marry as soon as they could,[15] and what marriage meant to them once it became legal.

"Rushing" to Legally Marry

On the first day after same-sex marriage became legal in Massachusetts, major news outlets reported that same-sex couples were "rushing" to marry.[16] Many even paid additional fees to be able to waive the normal three-day waiting period and marry as quickly as was feasible. Yet the term "rushing" suggests that same-sex couples were not taking their time to make marriage decisions and that they were not yet ready to do so. In reality, this seeming "rush" to marry needs to be understood in a context in which many same-sex couples already had marriage-like commitments to one another or had already been planning to marry.

Of the twelve participants who had already had commitment ceremonies before it became legal, ten of these were still with the same partners by the time legal marriage became available, and eight of them legally married within a couple months of it becoming possible.[17] For example, Beth and her partner, who had had the big Holy Union ceremony in the mid-1990s, legally married as soon as they could in May 2004. She said the decision required no discussion, explaining, "I think we just knew we would get married." She was typical of this group in the way she articulated getting legally married as both obvious and inevitable, and requiring little conversation. They were "already married," so why not also make it legal?

Those who were already in marriage-like relationships offered three main reasons for quickly deciding to make it legal: wanting to be part of history and the first group of same-sex couples to legally marry, worrying that their rights might be taken away again, and feeling as if they had already waited a long time to get the legal recognition they deserved. After Caroline and her partner had their Holy Union ceremony in 2000, they started referring to one another as "wife" and regarded themselves as married. Yet Caroline wanted to line up with her partner to get their marriage license the first night legal same-sex marriages were offered. Her explanation captures all three reasons:

> I mean, we had a sense of the historical significance, so there was that personal feeling of "we want to be a part of this" and then there was the part that "they could take this away tomorrow" so we wanted to get it quick. But if was also just that we had already been married, we considered ourselves married for three years and we felt like we'd been waiting for three years to make it legal, but some couples had been waiting sixty years for this day.

Ricardo, a fifty-two-year-old, echoed a similar sense of urgency. He and his partner had already been together twenty-four years when marriage became legal. They had participated in the ACT UP marriage ceremony demonstrations in the 1980s, in which they had exchanged rings and said vows in a communal commitment ceremony.[18] They had "taken it seriously" as a marriage-like commitment and had already obtained a domestic partnership. Ricardo explained that, ideally, they would have wanted to wait another year so that they could get legally married on their twenty-fifth anniversary, but they did not feel they could take that risk, and so they married on Pride Day, four weeks after same-sex marriage became legal. Ricardo explained that they felt they "needed to move pretty quickly before Romney closed the door again" and felt "nervous with all of the political back-dooring."[19] Despite the rush, they were more than ready. There had not needed to be any discussion about whether to make their marriage legal. As Ricardo put it: "Marriage was just always what we had wanted."

How Legal Marriage Was Different

Though varying experiences with different meanings, what united commitment ceremonies, domestic partnerships, and civil unions was that none of them were equated with full legal marriage. I never heard any Marriage Embracers say that because they had already entered these other statuses, legal marriage was no longer necessary or desired. They had not waited around for legal marriage to enact marriage-like commitments, but neither did they eschew its significance when it became available. So how did those who had already had commitment ceremonies, domestic partnerships, and civil unions understand legal marriage as similar to and different from what they had already done? As I show next, what legal marriage meant to Marriage Embracers, and the ways in which they conceptualized it as distinctive, largely depended on what forms of alternative marriage practices they had already engaged in.

ANOTHER MARRIAGE, THE SAME THING

Comparing commitment ceremonies and legal marriages, it is clear both types of marriage were motivated by much the same driving force, namely, a desire, even a need, to publicly declare and celebrate love and commitment. This makes sense—if one embraces marriage for its cultural power to demonstrate love and commitment, then why not take the opportunity to do so again when it becomes legal? Ann had already had a commitment ceremony and civil union with a previous partner, and the experience of that painful breakup had left her somewhat reluctant to ever marry again. Yet she and her new partner of two years decided to legally marry after a health crisis put her partner in the hospital. This was not because of any need for legal benefits, but because it prompted an emotional response in Ann and stirred up the same needs and desires she had always felt—to be connected to her partner through marriage. Ann explained, "Emotionally, it was like the same thing [as when I had married before], like I had to have this. I had to have a public ceremony. It was just the same. It came from somewhere that was not talking through my brain." It was not a rational decision made because of a need for legal rights or benefits, but rather a deeply felt and long held emotional need for marriage. This time around, marriage just happened to be legal.

Although those who had already had commitment ceremonies wanted to publicly declare their love and commitment again when they legally married, many were content with smaller, less formal celebrations. Ann and her partner "did not do wedding dresses or a church or anything like that," opting instead to have a more "informal celebration" with friends. Importantly, a big wedding felt less necessary due to the fact it was legal; she explained, "This time we had the law, so I didn't have to come up with a ceremony. We were going to have this legal marker, and that was the function of it for me." The legality of the marriage lessened the need for a large ceremony because the law publicly declared them a married couple in the same way a wedding ceremony had before it was legal. Legal and cultural dimensions of marriage ultimately served the same function, offering public recognition of commitment. In a similar way, Theresa, who legally married a decade after having a big commitment ceremony, described the wedding she and her partner had for their legal marriage as "more of a formality." She said, "We wanted to celebrate it, we wanted it to be public," but "we went for much more of [a] simple backyard ceremony with no music or anything, just vows." This was both because a big wedding seemed less necessary to her now it was legal and because they had already done one before.

Regardless of the size or nature of the wedding or celebration, those who had already had commitment ceremonies tended to conceptualize their legal marriages as extensions of the marriages they already had—more like a renewal of vows than something completely new. Tricia, a sixty-two-year-old woman, and her partner had had a commitment ceremony four years into their relationship, just a year before marriage became legal. She had heard rumors that legal marriage might be in the works but because she had not believed it would ever happen, she and her partner had gone ahead with their commitment ceremony. When same-sex marriage became legal just a year later, they still wanted to legally marry and had another big ceremony to celebrate. However, she insisted that their "real" wedding anniversary was the date they had had the commitment ceremony, and they continued to celebrate that rather than the date of their legal marriage. In her mind, legal marriage did not replace her commitment ceremony, but rather added on to and merged with it. This was also evident in the way she organized her wedding photographs. The two events were so connected in her mind that when she showed me her wedding photos, they were all mixed together, and she sometimes had to think about which event was which. Respondents' conceptualization of legal marriage as an extension of their preexisting marriages was further represented by the fact that several people made decisions to wear the same outfits or use the same vows for both events. These were conscious decisions to symbolically connect their commitment ceremonies and legal marriages together as different stages of the same union.

At the same time, those who had already had commitment ceremonies sometimes also saw their legal marriages as opportunities to enact new symbolic or ritual elements of marriage that they hadn't included in their weddings the first time around. Legal marriage was a way to take their preexisting marriages to a new level or to enact new symbolic gestures in celebration of them. Some, like Theresa, used the opportunity to get "ring upgrades," as she had never had a diamond before, but made sure to wear both the wedding ring from her commitment ceremony and the new one. Others stressed the symbolic importance of switching their rings from their right to their left hands upon marriage.[20] Some, like Tricia, saw it as a chance to add a religious dimension to their marriages because they had not married in a place of worship for their commitment ceremonies and wanted to use legal marriage as a chance to celebrate with their religious communities. Tricia and her wife also decided to change their names when they legally married, something that they had not done before and was now much easier. In these myriad ways, legal marriage was conceptualized both as an extension of the marital unions they already had and as an opportunity to include additional symbolic or cultural marriage practices in the event. Put simply, for these Marriage Embracers, legal marriage was a chance to embrace more marriage experiences.

TWO KEY DIFFERENCES: LEGAL RIGHTS AND SOCIAL RECOGNITION

Conceptualizing their legal marriages as extensions of their preexisting marriages did not mean that LGBQ people who had already had commitment ceremonies understood legality as irrelevant or unimportant; it was just that legality was not typically the basis for how they thought or spoke about their decisions to legally marry. Once they were legally married, though, they identified two key ways in which legal marriage was qualitatively different from their commitment ceremonies. The first, and most obvious, was the importance of having access to rights and protections as a couple. Caroline argued:

> We had only been married [through the Holy Union ceremony] a couple years when marriage actually became legal. We married because we love each other, that's the main reason, and we wouldn't have got married just to be married. But at the same time the benefits part can get left out of these discussions. You know, when you're legally married you have a right to visit in the hospital when they're ill, you have a right to inherit certain things, you have a right to adopt jointly. There are all these rights that you have that you don't have when you're just [*pauses, trying to think of the words*] a couple of partners.

Legal benefits and protections may not have been at the heart of why they legally married, but they were certainly important and appreciated. Beth put it this way: "Whatever else, it was important to get legally married too because we've commingled our lives and finances. And what goddamned little we have I want to protect. You know?"

It's important to recall that although alternative marriage statuses, such as domestic partnerships and civil unions, offered only partial access to legal marriage benefits, so too did marriage when it first became legal. Until the Defense of Marriage Act was overturned in June 2013, married same-sex couples had access only to state-level benefits, meaning that the legal gains from marriage were in fact relatively limited for the first nine years. That 68 percent of all resident same-sex couples in Massachusetts had legally married by 2010[21] despite not having access to federal marriage benefits is telling. For some, although legal gains were limited, they were still appreciated and necessary. They married to get health insurance or visitation rights, for example, even though they knew it would not help them with estate planning or federal taxes. But for most, tangible rights and protections did not matter as much as the intangible cultural gains they expected from marriage—specifically, greater social recognition and legitimacy as a married couple.

Social recognition and legitimacy were key distinctions made between commitment ceremonies and legal marriage. Most felt their commitment ceremonies had been successful at gaining them greater acceptance and recognition as a couple from their families. But those events had not helped them achieve broader social status or legitimacy as a married couple. Only legal marriage had the power to do that. Theresa told me:

> I don't think it changed much as far as family was concerned because they had already seen us as married from the other wedding, but as far as being in public and being able to say "I'm married," well we weren't sure it was going to make any difference, but it did actually make us feel different. Just because it's legal now, it's more acceptable.

This distinction between family and social recognition was echoed by many others. Caroline expressed it astutely when she commented that whereas their Holy Union had been "for their families and the two of us," the "legal marriage felt like it was for all LGBT people." Being legally married made LGBQ people feel equal and included on a broader societal level in a way that a commitment ceremony could not have. Like others, Caroline described it as "feeling like we could hold our heads up high," and not having to worry so much about holding her wife's hand, or calling her "wife" in public. She said, "We know we've been equal the whole time, but now we are legally married, everyone knows it. It's unbelievable what a difference that makes."[22]

FINALLY, A WEDDING, WITH FAMILY

So far, I have only been discussing how those who already had commitment ceremonies understood and experienced legal marriage. Those who had already had domestic partnerships or civil unions but no prior commitment ceremony differed in their reactions to gaining access to legal marriage. The primary difference was that, for the most part, they had not already had a wedding nor ever celebrated their marital commitments publicly with others. Because their domestic partnerships and civil unions had been private, or very small, events, legal marriage represented an opportunity to finally have a celebration with family.[23] Whereas domestic partnerships and civil unions had primarily been about gaining some legal protections or benefits, or being formally recognized by an authority figure, legal marriages were more centrally about public celebrations of commitment. Those who had already had domestic partnerships and civil unions, but not commitment ceremonies, therefore typically took a little longer to legally marry because they wanted to plan weddings—tending to get legally married within the first year rather than first few weeks or months of it becoming legal.

When I asked Patrick why he wanted to get legally married to his partner of fifteen years once it became available, he acknowledged the legal gains but focused on the opportunity to make a public commitment and gain recognition from family and friends.

> The [added] legal protection, I definitely see value in that. But it was also the social thing that—I mean, I was never sure how far in my extended family people knew about it [my sexuality]; there are lots of cousins and aunts and uncles that I very rarely see, maybe once a decade sort of thing. So certainly, throwing a wedding and inviting the whole family is one way to make sure everyone knows. [*laughs*]

Patrick got out his wedding album for me to look at while we continued talking. Showing me photos of his family, he told me that he and his partner waited about a year to get legally married because they "were concerned about getting family in from out of town and wanted to make sure that everyone could make it." His focus on the importance of having family celebrate with them was also clear when he explained that although he and his partner had both visited one another's families, their families had never actually met one another before. Legal marriage empowered them to have a wedding and make new family connections.

Bill, a sixty-one-year-old man, and his partner had been together for seventeen years before legally marrying, and they had already had a civil union in Vermont four years before legal marriage became available. But they had not invited anyone else to celebrate that with them. Having a more formal wedding and sharing their marriage with family was therefore key for them when they got legally married. As Bill put it,

> I think [the legal marriage] was just to have that solid commitment and the family piece. It was the family really. I think [my partner's] family in particular, his sisters got married and he wanted to have a wedding like they had. He

wanted the prime rib and he wanted the pasta dishes, so we had it in a church and it was done really, really well. We had the limo and went out and did all the pictures around a pond. Tuxedos. . . . I think the family being there was a big one for him. It was good for me too.

Thus, for Marriage Embracers who had already had a domestic partnership or civil union but no commitment ceremony, legal marriage offered them not only additional legal protections and benefits, but also a chance to gain family recognition and legitimacy in a way that had not seemed possible before.[24]

What legal marriage meant to Marriage Embracers depended in part on what forms of alternative marriage practices they had already engaged in. Those who had commitment ceremonies tended to discuss legal marriage as a way to add on legal rights and social recognition, while those who had domestic partnerships and civil unions tended to see it as a way to add on family recognition. In this way, legal marriage was a package deal, offering all dimensions of marriage and allowing Marriage Embracers to embrace it for whatever aspects of marriage they still needed and desired.

However, the meaning of legal marriage also depended, in part, on one's life-stage when gaining access to it. A couple of people who had already participated in other legal marriage-like statuses ultimately decided those were enough and did not add any kind of celebration for their legal marriages. For example, despite Nora's dissatisfaction with her previous civil union experience and the fact they had not invited family to celebrate it, by the time marriage became legal she experienced no real need for a do-over. Rather than "rushing to marry," she felt little need to do so at all. In a legal twist of fate, she and her partner moved to Massachusetts from Connecticut in 2009 right around the time that the Connecticut legislature decided to automatically convert all civil unions into legal marriages.[25] This meant that her civil union automatically became a legal marriage, and no further action was required. Though they could have planned a wedding to celebrate the transition, they decided not to. In fact, she recalled that all she and her wife had done to celebrate was "give each other a high five" and "make a funny Facebook post about it!" She explained, "By that point, we were six years into parenting and that's what our lives were all about. It becomes less about you and more about your commitment to your kids. We have a great relationship, but our relationship is very much about our kids now." Though they had never experienced a wedding, and Nora had previously wanted one, by the time same-sex marriage became legal their lives had moved on. In this way, legal same-sex marriage allowed some Marriage Embracers to have the kind of wedding they had always wanted but came too late for others whose priorities had shifted to other things.[26]

Bringing Marriage to Life

The Marriage Embracer group also includes LGBQ people who had always wanted to marry prior to same-sex marriage becoming legal but had not, and probably would not have, gone so far as to actually enact marriage through a commitment ceremony or alternative legal status before legal marriage became available. They imagined getting married and aspired to it. They talked about marriage regularly with their partners and others. Seven of them also followed the cultural script and marital practice of exchanging rings as a sign of personal commitment to one another. Not being able to legally marry did not stop them from fully embracing the cultural *idea* of marriage. Yet, unlike those who had already entered alternative marital statuses, this group needed legal recognition to transform marriage from an idea or symbolic gesture into a lived reality—something they would actually do.

NOT SETTLING FOR SECOND-CLASS STATUS

Negative feelings toward other marriage options partially explain why these Marriage Embracers did not act on their marital desires and get married before it became legal. Those that had commitment ceremonies, domestic partnerships, and civil unions had accepted whatever form of marriage was available at the time, using them to gain some dimension of marriage but knowing it was far from perfect. By contrast, these other Marriage Embracers refused to settle for anything less than full, legal marriage. They had considered commitment ceremonies but concluded that they felt "second-rate" or "not real" and so did not want to get married that way.[27] Harriet, a sixty-four-year-old who had been with her partner thirty-one years before getting married, recalled having once "toyed" with the idea of a commitment ceremony after going to one, but then changing her mind upon further reflection:

> But for me the commitment ceremony, which was held in an Episcopal church, was claustrophobic. I thought, "This is tragic. These two people have been together all this time, and their church where they are so active and so loyal won't recognize their right to marry." And I just thought, "I will never settle for that."

For Harriet, her friend's commitment ceremony ultimately represented settling for something less than the real thing.

Many also bemoaned the lack of equality and the second-class citizenship status that civil unions symbolized. Talia, a forty-seven-year-old who had been with her partner eight years before marriage, felt insulted by the option of civil unions. To her, they felt like someone saying, "We'll give you the legal rights, but don't call it marriage, because that taints our experience of our own relationship; you can't have that label, it's too good for you." These Marriage Embracers understood that there is a "hierarchy to marriage" and had not wanted to accept anything other than the real thing.[28]

MAKING MARRIAGE TANGIBLE

Negative feelings about other marriage options offer only a partial explanation for why it took full legal marriage for large numbers of same-sex couples to actually marry. Even those who felt less negatively found themselves making much faster and easier decisions to marry once it became a legal option. It was as if marital desires that had lain dormant immediately sprang to life once they became a legal option. Matt, a forty-two-year-old, had gotten together with his partner in the early 1990s and they had started talking about marriage almost right away. He told me, "Marriage was definitely always part of the discussion for sure. We had talked about having a commitment ceremony years before gay marriage was ever a blip on the cultural radar." They had talked about "where we would do it and who would be invited and what kind of format it would have." Yet they "just never really sort of got around to it." This was not because of any antipathy Matt felt toward commitment ceremonies. He did not really know why they hadn't already married, but listed several possible reasons, including his "disillusionment with the Catholic Church" (eliminating the option of having a church wedding), that they "got busy with other things," and "that they didn't have a lot of money to have a big party." And so, he said, "Marriage was just kind of on hold." Yet when marriage became legal all those reasons not to do it immediately disappeared, and they "just knew" that they "had to do this as soon as possible."

Gaining access to legal marriage also prompted Hannah, a thirty-nine-year-old woman, to take more definitive action on her marriage plans. She and her partner were together seven years before marriage became legal. They had already "talked about the possibility of having some sort of commitment ceremony" and had even started to meet with rabbis to see if they could find one who would marry them. But their plans were still "all very vague and unformed." In fact, when a rabbi had congratulated them on their engagement Hannah's reaction had been to ask her partner, "Are we engaged?" Laughing at herself, she recognized that "obviously if you're showing up to a rabbi to talk about the possibility of getting married, they assume you're engaged!" Yet she admitted that she had been unsure about their status. Gaining access to legal marriage made what they were doing clearer and helped them more formally "decide to do this":

> I definitely think that the timing of marriage equality helped solidify that, clarify it. I guess having access to it sort of changes your perception of what the options are. I mean, I know some couples have commitment ceremonies anyway, but you know, then you're totally kind of creating your own thing and it's very clear it's different, whereas now you [think], "Oh, it's legal, you could do it."

Like Hannah, lots of Marriage Embracers described their marriage plans before it was legal as "unclear" and "uncertain." When it became legal, marriage became more "concrete," "defined," and "solidified." Legalization certainly did not introduce the idea of marriage to them, but it did make it seem like a more tangible option.

Cultural sociologist Ann Swidler's analyses of the way in which people draw on culture help explain why it took legal marriage to catalyze marital action among many Marriage Embracers. She suggests that people have cultural ideas "on file" as parts of their repertoire of knowledge and experience, or cultural imaginations, but that they only draw on them when an appropriate situation arises.[29] Here, the appropriate situation was being able to marry legally. They could have married in some other way, but legal marriage made getting married seem like a more real option, helping them turn their marital aspirations and plans into action. As Swidler so aptly puts it, "Institutions, or the capacity for action that institutions create, may help make ideas real."[30] It was much easier to enact marriage in the context of legality because it provided greater certainty and clarity about exactly what they were doing.

TAKING LOVE AND COMMITMENT TO THE NEXT LEVEL

The option to marry legally did not prompt these Marriage Embracers to marry because they needed the incentive of legal benefits or rights; rather, legal marriage catalyzed marital decision-making because it cemented the relationship between marriage, love, and commitment. Like others, Matt and his partner (who just "never got around to getting married" until it was legal) attributed their decision to marry to "love."[31] He and his partner were both lawyers and well aware of the legal benefits and protections they would gain from legal marriage. Yet these were not the deciding factor:

> I'd say that it [legal benefits] was a factor, but it wasn't *the* factor. I mean, I wanted to get married of course because I was in love with him. A lot of it was

that like giddy silliness of just wanting to be with this guy forever and ever, and that was the main overriding thing for sure.

This might seem counterintuitive: if love was a primary reason for getting married, why did it need to be legal for these Marriage Embracers to do it? As already discussed, negative feelings toward alternative marital options offer a partial explanation for their prior reluctance to marry. But they also perceived legal marriage as offering the truest, most tangible expression of love and commitment. However much they already loved their partners and however committed they already were to them, the only available cultural script still upheld legal marriage as the real deal—the strongest form of love and commitment one could participate in. Not ever believing they would have access to legal marriage, Marriage Embracers did not wait for it in order to fully love or commit to their partners, but they had still internalized the script.[32]

Robert, fifty-one, and his partner had met in the early 1990s, dated for a while, and then split up. They got back together in 2000, adopted a son, and legally married in 2004. Explaining why they had wanted to get legally married, Robert said:

> It really shows total commitment, and it's more binding. It's more of a relationship. Of course, we also wanted to do it because we had a son, and we owned property together and that kind of thing. We just wanted to make it legal all around. But [it was] really to further cement our relationship.

Here Robert acknowledges that there are legal gains from marriage, but stresses instead that legal marriage gave them a way of demonstrating commitment in a more total, binding way. Many others spoke about the ways in which legal marriage represented a distinct kind of love and commitment. Legal marriage was not regarded as just one way of showing love or commitment among many equal possibilities; rather, it was the ultimate show of these things. Steven, a thirty-six-year-old who had been with his partner nine years before legally marrying him, described it as "kind of like in education with a terminal degree—it's your terminal relationship status and you can't go any higher than that."

Conclusion

The experiences of Marriage Embracers reveal, or at least remind us of, something that has become harder to see in a post same-sex marriage world: that as an institution, marriage had the power to shape same-sex relationships even when they were excluded from it. Even before same-sex marriage was legalized, many LGBQ people had already internalized cultural scripts about what marriage meant and was capable of. It had already taken on a wide range of cultural meanings for same-sex couples, including as a romantic ideal to aspire to, a public celebration and demonstration of commitment, a means of partaking in cultural and religious traditions, a way of gaining recognition and support from family and friends, and an avenue for forming new family connections and relationships. At a regulatory level, marriage also already had institutional power through the availability of domestic partnerships and civil unions. These represented the closest legal status LGBQ people thought they would ever get to the "real thing," a means of obtaining some of the rights and protections typically reserved for married couples, a kind of insurance policy for obtaining social recognition as a couple and family if ever there was a need for it, and a means of having some legal authority, such as a justice of the peace, declare their relationship legitimate.

The institutional power of marriage only grew with legalization. Despite the wide-ranging sources of power marriage already had prior to legalization, Marriage Embracers recognized the distinctiveness of legal marriage. They were acutely aware that only legal marriage combined all the cultural, social, and legal possibilities of marriage as a package deal; with legal marriage, they could have it all. The cultural scripts they had already internalized also felt more real and achievable with the weight of the law behind them. Only legal marriage could help these already committed couples gain widespread social recognition and legitimacy as a married couple. Only full legal marriage offered them access to the most culturally understood, recognized, and valued form of love and commitment. As the sociologist Kathleen Hull argued in her theory of law as an influential cultural structure: "The law of the state has a unique cultural force that paradoxically both transcends and connects with the specific rights, benefits, and protections afforded by legal marriage."[33] In these ways, the power of marriage as an institution is both old and new, existing before legalization and growing with it.

Looking at the experiences of Marriage Embracers before same-sex marriage became legal, we see LGBQ people displaying both freedom from the law and reliance on it. They had the ability to use the institution of marriage consciously and selectively to try to gain personal and social benefits from it, but they also relied on the law to bring marriage to life and make it feel like a real possibility, with more concrete, cultural meaning and significance. We see both agency and constraint, with strategic uses of marriage before and after legalization as well as a deeply ingrained reliance on marriage in their relationships.

As we will continue to see in the next two chapters, there is no one "gaining marriage" story. Marriage Embracers experienced legal marriage in diverse ways, assigning it varying meanings, because they had already conceptualized and integrated marriage into their relationships differently. Some of them saw themselves as already married and legal marriage as an extension of what they already had, while others experienced their marital desires springing to life and feeling achievable for the first time in the context of legal marriage. And the meaning and significance of legal marriage varies further when we consider other groups of LGBQ people, whom I call Marriage Rejecters (chapter 2) and Marriage Assumers (chapter 3). Each group helps to illuminate the complex, multifaceted ways marriage works as an institution, and the power of legal marriage to reshape same-sex relationships.

2

Marriage Rejecters

Navigating the Pulls of Marriage

When I met Tamryn, a twenty-nine-year-old woman, for our interview, she wanted to assert her rejection of marriage quickly, just in case I had misunderstood her willingness to participate in the study as indicating support for the institution of marriage. Rather abruptly, she said, "I think I should tell you that I have a lot of ambivalence about marriage. It just doesn't make sense to me that we would want to make our relationships look like heteronormative relationships, which are fraught with problems." Tamryn explained the "ambivalence" she felt toward marriage as having emerged from a long-standing engagement in queer politics, both in college and afterward, and her sense of belonging and involvement with communities of "other radical queer women." For her, the political and personal practice of being queer was fundamentally at odds with the institution of marriage. She used the term "partner" throughout the interview and was not wearing a wedding ring (something she told me she would "never do" because it was a "patriarchal symbol of ownership"). As such, the casual observer would likely have assumed Tamryn was not married. Yet Tamryn was, in fact, legally married.

Bob, a forty-nine-year-old gay man, also wanted to emphasize that he rejected marriage, but he did so on different grounds than Tamryn. Whereas Tamryn rejected the idea of marriage as an institution that any queer person should want to be a part of, Bob rejected the idea that he and his partner of eleven years needed marriage to be committed to one another. He said, "The marriage thing, I just don't think it matters for us. We love each other. We've clearly already committed our lives to each other. And we managed to do that in the midst of society telling us to fuck off. I can't get too excited about society now saying 'OK, you're all right.' Personally, for us, we don't need marriage." But, like Tamryn, Bob was also legally married. Why did Tamryn and Bob, and others, espouse rejection of marriage but end up getting legally married anyway? Why did their marital actions depart from their beliefs and feelings toward marriage? And how did they reconcile and live with this disconnect? These are the questions and puzzles at the heart of this chapter.

Tamryn and Bob both belong to the group of LGBQ participants I call Marriage Rejecters. In the last chapter, I focused on Marriage Embracers—those LGBQ people who had already aspired to or enacted marriage before it was a legal possibility. But not all LGBQ people desired marriage, or even cared much about it; some outright disdained it. Marriage Rejecters rejected marriage as unnecessary, undesirable, or even inappropriate for their relationships. Rejecters had completely different feelings about marriage than Embracers and were therefore positioned to experience marriage very differently when it became legal. But they were not necessarily freer from its institutional power. Comparing across groups allows us to see the diverse, yet equally powerful, ways marriage shapes the lives of LGBQ people.

Of the 116 people who took part in this study, 28 were Marriage Rejecters. Their stories and experiences are important for understanding the complex interplay of agency and structure in marital experiences. Whatever they might have thought or felt about marriage, their ideas and feelings did not occur in a social and cultural vacuum. Marriage Rejecters had to grapple with the same social and cultural forces and pressures around marriage as anyone else, and many were ultimately pulled into, or at least toward, the institution they rejected: half got legally married, and many others thought they were "likely" to do so in the future. They were pulled into marriage through a range of instrumental, normative, and cultural mechanisms. Disinterest in, even disdain for, marriage proved no match for its institutional power.

The experiences of Marriage Rejecters also help illuminate the ongoing mental labor involved in gaining access to legal marriage and the work involved in resigning oneself to the power that it has over one's relationships and lives. For all the groups described in this book, marriage is a form of work. The Marriage Embracers described in chapter 1 did the work of reimagining their long-standing preexisting relationships after marriage became legal and of combining the many cultural and legal dimensions of their marriages together. The Marriage Assumers described in the next chapter engaged in the work of preparing and planning marriage and of carefully adhering to narrow marriage scripts. The Marriage Rejecters in this chapter did the work of coming to terms with entering an institution they previously wanted little to do with and of grappling with the power that it had over their lives and the lives of LGBQ people more generally. This marriage work was ongoing and challenging more than a decade after marriage had become legal.

It might be tempting to lump all Marriage Rejecters together under the category of marriage haters. But that would be an oversimplification. Marriage Rejecters were a varied group. They rejected marriage to differing degrees and in differing ways. Broadly speaking, there were two distinct groups of Marriage Rejecters. As I describe below, Bob represents what I term Personal Marriage Rejecters, while Tamryn represents Intellectual Marriage Rejecters—each rejected marriage on different grounds. As I will show, there is also variation in the reasons some Marriage Rejecters ultimately decided to marry, with Rejecters being pulled into marriage through different social, cultural, and relational mechanisms. Moreover, there is clearly much variation in the ways Marriage Rejecters felt about being pulled into and toward marriage, with some being able to move from rejection to marriage relatively easily, while others continued to actively struggle with the decision.

Personal Marriage Rejecters: "Been There, Done That, in Other Ways"

At first glance, this subset of Marriage Rejecters could sound like the Marriage Embracers described in chapter 1. Like Embracers, most had already sustained long-term, committed relationships prior to gaining access to legal marriage, and they were relatively older than the Assumers described in the next chapter (at least in their forties, but often in their fifties or older). Like Marriage Embracers, they had also never imagined that they would have access to legal marriage in their lifetimes. For example, Bob said, "I never even thought about marriage! I grew up into my thirties, I guess even into my forties, never thinking that such a thing would really be possible. I come from a different time where it's just kind of—that wasn't expected or possible." However, whereas Marriage Embracers still cared deeply about marriage and found ways to embrace it without legal access and recognition, Personal Marriage Rejecters rejected marriage as unimportant for their own personal relationships. They rejected the widely held cultural belief that marriage would represent a distinct or higher level of relationship commitment between them and their partners. Instead, they conceptualized meaningful commitment as possible outside of a marital model. In fact, they were proud of the relationships they and their partners had created and sustained together, and they could not imagine how getting married would strengthen what was already a solid and secure commitment.[1]

Recall from chapter 1 that Marriage Embracers who had commitment ceremonies felt "already married" before getting legally married. No Marriage Rejecters had participated in a commitment ceremony, yet many of them also already felt "essentially married." But whereas Marriage Embracers felt this way because they had had a wedding-like ceremony, these Marriage Rejecters felt already married because they believed that the kind of commitment they had created was equal to, and essentially the same, as any marriage. For example, Dennis, a fifty-three-year-old unmarried man who had been with his partner for thirteen years said, "I think marriage *is* the sense of commitment. We have almost what you would consider a marriage. We just don't have the public declaration." In his mind, because they were committed, they were for all intents and purposes essentially married. Others also emphasized that it does not take a legal bond or wedding ritual to create a marriage; commitment itself makes a marriage.

As I will discuss, many Marriage Rejecters did ultimately end up getting legally married. But they rejected the idea that their relationships needed legal marriage, and they were very careful to emphasize this point. Bob described his partner and himself as "happily married before we were officially married." He said, "We've done this on our own, and it's *our* commitment. It's our world, in a way." Jenn, a forty-one-year-old who had been with her partner sixteen years before marrying her, put it this way: "We were essentially married already. We felt like the commitment was already there. People say that breaking up is so much harder once you're married, but breaking up had never crossed our minds; it wasn't a consideration anyway." Jenn wanted to stress that same-sex couples in long-term relationships did not need institutional barriers to breaking up. No specter of divorce was needed for them to stick things out. In fact, to her, it was their preexisting sense of commitment that explained why they had "waited so long to actually legally get married." This idea is borne out in the survey data as well. The longer LGBQ people in this study had been with their partners, the less importance they placed on getting legally married.[2]

Yet this insistence on not needing marriage to be committed was also a response to institutional exclusion. Many Personal Marriage Rejecters also emphasized that they had maintained committed relationships while being *denied* access to marriage. Because they had succeeded in a context of institutional exclusion, the cultural idea that marriage symbolized the highest or most sincere form of commitment was offensive. Thus, their rejection of the idea that they needed marriage stemmed both from a celebration of their ability to create successful relationships outside a marital model and a more visceral reaction resulting from being excluded from the institution for so long. Terrence, a fifty-one-year-old unmarried man who had been with his partner for twenty-five years, exclaimed, "We were so committed anyway we didn't need that extra piece of commitment. We were both like, 'Damn it, all these years we weren't allowed to get married and we have this really committed relationship. Why do we need it now?'" Terrence laughed as he admitted, "It's funny because we want to celebrate in terms of having the right, but it's also like we're a little pissed about it too."

Just because they rejected marriage as unimportant for their own personal relationships, Personal Marriage Rejecters did not reject marriage wholesale as an institution. This is what distinguishes them from the Intellectual Marriage Rejecters I describe next. Personal Marriage Rejecters often spoke simultaneously about the importance of marriage for *other* LGBQ people or for LGBQ people more *generally*, alongside its unimportance for themselves. Dennis considered it this way:

> I mean, in a way I still think of marriage as a kind of blessing. If we were to change our mind tomorrow and decide we want to have a nice big gathering marriage out in the backyard, then we should have the right to do that. So even though we may not partake of it, I think it should be a right that I should have. And so, do I feel like marriage has had any impact on me or my relationship? No! But I hope it does for other people!

Similarly, although Terrence maintained that "marriage just didn't feel important" for him and his partner, he said that it "felt amazing to know that you could do it if you wanted to" and described how happy he had been for his friends who had wanted to marry. Likewise, Judy, a fifty-year-old woman who had been with her partner for seventeen years, "never had bride dreams" herself and rejected marriage as irrelevant for her own relationship. Yet she wanted to make clear: "Certainly for the people who were doing it, I was really happy for them. It's just that no matter how happy I was for other people, I definitely didn't think, 'Oh, should I get married now?!' I mean, we felt so married anyway."

Personal Marriage Rejecters sometimes also made a generational distinction, seeing marriage as something more important for younger generations of LGBQ people than for their generation.[3] Ted, a fifty-one-year-old man who had been with his partner for twenty-two years, put it this way:

> Part of it, for me, feels like a generation divide where I sort of sit between two generations. I think the issue is how we approach relationships. The decision to marry is a different one for folks like us where we have been together for so long in a non–marriage equality world that it's just a whole different thing. I think we really just don't feel it applies to us. We have a relationship where marriage isn't going to bring anything or take away anything. I mean, we would have to put some energy into it, and it's not where we want to put our energy. As opposed to a younger couple today where the solemnification

of things through marriage is more front and center, you know? We've been there, done that in other ways.

Ted conceptualized marriage as a particular "approach" to relationships that felt more difficult to integrate mid-way through or later on in the progression of a relationship; it was something that seemed less necessary the longer one had sustained a relationship without it.

Other Personal Marriage Rejecters also spoke about legal marriage as coming too late in their relationships to make much difference for them personally but as something they could completely understand making a huge difference for younger LGBQ people. Bob described marriage as "a legacy to the coming generations of young gays and lesbians." Though he was personally disinterested in marriage, he felt glad to have been able to witness legal marriage in his lifetime, even going so far as to say that the challenges he had faced being gay by not having access to legal marriage now felt more meaningful knowing that other, younger, LGBQ people would not have to experience them.

> Whatever real discomfort and challenge I had to go through in my life, and so many other gays and lesbians have had to go through in their lives, I just feel like that has been a big purpose in my life to just witness marriage. It's given my life a lot of purpose, which otherwise, I would think, wow, why did I have to go through that much pain and suffering just because of this inborn tendency. At least now I can kind of, at almost fifty years of age, I can look back and say yeah, take a big sigh, [sighs] wow. That was hard to go through, but we've come out the other side, and things are going to be better for gays and lesbians from now on.

Marriage gave Bob "a lot of hope" that younger LGBQ people would not face the same kind of discrimination that people in his generation had.

James, an unmarried fifty-seven-year-old man, who had been with his partner for seven years, also personally rejected marriage for his own relationship even though he was supportive of marriage equality for other, younger, same-sex couples. He explained, "I'm very old school, having been around in the earlier days, and been in that world when only straight people got married and marriage was not a gay thing. It was something that straight people did, and we had our own way of having relationships." Yet he thought that marriage made much more sense for younger LGBQ people whose relationships he perceived as already looking and functioning more like heterosexual ones. "I would definitely be in a different frame of mind [about getting married] if I was younger, or if I wanted to have children. Marriage is for the younger generations," he said.

Intellectual Marriage Rejecters

Personal Marriage Rejecters had all experienced long-term committed relationships without having access to legal marriage and felt strongly that they did not need marriage to be committed to their partners. Intellectual Marriage Rejecters were a more varied group with regard to relationship duration and age, and they rejected marriage on different terms: not only as unnecessary for their personal relationships, but also as undesirable; and not only for them personally but for *all* same-sex couples. I call them Intellectual Marriage Rejecters because they rejected marriage on intellectual grounds, citing theoretical critiques of marriage—as patriarchal, hierarchical, oppressive, and heteronormative. They tended to be people who had been exposed, either during college or in their communities, to a more radical form of queer politics that had challenged existing norms for expected couple and family relationships.

Today, "queer" is an umbrella term used to encompass a range of sexual and gender identities that fall outside heterosexual norms, but queer politics is characterized most fundamentally as anti-assimilationist—representing a desire not to fit into mainstream heterosexual culture and instead advocating for new ways to restructure society.[4] The mantra "We're here, we're queer, get used to it" has been used as a rallying cry in queer movements to epitomize the idea that queer people must boldly challenge and disrupt existing structures and ideas.[5] The fight for legal marriage rights raised a number of concerns among queer scholars, but many focused on the idea of normalization:[6] the process by which heteronormative models of behavior (including, but not limited to, marriage, monogamy, and childrearing) would come to be seen as increasingly normal and desirable to LGBTQ+ people, undermining the potential of queer politics. Queer scholars and activists worried that same-sex marriage signaled what the theorist Lisa Duggan refers to as "the new homonormativity:" that it would establish the dominance of a heterosexual norm even within the lives of LGBTQ+ people, mark "the final assimilation of LGBT people into mainstream culture," and "sound the death knell of LGBT/queer culture."[7]

The Intellectual Marriage Rejecters expressed some version of these scholarly and activist critiques that they had learned from college courses, queer literature, or community activism, but the specifics of each Rejecter's critiques varied. Taken together, however, Intellectual Rejecters can be categorized as belonging in one of two groups. The first, smaller group, saw marriage as a complete "sellout" for the LGBTQ+ community: it was something to be rejected wholesale. But the second, larger group, applauded marriage equality as a social justice success while seeing it as a queer failure, expressing concerns about the effects of marriage equality on relationships that fall outside expected (heterosexual) marriage norms.

A SELLOUT

These were the most hardcore Intellectual Marriage Rejecters, rejecting marriage as an undesirable goal for the LGBTQ+ community. They could not understand why LGBTQ+ people would want marriage or aspire to it. Tamryn had been in college when same-sex marriage first became legal. She had been deeply immersed in queer politics at the time and continued to mostly engage with communities of queer women. She told me:

> I was very engaged in queer politics at college. I led the Queer Student's Organization. Marriage was a big deal! We were all talking about it. Going to rallies and stuff. I still remember reading the *Dykes to Watch Out For* [comic] strip when it happened.[8] You know, the "Will you do the honor of hegemonically re-inscribing and destabilizing hegemonic discourse with me?"

Tamryn understood the goal of marriage as "being able to live a normal life" but had always questioned "whether or not leading a normal life is really the best goal" for LGBTQ+ people.

Others in this group said they had already experienced living the so-called normal life and had not been especially happy doing so. As such, they could not understand why LGBTQ+ people would want to aspire to such "misery" when LGBTQ+ culture offered alternative, better ways of doing relationships and family life. Take John, for example. He was a fifty-three-year-old man who had previously been married to a woman for over twenty years because he "was raised thinking that was what you should do." He had been with his current same-sex partner for two years. Now that he finally felt free to embrace his sexuality, he vehemently rejected the idea that he "should get married" again. As he had "embraced more and more of the gay male culture," he came to reject "the idea that gay people are just like straight people and the idea that we should be allowed marriage just because they have marriage or have this right because we're all the same." John said, "I'm really nervous about the imposition of heteronormative standards on the gay community. You know what, we don't have to do that. We don't have to follow that model."

Becky, a thirty-seven-year-old unmarried woman, had also lived what she regarded as the "normal life," but with a same-sex partner, and had not been happy in it. Prior to her current relationship of three years, she had had a child with a previous same-sex partner and ended up in a very marriage-like relationship, which she had eventually experienced as depressing and difficult to get out of. Now she was in another relationship but enjoying the less nuclear, dyadic co-parenting arrangement she had with current and ex-partners. Becky described herself as generally "nonconformist" and as having "never wanted the white picket fence," and she could not understand why lesbians would want marriage. She said:

> Have you ever seen that *New Yorker* cartoon? It has two people in bed, like a husband and wife in bed, and they are reading a headline in the newspaper about that gays have the right to marriage and the caption is something like, "Oh, good, now they can suffer just like the rest of us!"[9] I sort of have a similar sentiment. I see marriage as this pretty insidious thing that I've never really wanted a part of. My ideal world is that there would be no marriage for anybody. There would be different rules of how you could establish emotional or sexual connections or economic commitments to other people; they'd be much broader than marital coupling.

But Becky now felt increasingly alone in that desire for less heteronormative coupling and family arrangements and frustrated to be "surrounded by lesbians who are choosing to get married."

These Intellectual Marriage Rejecters saw marriage as a sad departure from the kinds of alternative relationships and families they had previously seen flourish around them in LGBTQ+ communities. Becky argued, "The worst thing is politically this makes a population of people who several decades ago were much more likely to have that kind of analysis of the family as a somewhat oppressive and limiting arrangement happier, in a way." She described it as "sort of like the opiate of the masses. It's like throwing people enough of a bone that they're happy with what they've got, but what they've got still sucks and that makes me unhappy." Ruby, a thirty-three-year-old woman who had been with her partner for eight years, similarly recalled all the conversations she and her friends used to have about creating alternative structures, including polyamory, being an "ethical slut,"[10] co-parenting with friends, and the importance of family protections and benefits not being tied to marriage. And now she bemoaned the fact that her friends were "giving up on this dream that we'd been creating of a world where we didn't need those kinds of rules and conventional structures to be happy." She said:

> The worst thing is that marriage really thwarts a more complex, critical conversation about what kind of structures for families are permissible and accessible, that it just limits our worldview; it reduces us back to this limited idea of what a family is supposed to look like, and that makes me feel kind of tired and sad.

Not only did these Intellectual Marriage Rejecters think other LGBTQ+ people had given up on more rewarding alternatives to marriage, but they also berated the fact that others had seemed to stop being critical of marriage as an institution—something they felt they had once been more thoughtful and vocal about. Ruby simultaneously laughed and sounded angry as she told me:

> [Everyone I know who married] seemed pretty pleased about the whole thing. [*laughs*] It's become so normative. Like, where is that critique? I'm not hearing those radical queer voices that used to be so loud in my ear, that were like, "Why are you capitulating to this hetero institution?" . . . Like, a friend was showing off her diamond ring, and I'm like, "Really? We're taking the whole kit and caboodle, we're not even critiquing the diamonds anymore? What?"[11]

These comments make clear that not only did these individuals vehemently reject marriage as an institution, they also increasingly felt alone and abandoned in their views. Tamryn emphasized this when she described herself as belonging to a "little pocket of radical queers" in opposition to the "mainstream LGBT community," which she saw as "heading towards marriage and wanting to live lives that are just like everybody else's—the 'I want my white picket fence and my 2.4 kids and a dog' group." She joked that the only radical gesture most other LGBTQ+ people now engaged in was "maybe wanting a Prius instead of an SUV!" Sounding sad and frustrated, she said, "I think that's where we're as a community heading. But that's not what I want."

A SOCIAL JUSTICE SUCCESS; A QUEER FAILURE

The vast majority of Intellectual Marriage Rejecters held more conflicting sentiments about marriage. They expressed support for marriage equality as an important social justice success on the one hand while wishing that the LGBTQ+ community had fought for something better, something queerer on the other. Zoe, an unmarried thirty-five-year-old woman who had been with her partner for nine years, celebrated the achievement of marriage rights as a form of equality while articulating intellectual critiques of marriage and sharing her version of a better alternative. Zoe described herself as a "left-wing feminist type" and jokingly said she had been "brainwashed" by feminism, explaining, "I've always been skeptical of marriage, you know, because I was brainwashed to be! I went to schools where people were thinking critically about the institution of marriage." In particular, Zoe critiqued the ways that marriage continued to be deeply patriarchal, describing the "sexist cultural narratives" that accompany marriage and the "gender roles" she felt got "pushed on you, whether you're gay or straight." She imagined an ideal, alternative form of marriage, one with a much more limited role: no more than "a simple contract to gain benefits and protections ... and with none of the deeply ingrained cultural meanings and gender narratives" that are typically attached to it. However, she understood that what was being offered was not an opportunity to redesign marriage, only to gain equal access to the institution as it was. She was grateful for the equal opportunity LGBQ people now had to marry, even though she herself had no interest in doing so. She maintained, "I think marriage is incredibly important as a social justice issue."

Other Intellectual Marriage Rejecters exhibited stronger, more ongoing struggles around marriage. It felt as if they were using the interviews to continue working through their internal conflicts over marriage. They battled between dueling sentiments, expressing joy and gratitude for gaining *access* to marriage alongside concerns about the *effects* of marriage on queer culture and community. Put simply, they questioned whether they could have their cake and eat it too. Could they gain equality and rights while also maintaining a distinct queer culture and the cultural and social benefits of not having marriage? Could they become part of an institution and still fight for something better? Some scholars and activists have argued that the fight for marriage equality actually created and sustained room for these kinds of debates.[12] But after marriage equality was won, these conflicts did not disappear. Marriage Rejecters' marriage stories make clear that many LGBQ people are still actively struggling to manage their feelings about the adverse marriage outcomes they now see long after marriage became legal.

Keith, a forty-one-year-old man, had "never conceived of getting married." By the time same-sex marriage became legal, he had "been really radicalized by college and graduate school" and was deeply involved in various forms of progressive activism and public service work. He said, "The idea of being married was like, who the fuck wants to imprison yourself like that? I viewed it as this completely confining normative institution that I wanted no part of!" Like Zoe, Keith's queerer ideal was a system in which marriage was associated with fewer privileges and less cultural hegemony. Keith was also concerned with achieving recognition for families that differed from the heterosexual status quo: "Why do we build in all of these privileges that accrue to that right, and then discriminate against people who aren't that thing?" Initially he had felt that marriage equality was a "step in that direction," in the sense of accruing less status and privilege to *heterosexual* marriage: "I didn't understand why straight people get to have that right and gay people don't get to have that. So, I believed in marriage as a matter of equality and antidiscrimination." But, in the years since it became legal, he had become increasingly concerned that other kinds of queer families were not achieving the rights and recognition they deserved:

> There's still a whole set of other questions about privileges and hierarchies and inequalities that we haven't thought through as deeply as we should as a movement. So marriage equality makes no sense to me because we just keep creating different notches in the hierarchy. Why would we want to create hierarchies within our own community in our attempt to have some kind of equality with the folks who actually created those hierarchies of inequality in the first place? What the marriage equality movement is on some level is about is that we want to be on top too. But that always means that there are going to be other people on the bottom. Like my friend who is in this polyamorous relationship—why should we be able to get a tax cut because we're not fucking as many people as he is? [*laughs*] It makes no sense.

Almost a decade after marriage had become legal, Keith was no longer sure that marriage was the step toward equality that he had initially thought it was.

Art, a forty-four-year-old man,[13] also worried that queer families were now being discriminated against more informally within the LGBTQ+ community as a result of marriage. From the 1990s on, he had "been involved one way or the other in organizing around relationship recognition," including for marriage rights. But he had hoped more diverse relationships would be recognized. When he had first come out in the 1980s he had felt "rescued by lesbian feminism" and had found it "hugely liberating" to have been "embraced by a deeply leftist feminist community." He lived in a housing cooperative and maintained an open relationship with his partner. He felt surrounded by other LGBQ people maintaining alternative relationships and family structures. For example, he described his neighbors as a "triad" of "three men in a long-term relationship" and his oldest friends as a "female couple who are co-parenting kids with a male couple." None of the queer families he knew had achieved any kind of formal relationship recognition, but Art felt that they had, until marriage equality, at least been widely accepted within the broader LGBTQ+ community. He explained:

> One really lovely thing about queer culture for many years is that although we were on the outside there were a lot of relationship structures, whether it was polyamory or triads or co-parenting or what have you or people who were single by choice, that were largely honored and accepted by the community.

Now, however, he said, "I have seen some evidence that that has started to change, and I fear how much more it's going to change." When probed for the kind of evidence he had seen of non(hetero)normative queer families being discriminated against in the wake of legal marriage, Art said that although he had not "seen concrete evidence of" stigma, he observed assumptions shifting, with most LGBTQ+ people assuming that same-sex couples want to marry, asking them repeatedly when they were going to, and expressing surprise and confusion over desires to live and love differently.

Art was far from alone in this perception. Almost every unmarried Marriage Rejecter told me how tiring it was to have to field questions about when they were getting married and why they weren't. They also believed that others now judged their relationships as less committed, deficient, and "in trouble" because of their decision not to marry. Zoe, for example, said:

> There are a lot of people I meet through [my job] and they are always wanting to know, "Are you getting married?" And sometimes I'm just not in the mood to describe the twenty different reasons it's not important to me! I always wonder about other LGBT people we meet who have made the decision to marry. I'm sure some of them are sad for us because they don't think we are committed.

Zoe admitted that as tiring as these conversations were, she still felt some pressure to try and articulate or prove her relationship commitment to people. She said, "I find myself always saying something like 'But we're ten years strong!' You know, something cheesy like that! 'We are pretty committed, we've been together a long time!' Something like that."

In addition to the general fatigue of having to explain their decisions, and commitment, to others, unmarried Marriage Rejecters felt that their unmarried status now signaled a kind of radical politics to other people, positioning them automatically at odds with, even a threat to, the LGBTQ+ mainstream. As Zoe explained, "I'm sure there are those [LGBTQ+] people who also think you aren't helping any of us by not getting married. So, I'm sure we make some people uncomfortable because of our choice not to." She implicitly understood that the fight for marriage equality depended on the idea that same-sex couples wanted to conform to heteronormative relationship standards. Not choosing to marry when the option became available therefore positioned them as a threat to the idea that same-sex couples are "just like" heterosexual couples. From an organizational perspective, there is broad scholarly consensus that the marriage equality movement "strategically embraced sameness" to win marriage rights, marking a historical shift in emphasis away from a collective identity based on difference, societal transformation, and sexual liberation, and toward emphasizing similarities to the heterosexual majority.[14] This shift to emphasizing "sameness" is now widely believed to be the cornerstone of the marriage equality movement's success. As such, although Zoe tried hard to "respect other people's choice to marry," she rightly perceived, and resented, the "irony" that other LGBTQ+ people were not so easily able to respect her choice not to.

Art explained the increase in stigma against non(hetero)normative queer families post–marriage equality somewhat differently. Rather than posing a threat to the ongoing marriage equality movement, Art perceived queer families as threatening LGBTQ+ individuals' ability to reconcile their internalized oppression. He argued that marriage offers those LGBTQ+ people who suffer from internalized oppression[15] a problematic means of resolving it, through the ability to believe and demonstrate that they are no different from heterosexuals:

> My fear around internalized oppression is that I think the way a lot of people try to deal with it is by making themselves more—gravitating more back towards—how do I say this? If you grew up queer and you are rejected in various ways, marriage allows you to come back to some of those sources of rejection and say "No, no, no, I'm just like you!" In that light, marriage feels like a way of creating some sort of reconciliation with parents, religious institutions, family, neighborhood, friends, whoever—and it may actually work too!

The fear, for Art, was that LGBTQ+ individuals who used marriage to manage their internalized oppression in this way would be "much less inclined to say 'Oh, by the way, my friends are still weird!'" Art astutely understood that access to legal marriage resolved the issue of internalized oppression on an individual level, by giving individuals access to a heteronormative institution, but failed to create broader social change that would help resolve it in the broader LGBTQ+ community, potentially making it even harder for those who did not want to emulate heterosexual family life to feel supported and valued.

Marriage Rejecters, like Art and others, were still actively struggling to work through their concerns about the effects of marriage on queer families and culture almost a decade after marriage had become legal, even while continuing to celebrate marriage as a social justice success. On top of these intellectual struggles, Marriage Rejecters also had to navigate complex feelings about their own personal decisions around marriage. Despite rejecting marriage, many of them nonetheless made decisions to get legally married. They had to come to terms with and validate these decisions to themselves and others.

Why Do Marriage Rejecters Get Married?

Considering their intellectual critiques and the unimportance they personally placed on marriage, the puzzle then is to understand why half of the

Marriage Rejecters had nevertheless legally married, and many others said they thought it was "likely" they would do so in the future. In fact, only one Marriage Rejecter expressed unequivocally that they would never marry and could never imagine any reason they would do so. There was then frequently a disconnect between the feelings and beliefs participants expressed about marriage and the decisions they ultimately made. This serves as an important reminder that rates of marriage do not serve as a reliable indicator of the feelings people have about it. Some LGBQ people marry despite having negative feelings toward or placing little importance on it. The experiences of Marriage Rejecters make clear the power that marriage has to shape relationship behaviors, compelling even the most critical and resistant of individuals to participate in an institution they might want little to do with.

As I outline below, Marriage Rejecters described being pulled into marriage through three key mechanisms: instrumental, normative, and cultural. These are not mutually exclusive. Any one person's experience could contain multiple or even all of these processes, and they overlap in complex ways. I distinguish them here only to offer clearer insights into the institutional processes at play. I include both married and unmarried Marriage Rejecters in the analyses below because I conceptualize them as being at different stages of a marital process, rather than as having qualitatively different relationships with the institution of marriage. To be clear, I am not arguing that it is inevitable that all Marriage Rejecters will get legally married. Rather, I argue that the myriad of factors operating to pull individuals into marriage are experienced by most, if not all Marriage Rejecters, regardless of whether they will ultimately end up marrying.

THE INSTRUMENTAL PULL OF MARRIAGE

Most Marriage Rejecters who decided to marry conceptualized marriage in instrumental terms—as a means of achieving some other practical end. This was not true of Marriage Embracers and Assumers. When Marriage Embracers and Assumers mentioned practical gains from getting legally married, they tended to do so only after being asked about them or quickly in passing. They were also usually quick to assert that they were most definitely *not* the primary reason they married, if they did. For most Embracers and Assumers, it felt culturally inappropriate to discuss marriage as an instrumental means of gaining rights and benefits, as if doing so did not imbue the institution with the necessary cultural reverence. For them, discussing marriage in instrumental terms risked throwing into question the love and commitment they had for their partners, as if both understandings of marriage could not coexist. Marriage Rejecters were just as in love with and committed to their partners but did not view marriage as necessary for those things. Most Marriage Rejecters would not have legally married if they had not perceived some real practical need for it. Moreover, describing marriage as *only* an instrumental decision to obtain some practical end allowed Marriage Rejecters to more easily rationalize and explain their decision to marry. After all, who could question one's need for healthcare coverage, hospital visitation rights, or power of attorney to make decisions for the person you love? Describing marriage in instrumental terms positioned the decision to marry as almost beyond their control—it became something they had to do, or something anyone sensible should do, in order to obtain necessary benefits and protections. Marrying was simply a smart, thoughtful decision based on practical reasoning.

Marriage did not solve all practical, legal issues for same-sex couples. As sociologists and legal scholars point out, same-sex couples continued to face a wide range of legal battles and discrimination in the post–marriage equality world.[16] Unfortunately, many same-sex couples incorrectly assumed that marrying would solve problems it did not and failed to foresee other new legal problems it created. However, the central point here is that many same-sex couples believed that marriage was a means to some instrumental end and were willing to enter the institution in order to gain it.

Age factored into this instrumental view of marriage. As they approached older ages, Marriage Rejecters started to look ahead and think about ways in which they might not be protected without marriage: If they got sick, would their partner be guaranteed hospital visitation rights? Could they list their partner on life insurance policies? How could their partner inherit shared property without facing unequal estate taxes? Would their partner easily be able to receive their social security benefits after they passed away? But, unlike Marriage Embracers (chapter 1), Marriage Rejecters typically felt little rush to marry. It was something they took time to think about, and they wanted to stress that they came to the decision after much consideration. They often reached the decision after their understanding of the legal implications of *not* being married had grown. Judy and her partner of seventeen years waited six years after same-sex marriage became legal before deciding to get married. She joked,

> We were so busy buying wedding gifts for other people we didn't have time to think about doing it ourselves! And going to other people's weddings really didn't make me feel like I wanted to do it myself. On the contrary, it probably just dampened my enthusiasm [for marriage] even more! [*laughs*]

However, when she and her partner decided to get wills drawn up, they started to take a more long-term view of their relationship, and this altered their thinking about marriage: "That made us realize what a big deal the legal system is. We knew we had to start thinking more about the legal implications of marriage." She also recalled that there had been "a couple of really high-profile cases of people not being able to get into the hospitals and stuff like that. We were getting older. We'd both been really healthy, but you start to have friends developing diseases and you know you want to protect yourself." When I asked Judy why she and her partner ultimately made the decision to marry, she replied, "Well, I think, [*laughs*] this sounds so kind of mercenary but really the legal issue was a lot of it. . . . At the time it definitely was around the legal issues and the hospitalization stuff and going to probate."

Jenn, forty-one, decided to get married in 2009, fourteen years into her relationship and five years after same-sex marriage had become legal. Her partner had always been more interested in marriage than she was and had asked her to marry her multiple times, but Jenn had always said no. She recalled, "[My partner] had asked me to get married again and again and again throughout the relationship. But I've never been like a big embracer of marriage. I'm able to feel that commitment without having something ceremonial." Regardless, over time the reality of Jenn's personal situation led her to the conclusion that marriage would solve many of their practical problems. She explained:

> As we progressed with the reality of me being self-employed, having a chronic illness, having to find different ways of having health insurance, I kind of concluded that—like, OK, there's some distinct legal and financial benefits to this. . . . It was a situation that was not sustainable—of owning a business, not being able to get my own health insurance (because I have a preexisting condition), and not being able to get on [my partner's] benefits unless we were married.[17] And we had been trying to have a child together for a while, and we started thinking, "You know, we are not legally married, and yes, second-parent adoption happens, but it's never a guarantee."[18] So there was this very practical reasoning, and I became more willing to consider it.

Jenn eventually agreed to marry her partner. In fact, she became so convinced that marriage would help solve many of the practical life problems they faced that they moved to Massachusetts (from a state that had not yet legalized it) specifically so they could get married.

Tamryn, one of the Marriage Rejecters I opened the chapter with, offered a similar narrative about why she ultimately decided to get married, explaining the decision as "very instrumental." She also emphasized that the decision was not a quick one, and that she and her partner had given a lot of thought to what marriage means and what they could use it for:

> We both really spent time thinking about things like "What is this institution constituted of and what are the things that we wanted to be able to get out of it, or that we think it's worthwhile for?" In terms of loving each other and living in a committed relationship and this and the other, the state doesn't need to be involved in that. What the state does need to be involved in is giving you certain legal benefits, and that is exactly how we understand that institution.

Tamryn's decision to marry emerged from serious consideration of the legal gains of getting married and the risks of not doing so. She was particularly concerned about the fact that her partner had been "disowned" by her father because of her sexuality. She worried about what would happen if her partner were to fall sick and her partner's father had the legal right to make decisions about her, while Tamryn would not. His ability to control her partner's finances would make it very difficult for Tamryn to afford to pay the rent and bills. Tamryn simply and forcefully stated, "Getting married was very much about getting me power of attorney so that [her father] could not have access to decision-making power or financial power for her." I probed Tamryn to find out why they hadn't tried to get her power of attorney without marrying, given how critical of marriage she was. She explained how much easier and cheaper it was to get that kind of protection via marriage: "Without marriage it's a whole set of expensive legal things that we would need to deal with, or we can go to the courthouse, pay forty dollars for a marriage certificate and then it's all done and it takes about an hour." Ultimately, the relative ease and affordability of the protection legal marriage offered her provided a good enough reason to do it. Tamryn did worry that they "might come to regret" the decision, but she felt confident that marriage would have no impact on the love they felt for one another, and so, for now, she thought she could live with it.

For Marriage Rejecters like Judy, Jenn, and Tamryn, decisions to marry happened when they finally got to a point at which they felt the risks or disadvantages of *not* being married outweighed their reservations about marriage. By contrast, Marriage Rejecters who made the decision to marry more quickly usually did so when their life situations changed in unexpected ways that made the need for marriage seem urgent—as the only means of maintaining or gaining access to a specific benefit or protection they immediately needed. Legal scholars have noted that after same-sex marriage became legal, many employers changed their policies to require partners be married to include them as a dependent for healthcare benefits.[19] This was an issue I heard about from several Marriage Rejecters.

Bob, the other Marriage Rejecter I opened the chapter with, explained that after moving to Massachusetts his partner took a new job and "according to his company, we needed to be legally married to get health insurance." They married within a week of him starting the job. He insisted: "We did it for very practical reasons, without much sentimentality." Bob did admit that he and his partner might have eventually decided to marry even if the healthcare situation had not necessitated it but said that they would have resisted doing so for longer without that impetus. Having seen firsthand the devastation the AIDS crisis had caused for same-sex couples in the 1980s and 1990s, Bob understood only too well the long-term risks of not having legal rights. He recalled:

> I worked with men who were dying of AIDS back in the early '90s, and I thought I was going to die. I thought everybody gay was going to die, because that's what was happening at the time. I remember men who had been with their partners for ten, twenty years dying and having the family come in and take the body, and take all of their possessions away from them. Their partners who had nursed them for years were shunned by the family, and the family came in and took everything.[20]

He explained that AIDS was "so seared" into his memory that it was always what he thought about when considering marriage. For Bob, and many men of his generation, marriage represented the assurance that "our rights aren't going to be superseded by some fictional family's right to say how things will be." It took an immediate need for healthcare to prompt Bob to marry, but given that marriage was the only means to gain secure rights as a family, Bob conceded that it was likely they would have eventually done so anyway.

Most of the unmarried Marriage Rejecters were open to marrying in the future *should* they develop a specific, practical need for it.[21] For example, Dennis said, "We're so committed anyway, marriage just feels like a public display. But if we had to do it we probably would out of sheer practicality. I can't help but know what the benefits are. I'm a pragmatist." Larry, a forty-two-year-old man who had been with his partner for fifteen years, also currently had no interest in marrying. Yet, somewhat "ironically," he and his partner had relocated to Massachusetts so that they could legally marry if they ever "needed" to. He explained that as they were "approaching their midforties" they were "starting to think about things like retirement." They had also experienced parental illnesses, which made them "stop and think more about the very nitty gritty legal aspects of sharing a life together and stuff." Those thoughts and conversations had made them more open to the idea of marrying in the future but, like Dennis, Larry stressed, "If we do get married, it will not be an emotional decision. That emotional decision to be together was made long ago. It will be purely a pragmatic and economic decision."

A few unmarried Marriage Rejecters articulated a more general sense that same-sex marriage did not currently offer enough benefits for it to make it worthwhile for them to get married yet. Recall that at the time of data collection, married same-sex couples only stood to gain state-level marriage benefits, as same-sex marriages were not yet federally recognized. Wendy, a fifty-one-year-old woman who had been with her partner twenty-three years, worked for the federal government and her partner worked for a national company, neither of which yet recognized same-sex marriage for the purposes of benefits. Wendy argued:

> So really, it doesn't mean enough for us [to do it] right now. We already have a commitment that marriage is supposed to represent. Why do we need somebody to—why do we have to go pay somebody to bless that? Until the day that it means something for us money-wise, then we say that's the day we're doing it.

Similarly, Terrence, who had been adamant that he and his partner did not need to get married to be a committed couple, told me, "I think we're definitely gonna reconsider [getting married] when it's a federal benefit because it will mean more, whereas right now it only means something in Massachusetts."

THE NORMATIVE PULL OF MARRIAGE

Marriage Rejecters did not always marry out of practical necessity. There were also normative mechanisms at play, pulling Marriage Rejecters toward and into marriage. These mechanisms were based on the influence of social expectations. Social interactions and internalized ideas about the "right thing" to do combined to make Marriage Rejecters feel as if they should be marrying, or at least considering it.

The first normative pull centered around social expectations regarding relationships and what makes one a good partner. In particular, it related to perceived expectations that they should make their partners happy even if that came at the expense of their own feelings. I describe this as a compromise mechanism. As should now be clear across chapters 1 and 2, older LGBQ people (in at least their forties) who had started relationships before same-sex marriage was legal were a varied group,[22] with some embracing marriage well before it was ever a legal possibility and others rejecting marriage as unimportant even after it became legal. As such, it should not be surprising to learn that feelings about marriage also often differed between same-sex partners. In fact, it was more common for one partner to want to marry while the other did not than for both partners to reject marriage. In these situations of unequal interest in marriage, compromise was necessary to maintain relationship success. As I discuss in chapter 3, compromises around marriage did not occur for Marriage Assumers, who were all younger LGBQ people in newer relationships that started only after marriage was already legal. Only older LGBQ people, who had already experienced love and commitment outside a marital model, felt able to make compromises around marriage. Among these older partners with unequal interest in marriage, compromise did work both ways: partners who desired marriage accepted they were not going to marry when their partners did not want to, and partners who did not want to marry were willing to do so when their partners really wanted to. Nevertheless, compromise leading *to* marriage was the more common scenario.

This compromise into marriage mechanism is explained by both instrumental and normative pulls. From an instrumental perspective, compromising to marry makes sense because while there are clear social benefits to marrying, there are few social benefits accrued to *not* marrying. Jenn (quoted above) falls into this camp. Jenn compromised and agreed to marry her partner after refusing for many years because she became persuaded by all the practical benefits of doing so. However, normative pulls are also important for understanding why some Marriage Rejecters ultimately compromised and agreed to marry. Marriage Rejecters found themselves more often agreeing to marry precisely because they did not place much importance on marriage. This might sound counterintuitive, but when one does not ascribe much relational or cultural weight to the institution of marriage, deciding to marry can be reconceptualized as a relatively low-significance event. Relationally and socially, an individual's negative feelings about marriage are regarded as having less significance than an individual's desire to get married. Disinterest in marriage has a long history of social association with immaturity, selfishness, and pathology,[23] whereas the desire to get married is seen as socially normative and important—deeply connected to maturity, legitimacy, and commitment. As such, the partner who wants to marry appears to gain more from marrying than the partner who does not want to marry stands to lose. Marriage Rejecters experienced relational pressures to agree to marry, because doing so seemed like the right thing to do, while not agreeing to marry when one's partner wanted to was interpreted as unnecessarily mean and self-centered.

Dianne, a fifty-two-year-old woman who had been with her partner fourteen years before marrying her, told me, "I just did not see the benefit of getting married—social or legal. I thought, 'Well, it's great that now people who want to get married can, but why would we? We have everything that we need.'"[24] By contrast, her partner saw marriage as an "obvious choice" and could not understand Dianne's lack of interest in it. Dianne expressed frustration and resentment as she recalled that "marriage was the one thing we ever really argued about." Yet she was ultimately persuaded that it was the right thing to do for their relationship: "Well, it was important to her and she persuaded me. I knew that it was really important to [my partner], and if it's important to her then it's important to me." Given the *lack* of importance Dianne placed on marriage and the magnitude of importance her partner placed on it, it came to seem foolish, stubborn, and selfish not to agree to marry, and not worth the ongoing conflict.

Like Dianne, Angie, a fifty-one-year-old woman, described a situation in which unequal interest in marriage created ongoing relationship conflict that was unlikely to be resolved any other way than marrying. Angie had already been in a heterosexual marriage prior to entering a same-sex relationship with her partner and had no interest in marrying again. Unfortunately, her partner, who had only ever been in same-sex relationships, felt very differently about marriage:

> So, she started talking about getting married as soon as we started living together, even when she first came to stay with me! And my reaction was pretty negative at the time. I remember vividly standing in my kitchen saying, "Why would I want to get married again?" And she was just crestfallen because she'd been waiting for this all her life, and here she was in her forties [thinking], "I could finally get married."

For Angie, coming out and entering same-sex relationships presented an opportunity to do relationships differently. For her partner, access to legal marriage was an opportunity to have the same kind of relationships heterosexuals had. Angie said, "At first, we agreed not to push it, but we had a lot of arguments about it, about why she did want to get married and about why I didn't want to. Not huge fights or anything, but certainly a lot of serious conversations." In the end, Angie recognized that this was something "[her partner] felt very strongly about" and agreed to marry. I asked her, "What would you say the worst thing about gaining access to legal marriage is?"[25] She replied, "She's not going to hear this, right? [*laughs*] I think it's the fact that because we could do it she was very insistent that we get married."

Dianne and Angie's narratives illuminate the kind of compromise mechanism that Personal Marriage Rejecters described: they were pulled into marriage when they put aside their own disinterest in marriage to avoid ongoing relationship conflict and succumbed to relationship pressures. Intellectual

Marriage Rejecters described the normative pull somewhat differently. They did not describe putting their critiques of marriage aside to avoid conflict. Instead, they described coming to feel that their critiques of marriage were silenced in the context of a romantic relationship. Intellectual Marriage Rejecters sometimes described having partners who were dismissive of their feelings about marriage, and who suggested that they were "only political" or "about making a statement" and therefore did not really matter, as if anything political could not be as sincere or meaningful as their own (positive) feelings about marriage. Keith, quoted earlier, astutely described this as premised on the cultural belief that the personal is (and should be) more powerful than the political. He had made his negative feelings toward marriage very clear to his partner. Yet Keith perceived that his partner remained perpetually confident that he would change his mind and they would get married.

> I haven't exactly asked him this, but I think from his perspective, I'm sure he thought that my opposition to getting married was *just* political. I think he thought—I tend to spout off about lots of things! And so, my "I'm never getting married" felt very political to him, because a lot of what I do is very political. But so, I think he felt "OK, sure, Keith has his politics around this, but *this is us.*"

Keith had a hard time separating the personal from the political, seeing them as one and the same. Yet he perceived that those who do not have political feelings about marriage are better able to "compartmentalize those things" and that they assume the personal should hold more weight. In the context of a relationship, normative pressures mean prioritizing the "personal" while deprioritizing any "political" critiques of marriage.

Another reason that some Intellectual Marriage Rejecters found themselves compromising and agreeing to marry is that the partner with more interest in marriage had a source of power they did not—the ability to propose and put them on the spot. Marriage Rejecters sometimes felt beholden to social expectations not to disappoint and embarrass their partners. As I show in chapter 4, proposals were relatively rare and undesirable among older LGBQ people in long-term relationships. So it is especially striking that when they did occur they were often used as a means of getting a less interested partner to agree to marry. When Keith's partner put him on the spot with a proposal, he found himself conceding in the moment, concluding, "I guess he really wants to get married, so we're going to get married!" This was also the case for Linda, a fifty-four-year-old woman and another Intellectual Marriage Rejecter. Even as a lawyer acutely aware of the instrumental benefits of marriage, Linda had not been interested in marrying. She explained, "I have a really strong feminist background, so I have that whole analysis of marriage as not really being necessarily a healthy institution." But Linda and her partner were on opposite ends of the political spectrum—she described herself as "radical feminist and very politically engaged" and her partner as "coming from [a] Republican background and not politically engaged at all." Linda joked that her partner used to refer to her as a "feminazi," teasing her about her feminist commitment to all things political. It should not be surprising that Linda and her partner did not see eye to eye on marriage. They did not fight about marriage, nor even discuss it much. Instead, Linda's partner simply surprised her with a proposal. And, caught by surprise, Linda found herself agreeing to marry. She said, "In that moment, I realized it clearly meant a lot to her to be able to get married. Marriage wasn't a big deal for me, and I really didn't feel like it mattered. It was important to me only because it was important to her." Linda reconceptualized her own feelings about marriage as not mattering, and the decision to marry as of therefore relatively low significance for her given how important it clearly was to her partner. She did not even think about saying no.

Given the cultural weight of a proposal in the popular imagination,[26] whatever one personally feels about marriage, there is still a widely shared understanding that to say no in that moment risks signaling a lack of love or commitment to one's partner, thus putting them in a very stigmatizing social situation. Without having also spoken to these Marriage Rejecter's partners I can't know for sure, but this pattern suggests the possibility that partners who want to marry might call their rejecting partner's bluff—trusting that if put on the spot that they would not want to hurt their feelings or embarrass them, even if this is only a partially conscious process. Regardless of the intent, these examples make clear that relationship expectations and the broader cultural weight placed on marriage serve to position those partners who want to marry as having more power than those who do not, and ultimately help push LGBQ people toward marriage in spite of their disinterest and critiques of it.

Some other Marriage Rejecters also described normative pulls in the form of peer influence. They told me how pervasive marriage had become, and the more they felt surrounded by marriage, the more it came to feel "normal" to them, and the less normal their unmarried status and critiques of marriage came to seem. They found themselves interacting with more people who were married and fewer who were not. And the more common same-sex marriage became, the more easily they identified others who seemed like them who were doing it, and the more easily they could start to imagine themselves also doing it—if *they* did it, then why not also them?

Take Megan, a thirty-one-year-old Marriage Rejecter, for example. She described herself as always having been "dead set against marriage." In her view, marriage was only "a bunch of government paperwork proving that two people live together for the government," while the "actual, real commitment is within two people who love one another." It "infuriated" her that people needed the government to "feel something that should come from within." She also rejected marriage on the basis of its homonormativity. "I tend to stray from the norm. I didn't want to get married because that's what's expected, that's what you're supposed to do in life . . . meet someone, get married, have children, work the rest of your life. Ugh, shoot me in the head, that's boring!" Megan insisted, "I was not someone who had ever dreamt of my wedding growing up!" But now she is engaged to her partner of three years. When I asked what had changed her mind, she put it down to peer influence: "In Massachusetts, marriage has become kind of expected. Everyone talks to you about getting married." Marriage talk became a ubiquitous part of her social interactions, and she could not help but be influenced by it. Megan made fun of herself, remembering how some friends started talking about bachelorette parties and she had started daydreaming about "Who's going to throw me one of those things? How do I get that?" But she also more seriously told me she had really struggled to accept how much she had been influenced by other people and how much her views had changed.

> I struggled with the idea that I wanted *more* than just a happy, committed relationship. I wanted that marriage thing which I had been dead set against. It was much more of a struggle for me 'cause I had been so vocally "I'm never doing this, this is bullshit, what the hell, you know, blah blah blah." [*animated, with a self-mocking tone*] So, then I was like, "Oh crap, I want to marry her!" [*laughs*]

This resulted in a tension between her intellectual critiques of marriage as an institution and her shifting personal desires to marry. Later, when I asked her what she thought the "worst thing" about having access to legal marriage was, Megan maintained that "it's that it has led to the expectation now for LGBQ people that you'll follow the traditional life path that you need to get married and have children." Yet she herself was being pulled down the very same socially expected path she critiqued.

Normative pulls into marriage coexisted alongside the seeming disappearance of queer alternatives. At the same time that same-sex marriages were becoming more visible, alternative LGBQ relationship forms became less visible, leaving those people who wanted to practice them feeling uncertain and alone in their desires to organize their relationships outside of a heteronormative marriage model. For example, Ruby said that before she had moved to Massachusetts she felt part of a community "full of activism and progressive thinking" and surrounded by people who adopted "variously structured households and families." She had always aspired to raise a child with a best friend instead of a romantic partner. However, since moving to Massachusetts she had found herself in a "much less queer world." She told me, "Being in Massachusetts I'm now swimming through a whole different set of social norms. Everyone is doing this very expected dyadic relationship thing and I don't have any real role models of other arrangements around me anymore." As a result, she felt much more alone in her desire to create alternative families and had started to think that they were unrealistic. And much to her surprise, she was also starting to "think about marriage with positive feelings." She admitted, "I'm embarrassed to feel so influenced by what's around me. I mean, I know I have to take responsibility for myself and for creating my own life. But I also would like to have more variety in the models that are around me. It's hard to do it alone." Peer influence in the context of legal marriage shifts Marriage Rejecters' views on marriage in two coexisting ways—increasing the visibility and pervasiveness of same-sex marriage examples and reducing the visibility of alternatives.

THE CULTURAL PULL OF MARRIAGE

Some Marriage Rejecters also found their feelings toward marriage shifting and softening in the years after marriage became legal through the cultural pulls of the institution. This was a slower, more complicated mechanism through which some Marriage Rejecters were pulled *toward* marriage, even if not directly into it. Only asking Marriage Rejecters why they decided to get married would not capture this process. These Marriage Rejecters had not decided to marry. Yet they found themselves gradually becoming more amenable to marriage when they had once been very critical of it as an institution.

For Intellectual Marriage Rejecters, critiques of marriage had come from an intellectual standpoint—from careful consideration of the drawbacks and limitations of the institution of marriage. However, once marriage became legal and something people were actually doing, it was no longer only an abstract institution to critique but something they regularly observed and experienced as a lived reality. Sometimes this resulted in a disconnect between their intellectual critiques and the personal experiences they had. Being able to get legally married was an immensely joyful moment for a lot of LGBQ people, and even the staunchest Marriage Rejecter found themselves getting pulled along by the collective effervescence of marriage moments, such as weddings.[27] That is because on some level even Marriage Rejecters had internalized cultural scripts about what weddings symbolize: a significant moment in the life course and relationship, love, commitment, stability, family inclusion, and social recognition. Given the dominance and strength of these scripts, whatever their own feelings about marriage as an institution, they found it hard not to feel happy in the lived marital moments they shared with others.

Intellectual Marriage Rejecters told me that they found themselves getting emotional and sentimental about marriage in spite of themselves, and much to their embarrassment, given that they had always been so publicly and vocally critical of marriage to others. Sometimes, this also resulted in teasing and ridicule among their friend groups. For example, Ann, a Marriage Embracer featured in chapter 1, chuckled as she recalled observing the reactions of her Marriage Rejecter friends at a wedding they all attended: "My hardcore activist friends all turned into water fountains [during that wedding]! They had spent years arguing that they did not want marriage! I guess being ready for it intellectually is not the same as being ready for it emotionally!" But the Marriage Rejecters I spoke to did not find it so amusing. They experienced their unexpected emotional reactions to marriage as troubling and were still struggling to come to terms with their softening feelings as they spoke to me.

Becky, who had initially told me that it made her "unhappy" to see other LGBQ people get married, perfectly captured the complex tension she experienced between intellectual critique and emotional reaction to this very intense cultural moment:

> There's part of me that intellectually didn't care about marriage, and even had contempt toward it. But at the same time, there was a more emotional reaction that made me happy. So, although I wish people would organize their lives differently, this is what they want to do and so of course it is sort of heartwarming, and I'm happy for people that they get to do this thing they seem to really want to do. Like, of course these news stories about these eighty-year-old women who had been together for decades and could finally get married affected me. Even though the more critical part of me is like ugh [*laughs*] there is also part of me that is able to be moved and *is* moved, whether I like it or not.

Her comment that she was emotionally affected whether she liked it or not also highlights how Marriage Rejecters came to conceptualize emotional reactions to marriage as something they often experienced as beyond their control. Even if Marriage Rejecters remained theoretically critical of marriage as an institution, they could not help but get swept up in moments of joy that marriage appeared to offer friends and acquaintances, or even LGBQ strangers.

Ruby, who had initially spoken of marriage as a sellout for the LGBQ community and as making her feel "tired and sad," also admitted that her "feelings on marriage were shifting." She too attributed this shift to seeing how happy marriage had made people she knew.

> I see the way my friends, my gay friends, who've gotten married—I see how meaningful it is for them and that has had a big impact on me for sure because they are so happy to have this possibility. I do think that living in Massachusetts and having more friends who are getting married is having an effect on me. My thoughts are evolving. I think that I'm trying to expand, I'm trying to be more open, less judgmental—to allow more room for my friends and colleagues and so on who are really made happy by this institution. [*laughs*]

Interestingly, Ruby also identified a sense that it had come to feel inappropriate to remain critical of marriage. In other words, it was not just that her feelings toward marriage were softening in response to shared cultural scripts and moments, but that it had also become less socially acceptable to be critical of marriage as an institution. Negative sentiments seemed out of place in light of all the positive emotions other people experienced in response to it. As such, Ruby had started to criticize her own critiques of marriage, describing them now as seeming "arrogant," "immature," and "selfish" given how much other people seemed to gain from it. She said, "In the face of all that pleasure my judgment is stopped short." In this sense, critical perspectives were softened by lived experiences of other people's marital joy, and no longer felt as socially and normatively appropriate. Here we see both cultural and normative mechanisms working in tandem to curb Marriage Rejecters' critiques of marriage and gradually to pull them into the institution.

Doing It My Way

Despite the fact that so many Marriage Rejecters ended up being pulled into the institution of marriage, they found ways to continue expressing their rejection of it. One of the most common was to reject wedding culture. This was a clear attempt to participate in marriage as an institution on their terms, in some kind of pared-down fashion, simply to gain a particular benefit of protection they needed or to make their partners happy while avoiding having to engage in the cultural expectations that went along with it. Having small or nonexistent weddings was one way Marriage Rejecters who decided to marry could maintain some sense of power. The institution of marriage might have pulled them in with instrumental advantages, or relational and peer pressure, but at the very least they could make it clear that they still wanted little to do with the cultural fanfare associated with it. Their partners might have gotten the upper hand in convincing them to marry but at the very least they could draw the line at a wedding. Regardless of the institutional forces that had pulled them into marriage, Marriage Rejecters almost always had very small weddings, or no wedding at all, opting for quick courthouse arrangements, very private services in their homes, or weekend elopements.

Marriage Rejecters wanted to emphasize how little time or money they spent on their marriage events, how little they cared about these events, the lack of "romance" or "sentimentality" they associated with them, and ultimately that whatever they did to get married did not constitute a wedding per se. For example, Tamryn, dryly told me:

> We went to a drive-through. It's basically on the side of the road. We made an appointment for April Fool's Day. We did exactly what was legally required and nothing more. I wore something very similar to what I'm wearing now. Jeans and a T-shirt. I had a roller derby bout that day, so we went, we did our vows in the morning, and then we tried to go and have breakfast, but I was in a rush and had to go, so she went and got breakfast with my parents and I went and got ready for the bout. [*laughs*] It was very not a big deal.

Several elements in Tamryn's narrative were common to how Marriage Rejecters emphasized that their marriage events were "no big deal," including that the events took place in locations that could not be considered formal or romantic, were fast and took little time, were preceded and followed by ordinary daily activities, and involved no more rituals or activities than was "legally required" (no rings, songs, costumes, honeymoons, etc.). Tamryn's decision to get married on April Fool's Day was an additional symbolic attempt to emphasize that they did not take getting married seriously and that the event held little sentimental meaning for them.

Whatever the desires of those getting married, certain formalities have to be adhered to, including having someone to witness the marriage and officiate it. However, most Marriage Rejecters opted to limit guests to only those formally and legally required. As Judy put it, "We invited the smallest group of people we could possibly get!" Sometimes witnesses were significant people in their lives, such as parents or siblings, but just as often Marriage Rejecters chose strangers or acquaintances to serve as witnesses. Moreover, most Marriage Rejecters also only told family and friends that they had married after the event. They did not want to be asked questions about the event, nor to feel pressured to make it more of an event than they wanted it to be. Judy said, "We really tried not to talk a lot about it beforehand. Our friends understand how private we are and that we were not going to do a big thing. But we also didn't want people to be offended. Right after we did it I contacted my parents and I told them." Linda similarly explained, "We didn't tell anybody we were going to do it. It just felt like it could be a more personal thing that way. Then it was really just about us I think." By marrying privately and then declaring themselves married more casually afterward, Marriage Rejecters felt able to marry their way, while maintaining a sense of control over how and why they were participating in the institution. They could attribute the meanings they personally wanted to attach to the marriage event and maintain a sense of freedom from broader cultural and social prescriptions about the right way to marry.

Yet even these moments of individual agency existed alongside social expectations and pressures to conform around marriage. Despite all of her attempts to reject wedding culture by marrying in a drive thru on April Fool's Day, and her insistence on not exchanging rings or engaging in any of the "symbols of ownership" associated with marriage, Tamryn nonetheless felt pressure to engage in wedding culture in other ways. For example, she felt she had no choice but to invite her parents to the event because they "would have been too mad" at her if she hadn't. She and her partner were now also planning on throwing a "big party to get all the people we love together." Tamryn was careful to distinguish that the "party" was "not a wedding." Yet she still clearly felt some need or pressure to hold an event that resembled a wedding. Tamryn explained this in two somewhat different ways. On the one hand, she said, "I think people would have been really disappointed if we didn't do anything," suggesting a kind of pressure to appease other people's social expectations around marriage. But on the other hand, she also spoke about it being "an excuse to get people together" that they "might never have again." Weddings are events that culturally allow people to join families and friends together, and there are few other events like them. Tamryn said she couldn't imagine other "circumstances under which [my partner's] brother and sister would meet my family" given how far away everyone lived. They wanted to bring their "communities together" and weddings—or "parties," as Tamryn insisted—provide a rare culturally validated way of doing so. As such, although Marriage Rejecters maintained agency and ongoing rejection by controlling the wedding event, they also sometimes found themselves more pulled into the wedding culture they professed to so vehemently reject than they seemed to realize.

Conclusion

Some sexualities scholars position LGBTQ+ people as having the power to resist, challenge, and selectively use institutions like marriage. For example, in her book *Queering Families: The Postmodern Partnerships of Cisgender Women and Transgender Men*, Carla Pfeffer describes ciswomen and their trans partners' decisions to marry or not as conscious, queer choices. Decisions *not* to marry are "normative resistance," conscious strategies employed to resist heteronormativity, while decisions *to* participate in institutions are examples of "inventive pragmatism," conscious uses of the institution to access social and material resources. It is certainly true that some LGBQ people are able to very consciously and deliberately engage with the institution of marriage on their own terms. Those Marriage Rejecters who had married, or who could imagine themselves doing so in the future, often wanted to emphasize that they were only engaging in the institution to get what they wanted or needed from it. Yet, overwhelmingly, the experiences of Marriage Rejecters illuminate the multifaceted ways legal marriage manages to pull them into an institution they had rejected and wanted to avoid. To me, this speaks more to the power of marriage as an institution than it does to the power of individuals to be able to resist and reject it.

The instrumental pulls into marriage were especially strong. So long as legal marriage remains uniquely tied to rights and protections, as the only means of achieving crucial benefits, the institution has the power to pull even the most ardent Rejecter into it. At some point one's need for rights and benefits are likely to outweigh individual resistance to the institution or make that resistance very difficult to maintain given the risks of doing so. Yet the data also underscore that the institutional pull into marriage is multifaceted, such that individuals get pulled into or at least toward marriage through multiple mechanisms. This means that even if one does not subscribe to the dominant cultural ideas surrounding marriage regarding its relationship to love, commitment, family inclusion, and legitimacy—as Marriage Embracers and Assumers do—marriage has several other tools at its disposal to draw individuals into it.

In part II of the book I examine what happens to those Marriage Rejecters who got legally married. Could they have their cake and eat it too? Is it possible to resist and reject the institution from the inside? Is it possible to do marriage differently, rejecting and challenging heteronormative marital practices, in private, through the kinds of dyadic relationship practices they engage in? For now, however, the experiences of Marriage Rejecters outlined in this chapter highlight the scope and power of marriage as an institution to impact even those who think of themselves as beyond its influence, as not needing or wanting marriage in their lives.

3

Marriage Assumers

It's Just What You Do

Clara, age twenty-nine, was one of the youngest married participants in this study. Growing up in Massachusetts, she had had a "secret girlfriend" during high school but had not come out as gay until her freshmen year of college. She had two "serious" same-sex relationships during college and eventually moved out of state with one of those girlfriends. They remained together for a couple years, but when they broke up Clara returned to Massachusetts. Clara had "always wanted to get married and have a family." She also never doubted her ability to do so. "All through high school and college" she had "felt really optimistic" about being able to legally marry one day. By the time she started high school, Massachusetts had already passed a "Safe Schools law for gay and lesbian students."[1] By the time she graduated college, Clara had "lived through everything from the safe school stuff to *Lawrence v. Texas*, and then marriage equality," and, to her, progress for LGBTQ+ people "just felt like it was an unstoppable force."

Same-sex marriage became legal in Massachusetts Clara's senior year in college. She came to expect it as an outcome for any successful, long-term relationship she had, and as something she would inevitably do. As she put it, "Marriage has been legal my whole adult life. So, I sort of was thinking of it as just a thing that I would do. It was always something I saw myself doing if I met the right person." In fact, Clara had planned on marrying her second college girlfriend. They got engaged at age twenty-two and planned their wedding, but then called it off when they broke up. Looking back, Clara said that although "it really sucked" at the time, she was glad they did not marry because she was "too young" and they were "not right" for each other.

Clara met the "right person" when she was twenty-five. Although she soon left to pursue a postgraduate opportunity in another state, Clara and her new girlfriend began to talk about marriage almost immediately. They agreed that being able to sustain a long-distance relationship was a good sign for their future. As soon as Clara returned to Massachusetts a year later, they moved in together. As she recalled, "At that point it was sort of like we were assuming we would eventually get married. Then it became 'When should we get married?'" They married the following year, when she was twenty-seven.

Clara did not offer any specific reasons for wanting to get married. Instead, it was just something she had always imagined doing and felt like an "obvious" next step in their relationship:

> I think it was pretty typical even of straight people. I mean, it was just the progression, from dating to being serious to moving in together to getting married. We were ready, we had committed to each other for our lives and we were planning the rest of our lives together and everything.

Getting married was also important for having children. Not only would she not have married someone who did not want children, but she said she would not have had children without being married: "I think it's a lot better in terms of rights and everything with kids, to be married. So, I would have pressed for that for that reason." Clara and her now-wife had a clear timeline for their family future: "We always said three to five years after we got married we'd start trying to have kids. Three years will be next May, so next fall we'll probably start trying."

Clara belongs to the group of LGBQ people in this study I call Marriage Assumers. A little over a third of the people in this study fall into this group (forty-one). They are predominantly young (in their twenties and thirties) and entered serious same-sex relationships only after same-sex marriage had already become legal. They had come out and formed committed relationships in a world in which legal same-sex marriage was possible, at least in Massachusetts. Their marital experiences are remarkably different compared to the other two groups of LGBQ people I have described—Marriage Embracers (chapter 1) and Marriage Rejecters (chapter 2). Recall from the previous chapters that neither Marriage Embracers nor Rejecters ever expected to legally marry. In stark contrast, Marriage Assumers took it for granted as an inevitable end point of their relationship trajectories. Moreover, marriage defined their relationships: they found it difficult to envisage long-term committed relationships or parenting in the absence of marriage, nor saw little point in investing in relationships that were not "marriage material." From incredibly early in their relationships, first dates even, they understood themselves as working toward marriage. Marriage was not only the end point of their relationships; it was the whole point. This was not true for either

Marriage Embracers or Marriage Rejecters, who were able to imagine and conceptualize love, commitment, and parenting outside a marital model. Yet despite the importance they placed on marriage, Marriage Assumers usually struggled to articulate clear reasons for getting married. Instead, it was just "what you do" when you love someone and are committed to them, have reached a particular stage in one's relationship, or want children.

In many ways, Marriage Assumers offer dating and marital narratives that sound indistinguishable from the average heterosexual.[2] On the surface then, they may not seem particularly interesting. But their experiences are a crucial lens for understanding the impact that legal marriage has had on same-sex relationships. The fact that this group of LGBQ individuals sound much more like the average heterosexual today than their LGBQ counterparts who formed committed relationships prior to the legalization of same-sex marriage matters in two ways. First, it suggests that having access to legal marriage early in one's life course is connected to a strong shift toward what the queer critic Lisa Duggan has termed "homonormativity": the dominance of heterosexual norms in the lives of LGBQ people. This shift was technically already well underway before same-sex marriage became legal. Back in the 1990s, conservative gay advocates for marriage stressed that LGBQ people were already "virtually normal" and wanted "to live ordinary middle-class lives,"[3] while queer critics bemoaned the fact that "nearly everyone, it seems, wants to be normal."[4] Clearly, gaining access to legal marriage rights was not necessary for LGBQ people to desire and enact homonormativity. Yet queer critics of marriage also worried that legal marriage would create "the final assimilation of LGBT people into mainstream culture."[5] The stark contrast between the marital assumptions, desires, and experiences of Marriage Assumers compared to their LGBQ counterparts in the Embracer and Rejecter groups offers empirical grounds for those concerns.

Second, the experiences of Marriage Assumers offer the strongest indicator of the institutionalization of marriage among LGBQ people.[6] Gaining access to legal marriage has fundamentally changed LGBQ people's experiences of marriage and the meanings they attach to it. In only a few years, new cohorts of LGBQ people have come to deeply internalize cultural ideas about marriage that Marriage Embracers and Rejecters did not, and they take it for granted in ways that they could not have even fathomed. The data in this chapter shows that, in less than a decade, among younger LGBQ individuals in new relationships, marriage had already become an institutionalized relationship experience: taken-for-granted, expected, widely conceived as the relationship norm, and required for relationship investment and success. This is all the more striking considering that at the time of data collection, same-sex marriage had not become legal nationwide.

The lack of variation we see among Marriage Assumers also offers another indication of institutionalization. When something is not institutionalized, people bring their own experiences, meanings, and feelings to bear on it. We saw this clearly in chapters 1 and 2. Although, broadly speaking, Marriage Embracers embraced marriage and Marriage Rejecters rejected marriage, the feelings they had about marriage, meanings they attached to it, and their marital experiences were incredibly complex and varied. But, as will become clear, this was much less true for Marriage Assumers. They shared much more uniform relationship trajectories and followed a widely shared cultural script about what was necessary to get to the point of marriage. And because Marriage Assumers subscribed to and internalized widely shared cultural ideas about the necessity and importance of marriage, they assigned more similar, simple, meanings to it—that it matters for love, commitment, and children. They drew on dominant cultural rhetoric about marriage but had not given it much thought themselves. In fact, after months of interviewing, I found that their responses were so alike that I could almost predict what their answers to certain questions would be. As you read this chapter, you too will notice the uniformity in language used around marriage—what it means, what it is for, and why it matters.

Always an Option

The historic event of same-sex marriage becoming legal in Massachusetts had little impact on Marriage Assumers. In fact, most admitted they could "not really remember it" occurring. Most had been in young adulthood at the time, in college or even high school. Some had not even yet come out to themselves or others as LGBQ. For example, when I asked Chris, now thirty-two, how he felt when marriage had first become legal, he replied, "So I guess to be honest I actually don't remember the moment that it happened. I was a medical student at that time; I pretty much had blinders on to most everything else." Then, thinking about the timing some more, he realized that he would not have even yet been out as gay then, adding, "No, because I came out in 2005 or 2006. So, I don't actually remember that moment, to be honest." But even among those who had already come out, many Marriage Assumers had not yet had any serious, committed same-sex relationship when same-sex marriage became legal, making the event seem somewhat abstract. Moreover, compared to Marriage Embracers and Rejecters, a much higher number of

Marriage Assumers were not yet living in Massachusetts at the time it became legal (a point I return to later). When I asked Vicky, twenty-five, how she felt when marriage became legal, she said, "I think I was out of state. So it didn't really hit home for me when everything happened. Plus, I think I was still thinking I'm gonna marry a guy. So marriage equality in Massachusetts didn't have an impact on me, not like it does now I'm living in Massachusetts."

Their sexual identity, relationship experience, and physical location when same-sex marriage became legal positioned Marriage Assumers to experience marriage equality as an insignificant historical event. Yet now that they were at different stages of their life course—out as LGBQ, married or in serious relationships, and living in Massachusetts—some of them looked back and wished they had paid more attention when it had first happened. A few even expressed guilt about the fact they had not appreciated its significance at the time. Ollie, thirty-two, said, "I know it probably should have meant more to me, but I don't think I was there emotionally yet, like you take it for granted, you know?"

By the time they were forming committed same-sex relationships, legal marriage felt as if it had always been an option for them. When I asked Kimberly, a twenty-six-year-old woman, if she had always wanted to get married, she simply replied, "I guess I always assumed that I would." And when I probed to ask her if she ever thought that she might not be able to get legally married, she said, "No, I was very aware of other things that I might struggle with. Like having children that were both legally ours and those kinds of things, but I think since by the time I came out I knew I could at least get married in Massachusetts that I didn't really worry too much about it."

Several Marriage Assumers moved to Massachusetts from another state precisely because they knew same-sex marriage was legal there. Liam, a thirty-three-year-old man, grew up in a state that he described as somewhere where "it is not OK to be gay." But marriage became legal in Massachusetts "right around the same time" that he came out as gay, and he met a same-sex partner he felt serious about shortly afterward. There was a marriage initiative on the ballot in his home state that would ban same-sex marriage. However, being able to witness marriage equality unfold in Massachusetts "in parallel" helped Liam "realize that marriage would be possible" for him. He had visited Boston only once before but began to apply for jobs there. After landing a job, he and his boyfriend moved there together after dating for less than a year. Liam explained how moving to Massachusetts and deciding to get legally married had gone hand in hand: "In pitching 'Hey, I'd like to move to Boston and you could come with me,' I pointed out, 'And that's a place we could eventually get married!'" He admitted that from that point on they almost assumed they would get married. "Getting married sort of took on an air of inevitability," he said. Others, like Chris, moved to Massachusetts by themselves but hoped to find a partner there. Looking back, Chris identified the role that legal marriage played: "I think on some level I was aware of the fact that this was a place where you could get married. This was a place that's more accepting. But I also hoped I would meet someone and fall in love and could get married."

These examples demonstrate the power of having access to marriage, even in just one state, for changing the ways LGBQ people imagined their futures and the kinds of assumptions they could make about what was possible in their lives. Once legal marriage was on the table, LGBQ people were quickly able to orient their lives around the new reality of having the option to legally marry.

Seeking Marriage Potential

In chapter 1, we saw Marriage Embracers embrace aspects of marriage over the course of their committed relationships, both before and after it was legal, but marriage was not the key defining feature of them. Their relationships felt secure, loving, and committed with or without marriage. By contrast, Marriage Assumers depended on marriage. It was an expected and necessary relationship goal, and they struggled to see potential in their relationships without the promise of it. Moreover, marriage usually defined Marriage Assumer's relationships very early on, in ways that neither Marriage Embracers nor Rejecters described, suggesting that having access to legal marriage has changed the ways in which same-sex couples date.

Marriage Assumers imagined and discussed marriage with their partners early in their relationships—some as early as first dates, but all within the first year.[7] They often described how new dates were instantly imagined as potential spouses and vetted as potential marriage material. Some even found ways to get marriage into first date conversations. Esteban, a thirty-four-year-old, described marriage as "giving you a way of talking more about the future" and as having "changed the terminology." He said that although he had always been "into long-term, future oriented relationships," by the time he started dating "as an adult" marriage had become "more of a conversation to have" when you met someone, and something people were "more inclined to talk about." When I probed to find out what kinds of things people might talk about when they met potential partners, Esteban responded that they might ask things like "Do you believe in marriage?" or joke "You know, I'm not getting any younger!" just to get the conversation started.

Casey, a forty-one-year-old man, had met his now-husband online in the winter of 2004, the same year marriage became legal in Massachusetts. He joked that when they finally met face-to-face about a month later, it was more of an "interview" than a first date. He understood this as connected to having the option to marry, adding, "I knew that I could marry this guy if I wanted to and so I certainly interviewed him! I mean, because I had known him for a minute and a half and I was asking him things like 'So, do you want kids?'" It was not that Casey wanted to have children or even to get married immediately; rather, it was that he wanted to have the possibility of doing so. With legal marriage now an option, he did not want to invest in a relationship with someone who was not imagining the same future. He explained:

> At that point I'm not sure I had even decided if I wanted to have kids! But I think I had decided that I wanted it to be an option to consider, and so my thinking was that if he was not interested in kids, because a lot of people don't want to have kids, well then, it's not going to be an option, so I don't want to go there at all if it's not an option.

As I describe later, for a lot of Marriage Assumers marriage and children were intimately connected in their minds. This was also the case for Casey. To him, it was obvious to him that if someone wanted to have kids, they would want to get married as well. He thought, "I didn't really even have to ask about marriage directly . . . because it is just there now."

Not all Marriage Assumers needed to determine marriage potential as soon as a first date, but most described establishing it as a shared goal with their partners relatively early on in their relationships, typically within the first year to eighteen months. Chris put it this way:

> So, for years, even before we got engaged, we had talked about how marriage was a goal for both of us. . . . We started talking about it after about a year and a half or so. We never sat down and discussed it, but we just talked about it from time to time, how it was important. So, I guess at a certain point in our relationship we had kind of chatted about it or mentioned it enough that we knew it was both something we wanted to do.

Nonetheless, as I elaborate on in chapter 4, marriage talk was a delicate balancing act. Marriage Assumers had to talk about marriage enough to establish that new relationships had marriage potential, but talking about it too much ran the risk of ruining the romance and "surprise" of a proposal.

While some, like Casey and Chris, described needing to know there was marriage potential, others articulated marriage as allowing them to more clearly imagine or "map out" a future with partners. Vicky said, "I think marriage changed the way I dated without me actually knowing it. Had I not been able to think about a future with marriage in it, I would've prolonged a partying phase instead of looking for someone that I could see myself raising a family with." Because she and her girlfriend knew marriage was possible, they had started "talking about engagement, marriage, and children" early on in their relationship. They had a clear and mutual plan that they "wanted to get engaged between about one and three years of being together."

Kimberly similarly described how being able to marry allowed her to imagine a future with her girlfriend very early on:

> So, she wants to be a heart surgeon, and it must have been about two months in that I started to get really excited because that sounds like a lot of money. [*laughs*] So I was just thinking about life, "Well, hypothetically, if we got married, we would be rich and that would be so wonderful." And so, I started thinking a lot about our future and actually mapped out, you know, "If we got married in this year, and then she became a heart surgeon in this year, then if I had kids in this year." Which is a plan we actually now want to stick to. [*laughs*] But so, I think it really made the relationship more serious fast. Because now I wanted to imagine all this stuff.

The potential to be with someone who could offer her a stable, secure future coupled with the ability to be legally married made Kimberly want to plan their whole futures together. But being able to assume that the relationship would end in marriage also had the effect of making new same-sex relationships take on an air of seriousness very quickly, and this resulted in new forms of tension and conflict for same-sex couples.

THE NEW DEAL-BREAKER

Because being able to imagine marriage potential had the effect of quickly defining new relationships as about marriage, this also meant that Marriage Assumers saw little point investing in relationships without the prospect of marriage. Marriage was considered essential for relationship success and longevity. As such, same-sex relationships that might have been considered worthy of investing in when legal marriage was not an option were now deemed as destined to fail if marriage was not on the table. For example, Lizzie, a forty-eight-year-old married woman, had been dating her first same-sex partner for two years when marriage equality began to seem possible. She and her partner were beginning to discuss moving in together, but the prospect of being able to get legally married made her pause and reevaluate the choice. She felt like she should check in with her partner and make sure the relationship was marriage material first: "I said to her, 'I don't really want to move in with someone who I don't think is potentially someone I would marry, so let's be serious about this. I don't want to just move in and see if it works and if not we split up then we go our own way.'" Luckily for Lizzie, her partner felt ready to commit to marriage.

For Marriage Assumers, any uncertainty over marriage, or unwillingness to commit to it, was taken as a sign that the relationship was unlikely to work out long-term. As such, they typically made marriage a deal-breaker early on, before making other commitments in their relationship, like moving in together, so that they would not "waste time" with someone who was not interested in marrying. Maria, a twenty-five-year-old unmarried woman who had been with her partner for a year and a half, put it this way: "I didn't want to start living with someone if it wasn't going anywhere." Interestingly, however, when her mom had asked her if her girlfriend was "the one," Maria had said that she did not know: "I don't believe there is one person for anyone. Right now, things are going great and it feels like this could keep going, but who knows what's going to happen. That's the best answer I can give right now." She needed to know that her relationship could result in marriage, even though she herself was not yet certain that she would want to marry her girlfriend. For Maria and Lizzie, and some others, the ability to make marriage potential a deal-breaker was empowering, enabling them to ensure they were in the kinds of relationships they wanted.

Yet the survey data reveals that about 40 percent of unmarried people experienced marriage as a source of tension in their relationships, reporting frequent arguments about it. Moreover, in the interviews, partner conflict over marriage was one of the most frequent responses to the question "What is the worst thing about having the right to legally marry?" Marriage Assumers explained conflict over marriage as resulting from a lack of confidence in the security of the relationship. They needed reassurance from their partners that they wanted to get married in order to feel secure in their relationships, and they interpreted their partners' disinterest in marriage as a sign that they were not committed. Conflict occurred when they did not gain the necessary reassurance about marriage from their partners. Esteban had started dating his partner in 2007. He was eager to get married and started bringing it up soon after they moved in together. But every time he did, his partner "would have a panic attack, get crazy, and start to hyperventilate a bit!" He understood that his partner had good reasons to be nervous about marriage—it was the longest relationship he'd ever been in, he came from a family of divorce, and he was worried about having to tell his unsupportive family they were getting married. Nonetheless, Esteban could not help but feel "offended" and "upset." He said:

> I was envisioning marriage as an option and so I was also thinking, "I don't want to be in a relationship that is not going in that direction. If this is something where he doesn't feel he can commit to me then maybe I don't want to be in the relationship." And this was also in the context of me having a lot of friends and colleagues who were getting engaged and married and I just felt like "Oh my god, what's taking so long? If it's not going to work out then I want to be single so I can pursue a relationship with someone who does want to make lifelong plans with me."

He tried to be patient and, luckily for him, his partner eventually came around to the idea, and even proposed to him. They married in 2011. However, along the way marriage had caused a lot of conflict. Esteban made it clear that had his partner not acquiesced he would not have stayed in the relationship.

Others were not as lucky as Esteban and had broken up with their previous partners over marriage. Raul was almost forty and living with a previous partner when marriage became legal. He and his partner had both been supportive of the movement for marriage equality and had even gone and spoken to their legislators about it. But when marriage became legal and he brought up the idea of marrying, his partner said he was not interested. For Raul "it was heartbreaking and eye-opening at the same time." He told me, "Everything was fine other than that, but I could not help thinking, 'OK, then, so then what am I doing with him?' Because I thought we were on the same track." Putting it bluntly, he said, "That was the beginning of the end, literally. For me, marriage ended that relationship." When he started dating again, Raul was careful to make sure that "it was someone who saw marriage as a possibility." Laughing, he confided, "Marriage became part of the checklist, along with whether they had any criminal background."

Mikey was twenty-six and in a three-year relationship with a twenty-year-old when marriage became legal. "Of course we started talking about marriage," but his partner didn't want to do it because he was still young and didn't want to "miss out on other opportunities" by marrying too soon. Having the prospect of marriage and starting to talk about it made Mikey question the relationship:

> It was then that I started to process the idea that [my partner] had a serious drinking problem and I was thinking I'm not sure we should get married. . . . I started to recognize at that point that maybe it wasn't going to work with him. So yeah, marriage had an impact on our relationship but not necessarily in the best way!

Since marriage became available, Mikey had become much more aware that he had "been making poor choices" about who he was "trying to make relationships work with." All these LGBQ people who had broken up with previous partners were now in other committed relationships. As such, they did not consider the fact that marriage had ended their previous relationships as a negative thing. Instead, they perceived marriage as having given them a new power to better evaluate and end relationships that were "destined to fail." Marriage helped "save" them from bad relationships, or even bad life decisions more generally.

These experiences differed significantly from those of Marriage Rejecters, who also often disagreed with their partners over marriage (see chapter 2). Marriage Rejecters disagreed with their partners theoretically over the importance of marriage as an institution or for their relationships but did not interpret those differences as indicative of a lack of commitment to them or the relationship. By contrast, Marriage Assumers assumed that a partner's (lack of) willingness or readiness to marry was indicative of their commitment to them. Marriage Rejecters were also usually able to reach compromises with their partners, either agreeing to marry to make their partners happy or having partners who agreed not to marry. Because marriage was less important than their partner's happiness, Marriage Rejecters acted as deal-makers around marriage. By contrast, Marriage Assumers were deal-breakers when it came to marriage, taking an all or nothing approach to their relationships. They were typically so dismayed by a partner's disinterest in marriage that the conflict allowed little room for discussion and negotiation. Marriage was more important than their partner's happiness, and they would rather marry someone different than compromise to save the relationship.

But Why Marry?

Given the importance Marriage Assumers placed on marriage in their relationships, one might imagine that they would have very clear ideas about why they wanted to get married and a lot to say about why it mattered so much to them. Yet these were questions they struggled to answer. When probed to think about why they wanted to marry, there were often awkward pauses or admissions that they had not in fact ever given the question much thought. For example, when I asked Catherine, a twenty-six-year-old woman who had been with her partner for a year and a half, why she wanted to get married, she said, "I've never really thought too much about why it's important to me to get married, I think it's just because I always imagined I would."

Sometimes, Marriage Assumers even looked at me somewhat incredulously, as if the question was absurd and the answer should just be obvious.

Again, this contrasted significantly with Marriage Embracers and Rejecters, who typically gave very thoughtful and precise answers about why they married. Having embraced marriage without it being legal, Marriage Embracers (chapter 1) were experts of sorts on marriage, acutely aware of the cultural and legal dimensions of it, and what could be gained from each. Marriage Rejecters focused instead very narrowly on specific legal gains and benefits to be had from marrying, stressing these as the only valid reasons for doing so. By contrast, Marriage Assumers typically did not directly discuss any social, cultural, or legal dimensions of marriage in explaining why marriage was so important to them. Instead, their reasons for marrying were much narrower, often not extending beyond their immediate relationship and what they wanted out of it. This makes sense; because marriage was assumed as the obvious outcome of their relationships, having broader social, cultural, or familial reasons to marry were not regarded as necessary.

FIRST COMES LOVE, THEN COMES MARRIAGE

Marriage Assumers typically responded to questions about why they wanted to get married by giving two somewhat different versions of a "that's just what you do" answer. The first version connected marriage to love and commitment: marriage is "just what you do" when you love someone and are committed to them. When Erin and her wife started dating in 2003, Erin was in her late twenties and same-sex marriage had not yet been made legal in her home state of Massachusetts. But by May 2004, less than a year into their relationship, she had the option to legally marry her partner. Erin told me that she immediately knew that they were going to get married—it was "just a matter of who was going to pop the question." When I asked Erin why she had wanted to get legally married, she acknowledged that she had not given it much thought but then articulated the ways in which marriage, love, and commitment were intertwined in her mind:

> I mean, the truth be told, I think there was a big part of us that just felt like this is what you do. It was kind of like when you love someone and you're committed to them, that's kind of what you do. And so, I think that was actually probably the biggest driving force, but also, certainly we love each other. We were committed to each other. I think we felt like first comes love, then comes marriage.

Erin simply took for granted that she and her partner would get legally married after such an option became possible. It was not something she felt she should do or had to do. Instead, she understood marriage as something obvious and inevitable that anyone would want to do if they were in a loving, committed relationship.

The second, even more common version connected marriage to the "natural progression" of a relationship: marriage is "just what you do" when you have been with someone for a while; it's the obvious next step in a relationship. Casey believed that having marriage "as an option from the moment" he met his partner made their relationship progression feel "generic." Because legal marriage was always on the table, he felt that their relationship inevitably followed a "typical boy-meets-boy kind of story about falling in love and all that usual stuff, a very generic story that's happened millions of times." He simply assumed that their relationship would follow a "typical" path toward marriage.

Words such as "evolution," "progression," "moving forward," and "natural next step" were frequently utilized to explain how Marriage Assumers got from dating to marriage, and why. Brianna, a married thirty-one-year-old, explained, "It just seemed like the next logical step [for us to get married] because we had the house, she had her degree. Just 'cause with life it's like progression. If you're with somebody that you love and you wanna do it, then you might as well get married." Jeff, an unmarried twenty-six-year-old man who had been with his partner for four years, connected this "natural progression" idea to both age and relationship duration: "It stands to reason that marriage is the eventual next step in our relationship. I mean, if you're in your late twenties or early thirties and you've been together for years, then this is the next logical step."

For those like Casey, Brianna, and Jeff who had only been young adults or in their early twenties when they had gained the right to legally marry, marriage was something they were always able to envisage as a normal part of their relationship progression. But for those who were somewhat older, what mattered for being a Marriage Assumer was whether or not they gained the right to legally marry at a point in their relationships and lives in which it could be incorporated as a typical "next step" and internalized as "just what you do" as part of the natural progression of things. Maggie (now forty) was thirty-four when she gained access to legal marriage. Unlike the younger Marriage Assumers, she said that "her generation" had not regarded marriage as "traditional" for same-sex relationships growing up. Nonetheless, because she had started a new relationship after marriage became legal and was still young enough to follow a typical (heteronormative) life course trajectory, she was able to adjust her thinking and internalize marriage as a "normal" thing to do. She explained, "So then by the time I was in my midthirties I was like, 'I can totally get married and have the very picket fence idea of a very nuclear family.' I can have a regular, normal relationship." She started dating her partner in 2009 and married her a year later. Now, just like younger Marriage Assumers who had grown up with access to legal marriage, Maggie believed marriage was "just what her relationship was about."

THEN COMES A BABY IN A BABY CARRIAGE

There was one reason for marriage that extended beyond the immediate couple relationship and which was more clearly articulated by Marriage Assumers: wanting to have children. Because Marriage Assumers were younger than the average Marriage Embracer or Rejecter, they were also much more likely to want to have children *in the future*, making this reason for marrying distinct to this group. Some Marriage Embracers already had children with their partners, but they did not discuss children as central reasons to marry. Most Marriage Rejecters did not have or want children.[8]

Assumers often spoke about marriage as "just what you do" if you want to have children. This was sometimes connected to religion and morality. For example, Rachel, thirty, said, "Not very long after we moved in together, I realized that it would definitely be important to her to get married if we were going to start a family. She's from a more conservative background, she went to church, and was very religious for a long time." Other times, the idea that one should be married to have children was loosely connected to social norms, a sense that it was just the "right thing to do" to be married when you have children. Eva, whose wife was currently pregnant with their first child together, said, "We knew that when we had kids that we wanted to be married." When I asked her why, she replied, "I don't really know. It just seemed like a good idea. Just seemed like the right order. [*pauses*] Yeah, I don't—I don't really have a good reason. It wasn't required, it just seemed like a nice way to do it."

However, some Marriage Assumers saw marriage as offering them greater legal protections as parents. Yet even here they did not refer to specific protections or rights that they would gain from it; rather, they had a vague sense that it was better to be married "in the eyes of the law" or "government" when they decided to have children, especially if they were not intending to be the birth parent. For example, when I asked Brianna "what were the main reasons you wanted to get married?" she gave this uncertain reply about the law, marriage, and parenting rights:

Kids. If everything goes according to plan, she's the one to give birth to our kids, so I wanted to be legally part of their life, I guess.

And what did you think marriage would give you in terms of parenting rights?

I don't know, just more rights as a parent. Cause I don't even know, do—if she has a child, if I still have to adopt? I actually don't know that. But I figured it would just make everything easier.

Brianna had been certain enough that marriage and children were connected legally for that to be a primary reason to marry, yet also deeply uncertain about the specific ways in which they worked together.

Sophie, a twenty-seven-year-old married woman, also articulated this kind of thinking well: "One piece that really drove us to get married that some of our friends hadn't really thought about is that we both really want to have children, and we want to make sure our children are protected as much as possible under every law humanly possible." However, when I asked her how exactly she thought being married would help them become parents or have more secure rights as parents, she admitted that she did not know:

Since we don't have any children yet, I don't know the actual intricacies of the law, but that's something that I just always felt strongly—being married and being parents has to be better in the eyes of the law than not being married. I know if one of us has a child we'd have to go through second-parent adoption regardless. I think, but I'm not positive, that it's easier if we're married. Who knows? I'm not really sure.

What one sees in Sophie's statement, like in those of others, is the idea that specific knowledge about the law was something most Marriage Assumers thought they could postpone finding out about until the time came to actually have children. Nonetheless, they took for granted that marriage and parenting were connected enough legally that wanting children was a good enough reason to marry. We also see an implicit, deeply internalized sense that marrying is the right thing to do legally, even without any specific knowledge of the legal implications of doing so.

Somewhat ironically, while Marriage Assumers assumed marriage would help them legally as parents, the law itself had not yet caught up. The kinds of assumptions that help heterosexual couples gain parenting rights did not apply equally to same-sex couples. For heterosexual couples a "Marital Presumption of Parentage" assumes that children born to a heterosexual married couple are products of that marriage and recognizes both members of the couple as parents. No evidence is needed for heterosexual spouses that a biological relationship exists between the man and child for the man to have legal rights, unless the presumption is rebutted by evidence proving that it is impossible for him to be a biological parent of the child. Because of the reliance on biological connectedness to dictate parenting rights, even after same-sex marriage became legal nationwide the same marital presumption was not extended to same-sex couples.[9] The specific laws surrounding same-sex parenting remain regionally varied and complex in many other ways too.[10] It is therefore not surprising that Marriage Assumers only had a vague sense that being married would help them, without grasping the specifics of what remained a complex legal situation. But they were not confused or overwhelmed by the legal landscape; they simply imagined marriage and parenting to be legally connected and assumed that legal rights in one domain would make it easier to navigate the other.

Several Marriage Assumers also believed that marriage would create a more secure and stable environment in which to raise children. This tended to be a reason articulated by those who had experienced some form of family instability themselves. For example, Casey, who had described a childhood of divorce, remarriages, and custody issues, and numerous family members who had children out of wedlock with multiple partners, had this to say after my question about why he had wanted to get married:

> We wanted to have a family. By then we knew we wanted to have kids.
> *And would you have ever thought about having kids without marriage?*
> No, I wouldn't have. Because I came from broken homes, rebroken, and broken a few more times! [*laughs*] So, I think I would have been hesitant. I think that I would probably be uncomfortable having children not feeling that there was an appropriate bond between us. I mean, like I said, most of my family is not married and has kids and that hasn't really gone very well for them. [*laughs*]

However, Casey also went on to make the point that being gay meant having the "luxury" of not having unplanned pregnancies and of being able to make a choice about the context in which to raise children. He understood that it can be "a lot harder for heterosexuals and for females, and a lot of work to make that choice if you're uneducated" and he wanted to make it clear that he "did not judge" people who had children outside of marriage or who could not achieve a stable relationship before having children. But he said, "Being that I was able to decide, I did feel that marriage was important."

Eva was one of those women whom Casey had described as not judging, having gotten pregnant unintentionally in a previous heterosexual relationship. Now her child was a teenager and she was married to a new, same-sex partner, and they wanted to have another child together. For Eva, the security of marriage was just as much for her as it was for the child they would have together. Having already experienced parenting alone, she did not want to do it again: "I would never have a baby not being married again. Being married I feel more comfortable with it. I'm not going to have to do this by myself. That was my big fear. It's too hard." In this way, the "security" and "stability" associated with marriage was conceptualized as both for children and for parents.

Lastly, some Marriage Assumers wanted to marry in order to create a clearer family unit. Eva said that before she married she had struggled to create the appropriate relationship between her girlfriend and her children and to communicate that relationship effectively to others. She had wanted her children, and other people, to see her girlfriend as family, not just her girlfriend, and she thought that marriage would help achieve that:

> Because I could call her my girlfriend but what do you call her to my kids? And we would be in meetings at my kids' school and it was awkward, you know it's nice now to be able to say "And this is their stepmother." So, I would say the biggest reason [we wanted to get married] is she felt like family. And I thought we should be a family.

Here Eva articulates an interesting tension between structure and agency: it already felt to her as if they were family, but she still perceived that marriage would help them achieve the status of family. This kind of subtle tension between structure and agency was apparent more generally in the fact that Marriage Assumers typically believed that *first* comes love, then comes marriage, and then comes a baby. In other words, they believed that they had to create love and commitment first, and once they had adequately done so, it was "natural" to get married and have children. However, they also believed that their relationships and families depended on the structure of marriage—that marriage was necessary for creating the kind of commitment conducive to having children and creating family status. As such, there was a kind of unresolved paradox in their narratives between what they felt they could achieve for their relationships and families without marriage, and what they believed they needed marriage for.

That children figured so centrally in their answers about why they had wanted to get married demonstrates that Marriage Assumers made assumptions about children as well as marriage. Although having access to legal marriage may not have resolved legal parenting rights for LGBQ people, it does seem to have begun shifting the ways in which they imagined and planned their family futures, with parenting and marriage becoming more interconnected and central in their minds. This supports emerging national survey data that reveals dramatic differences in expectations around family building between LGBTQ+ millennials and older generations of LGBTQ+ people, and it emphasizes the central role that access to legal marriage plays in shifting ideas about marriage and parenting across generations.[11]

Marital Readiness

Let's pause and imagine the average Marriage Assumer for a minute. She came out and started dating same-sex partners after legal marriage was already possible. She always assumed that she would get legally married one day. Knowing that her relationships have marriage potential matters to her, and she has vetted her partners for marriage interest and commitment early on, making it a deal-breaker. She does not know exactly why marriage is so important to her. Instead, she feels it is "just what you do" when you love someone and are committed to them. She also wants children, and she feels strongly (but rather abstractly) that marriage is important for having them. She has been lucky enough to find a partner who feels the same way. But how does she know when it is the right time to get married?

Given how much assurance Marriage Assumers needed early on in their relationships that their partners shared their desire for marriage, one might guess that they would want to get married quickly and early in their relationships. However, this was not typically the case. It was usually only the front end of their relationships that progressed very quickly toward marriage, and then their relationships slowed down. Marriage Assumers described relationships that moved quickly from meeting to dating and moving in together, with marriage "on the table" from the beginning.[12] But most did not actually make fast decisions to marry. Instead, they followed the kinds of trajectories that family sociologists find are common among young heterosexual couples: treating marriage as a "capstone," the last brick to be put in place only after all other life and relationship goals have been achieved.[13]

Forty percent of Marriage Assumers in this study were not yet married, but all saw themselves getting legally married in the future.[14] They were not as fast to marry as their older counterparts who had been in longer-term relationships in the Marriage Embracer group (chapter 1).[15] Marriage was regarded as the crowning achievement of their relationships, and it was something they were consciously working toward. This meant that although Marriage Assumers all expected to marry, they were not willing to "rush into it." For a few, it was just about getting to the right age. Catherine, who was twenty-six, thought that the only thing holding her back was her age, explaining that she was "just still too young for it now" but that she'd be open to thinking about it "in six months or a year." Erica, who was twenty-four years old, also felt too young to marry her partner. Her partner had proposed to her impulsively after an argument when she was twenty-two and she had initially said yes, but she called it off after a couple of weeks because she "felt very young, very twenty-two and not ready." But for the vast majority of Marriage Assumers, something more had to be achieved to get to the point of readiness for marriage.

One common theme was taking the time to ensure compatibility with partners and work through relationship issues. These kinds of narratives about marital readiness reflect adherence to what the sociologist Ann Swidler calls "prosaic" scripts about love—the idea that "the kind of love that leads to marriage" should not depend on irrational feelings but "on compatibility and practical traits that make persons good life partners."[16] Although Marriage Assumers believed marriage required lifelong work, they simultaneously thought one should feel certain about compatibility before marrying. This meant that Marriage Assumers typically used other relationship commitments, such as living together and even buying houses together, to test their compatibility. For example, Travis, an unmarried but engaged twenty-six-year-old, said that first they had needed to move in together and "test the waters" and only once they were "successful in that arena" had they felt ready to get engaged. Some referenced horror stories about other people who had not taken the time to test compatibility before tying the knot as a way of explaining why they were taking their time. For example, Brianna and her partner had bought a house together and got engaged after three years, but they took seven years to feel ready to actually get married. When I asked her why they had waited to marry, she said:

> I had a couple of friends that got married right away. [*laughs*] And they're all divorced now. One had been with her partner for like six months and they were like, "Yes! Let's get married" and they're now divorced. She's getting married again in a couple months. My other friend had been with her partner for a couple years and they—just didn't work out!

Having witnessed other people make what she presumed to be rushed decisions to marry, Brianna was not willing to make the same mistake herself. She felt confident enough in the long-term success of her relationship to commit to buying a house and getting engaged, but she wanted to really ensure compatibility before tying the knot.

Most Marriage Assumers also believed that they should work to resolve any serious relationship issues before marrying. Being willing to work through issues was a quality that had initially attracted Josh, a forty-year-old man, to his partner. He said, "I could tell he was resilient. He was someone that we'd be able to build a life together. We would make things work." Nevertheless, the beginning of their relationship was "crazy rocky," and they broke up about a year into it and then got back together. It took seven years for them to get to the point of readiness for marriage. Josh explained, "There were some things in our relationship that I think we really needed to work on. Trust, and I just needed to be confident that this was somebody that I really wanted to spend the rest of my life with." Ultimately, Josh thought he felt ready to marry before his partner, but he made "a conscious decision" to hold off until he knew for sure that they were both on the same page. Despite the difficult times they had, Josh said, "I always truly believed that we'll be together forever." In other words, he never really doubted that they would get to the marriage finish line, but the reverence with which he treated marriage meant that he was also not willing to rush to get there.

However, taking one's time to achieve marital readiness could feel risky for Marriage Assumers, who needed to feel assured their relationships were definitely headed toward marriage. They were loath to invest years in a relationship if they might not get to the desired finish line. One strategy they utilized was what I call "locking it down, then slowing it down." This was a kind of middle-ground capstone approach. They gained the much-needed commitment to marriage early on by getting engaged or exchanging rings, but then did not actually marry until they had laid all the necessary relationship groundwork. In fact, a fifth of unmarried participants who said they were likely to marry their partners were already engaged to them, and a further 40 percent had already exchanged rings with their partners to symbolize their commitment. This suggests an eagerness to symbolize commitment to marriage early in relationships. Whereas before same-sex marriage was legal same-sex couples exchanged rings to show commitment because they could not get married, for Marriage Assumers rings were frequently used as a precursor to marriage. And they were typically exchanged near the beginning of the relationship, suggesting that marriage is now incorporated into same-sex relationships at an early stage of relational development. Then, having locked down their marital commitment, Marriage Assumers slowed their relationship trajectories down in order to adhere to cultural ideas about marital readiness.

Vicky is an example of this "locking it down, then slowing it down" capstone approach. When she first met her girlfriend, she was only twenty-three, and her girlfriend was in the process of beginning to exit another same-sex marriage. Vicky felt very young and inexperienced and "not ready for anything serious" but quickly found herself "seriously attached" to her new girlfriend. When her girlfriend started divorcing her then-wife a few months after they met, Vicky gave her a "right-handed ring" to signify her commitment to her. She told me, "It was the first time that I've spent a significant amount of money on somebody. I couldn't obviously be there for the actual divorce, but I wanted her to know that I was emotionally there. It was more of a sign that I wasn't going anywhere." They moved in together after five months of dating, and her girlfriend officially proposed after a year. Vicky admitted that her friends had warned her that they "hadn't been together long enough," but they had been eager to lock down the relationship early on. Now they were engaged, Vicky was keen to start slowing things down. She confided, "[I felt], 'OK, we're going too fast, we need to slow it down.' " They had made "no concrete plans for the wedding yet" because they wanted "to build as good a relationship as possible before taking that step." Vicky wanted to give their families time to get to know one another too and felt that "that just takes time and can't be forced." So, although Vicky and her girlfriend had followed their hearts and sought marital commitment quickly and early in their relationship, their devotion to doing marriage the right way also meant that they were not willing to rush into it.

To my knowledge, this kind of "locking it down, then slowing it down" strategy is not something existing scholarship has identified among heterosexuals. But otherwise, Marriage Assumers appeared like the kind of "marital planners" family scholars have identified as typical of most young heterosexual couples.[17] They were delaying entry into marriage in response to an elongated transition to adulthood and regarded achieving other personal and professional goals as perquisites for marital readiness. Marriage Assumers articulated two somewhat different versions of the marital-planner approach. The first centered mostly on personal fulfillment.[18] Marriage Assumers believed that one should focus on achieving individual educational and career goals prior to marriage and that good partners should support you in doing so. They spoke about such educational and career goals as if it was obvious that they should be accomplished prior to marriage, but without ever really explaining why. Jo (thirty-two), who was with her partner ten years before marrying her, said that when marriage had first become legal she was too young to focus on a "major life goal" like marriage: "I was like twenty-three or twenty-four . . . and I was really busy traveling and drinking too much and just not really focused on major life goals!" But then their lives shifted to launching educational and career goals, and they spent several years living long distance as they gave each other the space to do so: "Then we were both in school, so clearly that wasn't the right time, as we both wanted to each get our master's degrees and stuff. So, marriage wasn't going to happen until after that." The implicit assumption was that marriage requires a kind of commitment and sacrifice that was incompatible with both the early "partying" stage of young adulthood and the kinds of dedication and flexibility needed to pursue postgraduate and early-stage professional career goals.

A second version of the marital-planner approach was less about first achieving individual goals and more about being able to contribute fully to marriage. Marriage Assumers spoke about ensuring they got to a secure place in their careers so that they were able to offer their spouses the kind of security they believed marriage required. Here, achieving particular schooling and career goals were more directly connected to ideas about marital success. For instance, Ryan, a twenty-nine-year-old man, felt that it was important he was in a secure, stable place with his career so that he could "uphold his end" of the marital bargain:

> I want to make sure that if I'm going to make a commitment to him then I'm making a financial commitment to sustaining a lifestyle. And so, I figured that once I'm in my thirties or once my career has found a steady financial stream I could count on [I'd be able to do that]. I didn't want to be married and struggling with stability, because to me marriage represents stability. Marriage will come when I have stability. Marriage is kind of the icing. I don't see it the other way around, that I'm going to get married and *then* it's going to be stable. I want to be in control of my own destiny and know that I got to wherever I am in my life for me and that I'm choosing to share that with someone else.

Seeing marriage as a financial as well as relationship commitment, these young unmarried people also stressed fiscal responsibility. Whitney, a twenty-three-year-old, said she would not consider marrying her partner until her student loans had been taken care of because they have to "be fiscally responsible to each other," and she did not want "money to become an argument for us."

Gender and social class dynamics are both at play here. Although both men and women mentioned the importance of being able to provide financial security in marriage, this was a more prevalent sentiment among men, as gendered cultural expectations still shape ideas about being a good provider in families.[19] Beliefs that marriage should only occur when one is financially secure are also class-based, putting marriage increasingly out of reach for those without good educational and career prospects.[20] Most of the LGBQ people in this study were securely middle or upper-middle class. As such, this typically represented only a short, temporary delay in marriage. Their young ages made their financial and professional situations feel less settled, but most fully expected to feel ready for marriage within a few years and were actively planning their lives to get to that point. However, some Marriage Assumers resented the longer-term class-based implications of the marital-planner approach. Ollie, a thirty-two-year-old man who had been with his partner for eight years, admitted that he had been "nagging" his partner about marriage for some time now and felt that class-based ideas about marital readiness were standing in the way.

> He knows I definitely want to be married. We've talked about the timing and eight years is a long time, but we don't have adult jobs yet. I understand he wants for us to both have steady jobs, and for us to have our own house or something. But I feel like I've come from a totally different background than he has. His parents are fairly comfortable, and my parents are on the poorer side, and all of my friends from when I grew up were poor. I think his family has different expectations of what needs to happen in order for people to get married. I know I'm never going to reach that. So realistically I don't think that it's going to happen and I worry that it's contingent on me getting to a certain career or something.

Ollie shared an insightful understanding of class-based differences in ideas about what goals have to be achieved to be ready for marriage. His partner's insistence on delaying marriage to meet goals that felt unrealistic had left Ollie feeling insecure about his commitment to marrying him: "Honestly, I can't really tell if he's just using this as some sort of excuse not to marry me." And it was reaching deal-breaker stage. Ollie's story is a useful reminder that adherence to cultural scripts about marital readiness has real consequences for relationship inequalities.

WHEN YOU KNOW, YOU KNOW . . . OR DO YOU?

The minority of Marriage Assumers who did not follow a capstone or marital-planner approach for deciding when to get married described their decisions very differently. They drew on "fairytale" language instead, believing that they had met "the one" and that "when you know, you know." Instead of a marital-planner approach, which relies on carefully working up to marriage, they felt that they had to follow their hearts and dive right in. Instead of believing that the time was right, they spoke about the person being right for them. When Heather, a thirty-one-year-old woman, described how she and her partner had gone from dating, to getting engaged, to married in the space of two years, she immediately offered an explanation based on mutual feelings that they were right for one another:

> We officially started dating in July of that year, got engaged the following spring, and then got married the following October. We both sort of felt like we had not been in a relationship like that before. We never got tired of spending time together, and we just connected on so many different levels . . . which

I don't think either of us had really had to that level before. We were both feeling like when you know, you know.

Swidler describes this as a "mythic" view of love: sudden, certain, and involving attributes such as a clear, all or nothing choice, and a unique other. She explains that these cultural myths about love persist in part because they are embedded into the institutional structure of marriage. The institution of marriage legally and culturally binds you to someone for life, making the mythic image of love true as a social reality, whatever the reality of your romantic bond. Moreover, the culture of love in its mythic form gives people a way of talking about the all or nothing consequences of choices they may be quite confused or ambivalent about making.[21] By drawing on language of "the one" and "knowing it felt right," these Marriage Assumers could assuage deeper uncertainty about marital readiness.

Nevertheless, uncertainty still came through in the narratives of Assumers who did not follow a marital-planner script. Marriage Assumers who let feelings instead of careful planning guide their marital decisions suffered from personal angst about whether they were doing the right thing as well as social anxiety about how others would judge them. Despite the cultural perseverance of mythic ideas about love and marriage, these Marriage Assumers were cognizant of the fact that their experiences ran counter to dominant cultural ideas about the right way to approach marriage. They knew that today, at least for the middle class, following one's heart is not widely considered the appropriate method for evaluating marital readiness. Maggie started dating her girlfriend in 2009, and they got engaged just a few months later. She described their relationship as like a "fairy tale," herself as being "head over heels," and both of them as feeling certain the other was "the one very early on." But she also admitted to having "two minds" about how quickly they got married:

> We're both children of divorce, so marriage makes me a little nervous. Part of me was like, "You need to know them for years and years before you even consider getting married," so only dating her for three months seemed crazy. But I figured I had never felt so loved in a relationship. And she's a nanny, and I've seen her with kids, so I knew I loved the way that she was with kids, I loved the way that she was with her friends. You know what I mean? I had two minds about it.

Maggie's anxiety was at odds with the part of herself that felt deeply that her partner and this relationship were different, and she wanted to trust those feelings. Maggie followed her heart, leaning into the mythic version of love, but still struggled to fully trust it, given both the social and personal reality of divorce and the cultural dominance of prosaic love as a more suitable basis for marriage.

The few Marriage Assumers who let feelings guide their marriage decisions also expressed shame and embarrassment. They understood that others judged them negatively for their decisions. Casey recalled how his friends had teased him for being so "lovey-dovey" with his now-husband when he first introduced him to them and for acting "as if they would be together forever" from the beginning. Embarrassed by how quickly they wanted to get engaged, they had decided to get "pre-engaged" instead, but "everyone just laughed" at them for that. Casey did not let his friends' ridicule deter him from following his heart. He and his now-husband moved in together after a few months, "pre-engaged" after six months, married within a year and a half, and started the adoption process to have children one year after marrying. Laughing, he said, "So it was like, bang, bang, bang, bang, bang. [*motioning that things happened in quick succession*]" He followed a very typical version of a mythic love script, which according to Swidler typically includes defiance of social forces and overcoming social judgment and barriers (think Romeo and Juliet).[22] Casey never doubted that his husband was "the one." But even years later as he is retelling his marriage story to me, he remains acutely aware that most other people in his life doubted his ability to make such a fast and certain decision.

The narratives of Marriage Assumers show that the institution continues to offer very clear cultural scripts for behavior, outlining the steps for what individuals should do to achieve marital readiness. There remain two dominant versions—one based on prosaic love and the other on mythic love—but the latter goes against social norms for appropriate behavior, at least among middle-class Americans. Thus, both the cultural and normative pillars of the institution (see introduction) work in tandem to guide something as seemingly personal as relationship progression.

Conclusion

The experiences of Marriage Assumers suggest that having access to legal marriage has radically redefined same-sex relationships. Considering the experiences of Marriage Assumers in comparison to those of Marriage Embracers (chapter 1) and Marriage Rejecters (chapter 2), both of whom mostly started their relationships before legal same-sex marriage was an option, we can see clearly how much same-sex relationships have changed. Marriage is now an assumed and expected outcome for new relationships. Whereas legal marriage shaped conceptions of what was possible for Marriage Embracers, it has shaped conceptions of what is expected and necessary for Marriage Assumers. Assumers espoused heteronormative cultural tropes like "first comes love, then comes marriage" and spoke as if legal marriage had always been there. It was taken for granted as "just what you do" when you love someone and are committed to them and as the obvious "next step" in the "natural progression" of a relationship. They further assumed that marriage and parenting were inseparable but with vague understandings of why. Yet having deeply internalized cultural ideas about the necessity of marriage also meant that this cohort of new same-sex daters struggled to conceptualize love and commitment outside of a marital model. They considered a partner's hesitancy around marriage to be a deal-breaker and were unwilling to invest time and energy into relationships without the assurance of marriage potential. Once in a relationship, other parts of their relationships and lives were evaluated through the lens of marriage: were they compatible enough with their partners for marriage? Had they achieved enough personal goals yet to get married? Were their careers and lives stable enough for marriage? Everything else became part of a broader marital master plan. Those that did not follow now-dominant cultural scripts for marriage and followed their hearts instead suffered personal angst and social shaming.

To be clear, this is not an argument that access to legal marriage has made same-sex relationships better or worse, only different. There were both gains and losses. Some Marriage Assumers found access to marriage empowering because it gave them information about how committed their partners were and enabled them to leave relationships that they saw as not marriage material. Nevertheless, access to legal marriage created new problems for same-sex relationships as well. Tension and conflict over marriage was common, and some relationships that may well have been successful when legal marriage was not an option were now considered failures. Marriage Assumers described a partner's disinterest, or even uncertainty, about marriage as a sign that they were not committed to them and the relationship, increasing relationship insecurities. Moreover, Marriage Assumers were much less willing to make compromises around marriage than their Embracer and Rejecter counterparts, who prioritized their relationships and partners' happiness over marriage.

To date, take-up rates of legal same-sex marriage have been high and fast, but some scholars have wondered whether they mostly represent a "backlog of couples who had lived together for many years" and who therefore took fast advantage of the opportunity to marry, while "younger couples may not marry in such large numbers in the future."[23] However, the data in this chapter paints a very different picture of the future of same-sex relationships. In less than a decade (even before it had become legal nationwide), marriage had already become an institutionalized relationship experience among younger

LGBQ individuals in new relationships—taken for granted, normalized, and internalized as the gold standard. Typical of institutionalized experiences, in some ways these Marriage Assumers gave marriage little thought. They were mostly unaware of the degree to which legal marriage was shaping their relationship choices and experiences and the meanings they attached to them. At the same time, they spent vast amounts of time thinking about marriage, allowing it to consume much time and emotional energy. They aspired to it, imagined it, planned it, and worried about it. They gave marriage a lot of thought on a personal level, but little thought as an institution. By contrast, both Marriage Embracers and Rejecters gave marriage *as an institution* a great deal of thought, interrogating what it meant legally, socially, and culturally, and they were much more aware of the ways in which gaining access to legal marriage was shaping their relationships. Marriage Assumers help demonstrate that once marriage becomes institutionalized, it becomes an invisible backdrop in the lives of LGBQ people.

As all LGBQ people now have access to legal marriage from the start of any new relationship, the marked differences across the groups I have described across these first three chapters will weaken over time. Moreover, as I will show in the next part of the book (especially chapters 5 and 6), some of these group differences become less pronounced after people actually get married, as LGBQ people with a range of premarital experiences find the experience of being legally married more similarly transformative.

PART II

Doing Marriage

4

Proposal Pressures

When I met Grace, she and her partner had just celebrated their seventeenth anniversary together. She was forty-eight, and her partner was fifty-two. She had started dating women toward the end of high school and came out as a lesbian during college. Back then she was a self-proclaimed "club girl" who "wasn't interested in anything committed." But by the time same-sex marriage became legal in 2004, Grace was forty and had been with her partner nine years. They had been through a lot already—experiencing the death of parents, losing jobs, trying to get pregnant, miscarrying, and adopting a child. They had also already exchanged rings in a private ceremony between the two of them, as a symbol of their marriage-like commitment. Though they had not invited others, Grace told me, "It was definitely something neither of us took lightly." Grace belongs to the Marriage Embracer group described in chapter 1, but only up to a point. She privately embraced marital rituals as important symbols of love and commitment, but she was not "one of those women who had always dreamed of a white wedding." For Grace, marriage was a "private commitment to make with someone" and not something she "needed to do in front of some religious body or in front of friends and family to feel valid." She admitted to occasionally watching "those horrible TV shows like *Say Yes to the Dress*" but was appalled by all the extravagance associated with weddings.

It is perhaps not surprising then that she and her partner got engaged to be legally married with very little fuss and fanfare. While driving, they heard on the radio that legal same-sex marriage was going into effect and got engaged right then and there. No one proposed, they just decided immediately to get married as soon as possible. Grace explained, "I think we just knew. I mean, I always tease her that I still haven't got my get-down-on-one-knee proposal—not that I'd ever expect that, but we joke! We didn't agonize over it; it just felt like the right thing to do." They went to get their marriage license that same day and were married five days later. Grace laughed as she recalled how she "hadn't planned anything at all." When her friends came to her house the morning of her legal marriage, they helped her choose an outfit from her closet, dragged her to get her first ever pedicure, and insisted she buy a bouquet of flowers to hold. Grace said, "It's not like I didn't know all those things [I should be doing]. I mean, I was my sister's maid of honor!" She just didn't care that much about what she was supposed to do and had not given it much thought.

By contrast, for Andy, a thirty-two-year-old Marriage Assumer (chapter 3), getting engaged and married the right way was very important. She, too, had come out as a lesbian during college but had only gotten together with her partner in 2005, a year after same-sex marriage had become legal. They dated long-distance for the first couple years, seeing each other only infrequently, and then moved in together. Andy assumed that moving in together meant marriage should follow closely behind. In fact, she immediately started making her desires for marriage known. She informed her partner that "*if* marriage were to happen," she wanted to be proposed to, and she even went so far as to say that "*if* you were to propose, this is kind of how I would like it"—though she was careful "not to talk about it too much and jump the gun." Andy got what she wanted: seven months later, her partner proposed.

> She did it pretty traditionally. She arranged a whole date for us, so we went out all day and then for a fancy dinner. I didn't know it was coming, actually. She wanted it to be a surprise. After dinner, we went for a walk and she got down on one knee and read a little speech and pulled out a ring. It was very traditional. She knew that was what I wanted. I wanted it to be formal. I wanted to be formally asked.

Andy was excited to plan all the logistics of the wedding, relishing in the details and decisions. She told me, "We spent a lot of time thinking about it and brainstorming ideas about the main ideas or feelings we wanted people to have when they went to our wedding." In fact, in Andy's opinion, although "the wedding day itself was obviously a big deal," planning the wedding was "just as important" because it led them to have all kinds of "deep conversations" about what mattered to them. Proposal and wedding planning entailed a lot of thought and work, but were considered important parts of the marital process, which ultimately brought Andy and her partner "closer together."

Both Grace and Andy cared about getting legally married and wanted to do it. Both considered the commitment of marriage to be important and serious. Yet Grace cared little about *how* to do it. She felt free to ignore dominant marital norms and scripts for getting engaged and married, and she felt able to do it on her own, in a more private, simple way. By contrast, Andy cared deeply about getting engaged and married the "right way." What explains why some LGBQ people cared so much about following existing engagement conventions while others gave them so little thought? And why does it matter?

This chapter focuses on one of the most socially prescribed and heteronormative marital moments—getting engaged—to examine how LGBQ people begin on the path of doing marriage. I show that the kind of freedom Grace exhibited to become engaged easily and casually has greatly diminished for same-sex couples. LGBQ people in newer relationships that began with access to legal marriage care about getting engaged "the right way," agonize over how to do it, and invest a lot of work into making it happen. They have internalized heteronormative cultural beliefs about what engagements symbolize about relationships. As Andy said, this has the potential to yield new benefits for same-sex relationships, such as opening up important conversations and bringing couples closer together. Yet trying to get engaged the "right way" also introduces new forms of work, stress, and inequality in same-sex relationships.

The Existing Engagement Script

How exactly should same-sex couples get engaged? This might seem like an odd question—perhaps even a patronizing one. Surely everyone knows how to get engaged? For heterosexuals, there is no shortage of models they can look to, with creative ideas for how to do it easily accessible on social media, in magazines, movies, TV shows, and websites like HowTheyAsked.com. Yet for all the seeming variation out there, heterosexuals get engaged in very similar ways. This is because they follow a widely shared and internalized cultural script outlining all the activities, behaviors, and meanings associated with proposals. It is an unwritten cultural guidebook that is understood and taken-for-granted by cultural insiders.[1] Of course, everyone enacts the script somewhat differently, bringing their own personalities and background to bear on it, but overall, there is more adherence to than departure from its main content.

Despite many changes to gender relations between young men and women in heterosexual relationships, research shows that they continue to follow a traditional and highly gendered script for how to get engaged. At its core, the script contains the following basic behavioral components: the man should propose to the woman; he should get down on one knee and present the woman with a diamond ring; he should make some declaration of love for the woman; and the woman should be (or act) surprised.[2] Of course, a dominant, powerful wedding industry shapes these kinds of desires for grand, romantic gestures. Event planning for proposals is a booming business. But these expected behaviors are also based on a set of shared gendered beliefs: that women are (and should be) more passive and men are (and should be) more aggressive when it comes to relationship progression; that women care more about commitment than men and that proposing is a way for men to explicitly demonstrate readiness to commit; that how one gets engaged is a way of gauging how in love a man is with a woman and the extent to which he deems her worthy of romance; and that the ring symbolizes a man's readiness to spend money on the family and ability to assume the marital breadwinner role.[3] Young heterosexuals exhibit discomfort and anxiety regarding any possible departures from the script and even perceive people who do not get engaged in the right way as having weaker relationships.[4]

But the people in this study were not heterosexual. Nor were they all young or in young relationships. They were not cultural insiders either, having been excluded from the institution of marriage until recently. As such, some of the seemingly simple, taken for granted ideas ingrained in the existing engagement script did not apply easily to them. They were in a situation the sociologist Andrew Cherlin describes as incomplete institutionalization.[5] Institutionalized behavior is habitualized, meaning one does not even think about it because clear norms guide behavior and become taken for granted as just what you do. But our society, which is oriented toward heterosexual relationships, provides little specific guidance for same-sex couples regarding marital behavior. Although a few people had commitment ceremonies already, and some had previously been engaged in different-sex relationships, the experience of getting engaged to be legally married to a same-sex partner was new and uncertain territory for everyone. According to existing theory, incompletely institutionalized situations increase the potential for stress, anxiety, and couple conflict. However, a lack of clear norms and guidelines for behavior can be liberating. It offers couples opportunities for doing things differently and forging relationships that are more in line with their values, beliefs, and needs. This, after all, is at the heart of the queer enterprise, which involves making "life choices distinct from those considered more socially expected, celebrated, and sanctioned," radically transforming society by resisting normalization.[6] In fact, most recent research with LGBQ people emphasizes the ways they are critical of normative relationship expectations and engage in conscious and active resistance to marital norms.[7]

Thus, existing research suggests same-sex couples should either be confused by the lack of clear norms for how to get engaged or be actively resisting them. But this research shows neither is true. Far from confusion about what to do or active resistance to doing it, the LGBQ people in this study either casually dismissed existing engagement expectations as irrelevant, with little stress or confusion, or took them for granted as the only way to do things. When they departed from existing engagement scripts, it was because they felt they did not apply to them rather than because they were trying to resist or challenge them. And when they adhered to existing scripts, they did so in deeply internalized ways, showing deep knowledge of and attachment to the details and beliefs underpinning them. Moreover, LGBQ people displayed much more stress trying to stick to the existing engagement script and get it right than they did from not knowing what to do or from trying to challenge it.

To Propose or Not to Propose?

The existing, heteronormative script promotes a romantic proposal as the ideal means of getting engaged. Yet only half of the LGBQ people in this study who had got engaged did so with a proposal, while the other half became engaged by means of mutual conversations, in which both partners discussed marriage and came to the decision to get legally married together.[8] They were not, however, randomly distributed across the proposal or no proposal groups.

Interestingly, gender played little role here. Because of the gendered targeting of the wedding industry,[9] we might expect women to care more about proposals as romantic gestures than men. Alternatively, because proposals are widely regarded as a means for men to show commitment to women,[10] women in same-sex relationships may care much less about proposals than their heterosexual counterparts. Yet the data does not support gender-based hypotheses, with men and women equally distributed across the proposal/no proposal groups[11] and gender playing very little role in determining which partner should propose, if there was a proposal.

Instead, the three broad groups I outline in part I of the book—Marriage Embracers, Rejecters, and Assumers—each understood the need for proposals differently. Being at varying life and relationship stages, and having distinct orientations toward marriage, positioned the LGBQ people in these groups differently regarding their need for and feelings about proposals. The longer a person had been with their partner and the older they were the less likely they were to have had a proposal as the means of getting engaged. Additionally, those who began their relationships before same-sex marriage was legal were significantly less likely to have had a proposal.[12] This cohort effect overlaps with the three groups I identify because Embracers and Rejecters tended to be older and in longer-term relationships that predated legal marriage, while Assumers tended to be younger and in shorter term relationships that began only after marriage was already legal. Nearly all Embracers and Rejecters regarded a proposal as unnecessary and unimportant for getting married. By contrast, almost all Marriage Assumers regarded a proposal as a necessary and important stage in their marriage experience.

EMBRACERS AND REJECTERS: PROPOSALS AS UNNECESSARY AND INAPPROPRIATE

It is not that Marriage Embracers and Rejecters were not aware of the same script for how to get engaged as Assumers. In this wedding-obsessed culture, one could not help but be exposed to it. As Grace stressed, she had been her sister's maid of honor and watched *Say Yes to the Dress*. Yet she had not internalized the script as relevant for her relationship. Marriage Embracers understood that proposals were a symbolic means for one partner to demonstrate readiness to commit to the other. But given that they were already in committed relationships, such a demonstration of commitment felt unnecessary. They also knew that proposals were meant to come as a surprise. But wanting to get married was no surprise given that many of them had already married in other ways. It was not the gendered presumption of a man proposing to a woman that failed to resonate with these same-sex couples, but the presumption of uncertain commitment and readiness for marriage.

In fact, proposals were a common source of jokes between Marriage Embracers and their partners. It was because they seemed so unnecessary that they could playfully joke about wanting one without risking their partners taking them seriously. Proposals symbolized something that only less committed, less sure couples would need to do. Gail, a fifty-six-year-old who had been with her partner twenty-four years when marriage became legal, told me, "I mean, we did talk about it, and in a joking way we proposed to each other, but it was just immediately for both of us, definitely for me, of course we're going to do this." When I asked her what she meant by proposing in a joking way, she replied, "Because there was no question for either of us of whether we were going to do it or not."

Even the few exceptions, when Marriage Embracers did have a proposal, illustrate how uncomfortable they felt with having to do so. For example, Patrick, a fifty-year-old man who had been with his partner for fifteen years, was much like his Embracer peers in thinking that he could simply have a casual conversation with his partner to get engaged. Unfortunately, his younger partner indicated he didn't feel the same way.[13] Patrick wearily recalled, "I mean, I was kind of playing with the idea of 'Should we get married?' and the one time I tried to bring it up conversationally, [he] was like, 'Are you proposing to me?' and then I kinda backed off because I wasn't sure I wanted to go there." When I asked Patrick why the idea of a proposal put him off, he explained, "I mean, I kinda felt like we'd been together for so long that it's something we could just talk about without going through—a sort of proposal." Feeling pressured to get engaged in a way that seemed inappropriate for their relationship, Patrick "backed off" and decided not to bring it up again for a while. Eventually, however, he realized, "[My partner] was waiting for me to do it. And if I hadn't got up the nerve to do it [*laughs*] it probably would have never happened." Patrick was nervous through the whole process and spent a long time "debating what to do" about all the details of how, when, and where to propose.

Marriage Rejecters usually ignored the heteronormative proposal imperative as well but for different reasons. In the existing heterosexual proposal script, there is an unstated assumption that both partners want to marry and have no reservations about marriage as an institution. The decision to marry centers only on whether each is ready to commit to *one another*, while interest in marriage more generally is taken for granted. But given Marriage Rejecters' reservations about marriage as an institution, having partners propose to them could feel pressuring and insensitive to their feelings.[14] Whether or not to marry was something to be worked out and negotiated between partners with thoughtful consideration. Decisions to marry were typically based on practical reasoning and needs that felt at odds with the seemingly required romance of proposals. Moreover, if they were ultimately persuaded to marry to achieve some practical right or protection, they wanted to avoid engaging in symbolic gestures that would make it seem they needed or wanted marriage for anything else.

Angie, a fifty-one-year-old woman, had a partner who was more interested in marrying than she was. They "had many serious conversations" about why her partner wanted to marry and why she did not. Her partner "agreed not to push it" by proposing, but at different stages of their relationship they kept "opening up the conversation again." Like many Marriage Rejecters (see chapter 2), Angie was eventually persuaded by the legal benefits of marriage. But she never considered proposing. Instead, they went to "talk to their lawyer" about the logistics of merging their lives. Like other Rejecters, she was not concerned about the romance of getting engaged and saw serious conversations about marriage as the only reasonable way to make the decision.

Whether they were so sure they wanted to marry one another that little or no conversation was needed (Embracers), or unsure about marriage as an institution and felt the need to engage in serious discussion with their partners about it (Rejecters), these LGBQ people considered a proposal to be an unnecessary and inappropriate means of getting engaged. They perceived the existing proposal script to be centered on a different kind of couple—one that has not already demonstrated commitment or for whom there are no reservations about marriage as an institution. The engagement experiences of Embracers and Rejecters fit with neither incomplete institutionalization nor conscious resistance theories about the ways new groups experience existing scripts for behavior. They did not feel unsure about how to get engaged and exhibited little anxiety about ignoring existing scripts for how to do so. The only time they experienced anxiety was when their partners were not on the same page as them, as with the case of Patrick. Neither were they consciously trying to resist the existing script in an effort to do marriage differently. Some had reservations about marriage as an institution, but they did not purposefully avoid a proposal because of concerns with heteronormativity. Although they had very different views of marriage, both Embracers and Rejecters felt free to ignore existing heteronormative proposal expectations.

ASSUMERS: ROMANCE AND MEMORY-MAKING

In stark contrast, Marriage Assumers exhibited little freedom to depart from the existing proposal script. And, for the most part, they did not want to. Instead, they frequently expressed strong desires for the kinds of proposals one is used to seeing depicted in popular culture. There was of course much variation in the particular ways these were enacted, with differing levels of formality, tradition, and innovation. Yet all the proposals were planned in advance by one partner and consisted of one person asking the other to marry them. Few explained their desire for formal proposals in any depth, or seemed to think their desires for one needed much explanation. Instead, proposals were described as just what one does, as what is "expected" and "appropriate" or what one "deserves" when they are in a loving, committed relationship.

When prompted, most explained their desire for a proposal by drawing on concepts such as romance or the need to make lasting memories. For example, when I asked Andy (introduced at the start of the chapter), why it was important to her that her partner "formally ask her" to get married, she initially had trouble answering, indicating how taken for granted the idea was to her. Then she emphasized her desire for the kind of romance one sees in stories:

I guess, [*pauses*] I don't really know why that was important to me! I guess I thought it was more romantic, you know? I think it's fine for other couples when they just have a conversation and then they are married and that's great, but for me I wanted someone to do sort of the storybook thing for just that one event.

Though Andy said it was "fine" for others to get engaged via conversations instead of a proposal, her response makes clear that she viewed this as a subpar way to get engaged and that she might judge couples who did so negatively.

Erin, a thirty-six-year-old who got together with her partner shortly before legal marriage became possible, focused on how important it was to create an appropriate memory of getting engaged:

We kind of would say these comments like, you know, "Oh, I love you so much. You're the one I want to spend the rest of my life with," you know, or "Will you marry me?" And I would be like, "Are you serious?" No, this is not the moment I'm trying to propose to you, you know? This is not the memory I want, of me coming out of the bathroom in a towel. [*laughs*] And so it was a lot of that kind of stuff over and over again. Because we kept trying to like figure out, this is not the memory. This is not the way we want to do it.

Erin and her partner clearly had moments when getting engaged came up organically in conversation, but they resisted those more casual moments and waited to get engaged until they could create the right kind of memory of it. Like others, both Andy and Erin explained their desire for romance and memory-making as emerging from their own personal relationship and individual desires. Yet at the same time, they believed that there was a "right way" to get engaged and aspired to create the kind of romantic memory they were used to seeing and hearing about. In this way, we can see their choices and behaviors being shaped by both social norms and cultural scripts: norms shaped their sense of what was socially expected and appropriate, while cultural scripts provided guidance for how to behave and the meanings associated with particular behaviors.

Looking at their experiences of getting engaged, the biggest difference across the three groups was not whether or not they had a proposal, but rather how much work was involved. Embracers were remarkably free from worry and work—they gave little thought to how to get engaged, they just knew they wanted to do it. Rejecters worried about whether or not to marry and felt anxiety about the decision, but they did not exert thought or effort around the intricacies of how to get engaged. By contrast, as I show next, getting engaged was an enormously effortful task for Assumers. I focus the remainder of the chapter on Marriage Assumers and their engagement experiences because this new generation of same-sex couples offers the most insight into the future of same-sex relationships and the ways gaining access to legal marriage has changed them.

Script Following as Relational Work

We rarely encounter portrayals of couples making careful decisions about whether or not to get married, nor having serious discussions and negotiations about marriage with their partners. We are led to believe that we should just know that we want to get married, and if our partners love us and are committed to the relationship then it should be safe to assume they will want to marry us too. Because proposals are regarded as a natural, organic outcome of the right kind of love and commitment, they are also meant to just happen, without someone ever needing to directly ask for one. In reality, however, proposals do not just happen. Instead, a great deal of work goes into achieving one. I identified three kinds of relational work that Marriage Assumers engaged in to achieve a romantic proposal: avoiding direct marriage talk; controlling spontaneous expressions of emotion; and creating the impression of surprise.

First, Marriage Assumers were very careful about the ways in which they talked to their partners about marriage prior to getting engaged. Marriage talk was a delicate balancing act, for while some conversation was necessary to let one another know that they were interested in getting engaged, too much conversation or too serious conversations could undermine the romance and surprise they wanted. They worked hard only ever to discuss marriage in seemingly casual or hypothetical ways. These indirect conversations were the means by which both partners could gain reassurances that they wanted to marry, and the one proposing could gain confidence that the other would say yes. Once the necessary assurance was gained no further conversation about getting engaged was appropriate, and the partner being proposed to must simply wait for it to occur.

Research shows that heterosexual couples avoid direct marriage talk with one another as well but posits this work as something only women do.[15] The idea is that women subscribe to the cultural idea that men are less committed and therefore fear that any marriage talk will be unwelcome by men. To be deemed worthy of being asked, heterosexual women must avoid seeming pushy. Yet both men and women in same-sex relationships avoided direct marriage talk and engaged in very similar conversational strategies to achieve a proposal. Their avoidance of direct marriage talk was driven by a general desire to achieve a romantic proposal. They had incorporated elements of the existing cultural script into their relationships without recognition of the gendered and heteronormative premises that typically underpin it.

Capturing the kind of carefulness with which these couples discussed marriage, Michelle, a twenty-nine-year-old woman who had been with her partner for a year, described how they regularly said things to one another like "How do you feel about marriage?" or "Would you be open with your parents about it *if* we got married?" These conversations allowed them to discuss the possibility of getting engaged abstractly without ever having to directly say they both wanted to marry one another. Michelle was well aware of what they were both doing, explaining, "[My partner] will just kind of casually say things about marriage, I think mostly because she just wants to know that I'm committed to her." Sometimes her partner even asked her more directly: "You're going to marry me, right?" but it would be said so nonchalantly that Michelle could answer it reassuringly without actually getting engaged to her yet.

It is this kind of talk that explains why Ryan, another twenty-nine-year-old, who had been with his partner for five years, could be "planning to get married" despite never having had a serious conversation with his partner about it. He said that from early on in the relationship they had "started talking about marriage in the hypothetical sense," having "conversations about what kind of lives we would want for ourselves, and kind of alluding toward marriage." Over time these conversations had evolved, so that now when they had them, they felt at liberty to ask follow up questions like "So we're serious about this, right?" or "We're thinking on the same page, right?"—"just as kind of more of an assurance that it [a proposal] will happen." As Ryan understood it, by the time it happens, "the proposal is expected. It is just kind of a formality, a moment that we can look back on when it finally happened."

In addition to avoiding direct marriage talk, couples engaged in another kind of self-policing work. They restrained themselves from spontaneous expressions of love that might lead to a premature proposal. As Erin described above, people sometimes spontaneously blurted out informal proposals to their partners. These were especially common when they felt strong emotions about their partners or found themselves in settings that seemed appropriately romantic. However, such spontaneous expressions of love and commitment were not regarded as romantic enough for a proposal because they failed to convey the seriousness and effort required. Examples of people's failure to control their emotions help illustrate the less visible work usually involved in doing so.

Jo, a thirty-two-year-old, told me a story about how she had "blurted out" a proposal to her partner at the airport after she had returned from an extended work trip. She said that "she had really missed her" and the sight of seeing her made her feel overcome with emotion. However, as soon as the words had come out, she regretted it. Laughing, she recalled how she had tried to make it seem more official and formal by "saying more nice things." Her partner said yes, but Jo felt bad that the situation was not appropriate for the type of proposal she thought her partner deserved. She explained, "I felt like she deserved something better than the 'I haven't showered, slept, or eaten' proposal, like a formal setting for handing a ring over." Jo even gave her partner a "twenty-four-hour take-back" period to change her mind and made sure to follow it up with a "more formal restaurant proposal" after she had bought her a ring. When I asked her why she had felt the need to do that, like others she focused on the importance of memory-making: "I think it's a nice memory that people want to have, and it gives it the significance that it deserves." She wanted to demarcate the moment and set it apart from the kind of regular, casual interactions she had with her partner, both to create a memory they could look back on and to identify it as a "significant" relationship transition.

Jo's partner had accepted her spontaneous proposal, but sometimes proposers were met with a partner's refusal, even if they wanted to marry them. Nate, a forty-year-old man, recapped a "funny story" of his failed proposal:

> We were staying at a beautiful bed and breakfast and had come in from the cold. We grabbed some hot cider and sat in the hot tub outside and it was lightly falling snow, it was very romantic, and I turned to [my partner] and said "What would you say if I asked you to marry me right now?" and he looked at me and said "I think I'd say yes," and I looked to him and went, "OK." [*sounds casual*] [*laughs*] That was it. He was so mad.

Although the setting was appropriately romantic, Nate had not planned to propose in advance. He knew that such a casual conversation would not suffice for getting engaged, but he had gotten carried away in the moment and had brought up getting married unthinkingly. The result was that Nate posed the marriage question too abstractly and casually, making his partner mad. They did not consider themselves engaged after this interaction, and to Nate's embarrassment, his partner "told everyone" about his inadequate proposal, making it clear that he expected something much more formal before he would accept it. Nate knew that "it had to be big" and promised his partner that he would ask him again in "the right way." Half a year later, he proposed more formally on their anniversary, having taken the time to write him a song with the proposal as the last refrain, and making much more of a performance of it. These examples show just how constrained the boundaries of the proposal script are and how much work is entailed in adhering to them. Narrow prescriptions for romance meant that both talking about marriage too directly and being too spontaneous threatened the achievement of a successful proposal.

Lastly, Marriage Assumers also engaged in relational work to construct the proposal as a surprise. Research with heterosexuals shows that, unlike in popular portrayals, proposals are actually rarely experienced as truly unexpected surprises. Rather, the proposal is a kind of public "frontstage" performance that ratifies a decision that has already been made "backstage" by the couple.[16] Elements of surprise are limited to "the details."[17] But here again, scholars typically point to a gendered process. It is heterosexual women who do the necessary "backstage work" to guide their male partners toward a proposal because men are considered in need of nudging to get it right. The same-sex couples in this book were engaging in very similar backstage work to ensure a proposal would occur, and then to fashion it as an unexpected surprise, but the work was usually being done by both partners together, and not just by female couples. Again, this shows that existing (hetero)normative marriage scripts can be internalized and incorporated into same-sex relationships, even when the gendered beliefs or practices underpinning them do not apply.

Travis, a twenty-six-year-old man, had started dating men right around the time marriage became legal. After dating his now fiancé for about a year and a half, Travis "knew [his partner] would love to be married" and felt ready to commit to him. They had successfully avoided direct conversations about getting engaged. But they had discussed it indirectly often enough so as to make the proposal essentially co-planned in advance. He recalled the backstage work that went into their proposal this way:

> There were a few times when we were passing jewelers and I would say "Do you want to go look at rings?" It was never explicitly said, "engagement" or "marriage," but it was invited. It was that type of invited feeling when talking about rings, so I knew that that was something he'd be open to. So, when I found a design for a ring that I liked, that I would want to wear for the rest of my life, I showed it to him. And I said, "What do you think of this design?" And he fell in love with it. And so at that point I was like, "So should we buy them?" [*laughs*] And he's like, "I'll buy yours if you buy mine." So we pulled out our laptops and we bought the rings! And so we didn't ask each other [to get married] at that point but we knew it was coming.

His description of the engagement being "invited" speaks to the symbolic meaning that rings carry. They drew on their shared understanding of what rings signify to signal their interest in getting engaged while avoiding direct conversation. Once the rings arrived in the mail, Travis and his partner went out to dinner at the same place they had had their first date. They had managed to communicate their intentions so effectively that both of them knew to take the rings with them and expected a proposal to occur. However, in this case, the high and obvious level of planning ultimately undermined the desired surprise, and Travis described the proposal as "not very romantic" precisely because it was so expected.

Travis's engagement represents an extreme example of backstage work. But even in situations where getting engaged was less obviously on the immediate horizon, the person receiving the proposal still usually had a good idea when it would occur. The fact that proposers often adhered to the script of proposing on special occasions, such as while on vacation or anniversaries, helped it to be easily anticipated. Rachel, a thirty-year-old woman who got together with her partner in 2008, told me that she and her partner had talked about marriage so many times that they "basically had a plan for when she was gonna propose." They "officially got engaged" on New Year's Eve three years into their relationship, and Rachel admitted that she "totally knew" her partner was "going to propose then." Similarly, Sophie, a twenty-seven-year-old woman, who also got together with her partner in 2008, confessed that because they had "been talking about marriage ever since we had been together" by the time her partner proposed two years later it was "completely expected." They were on vacation and as soon as her partner suggested they "sit out on the porch and watch the sunset" she knew "this is when she's going to do it!"

Despite being so expected, surprise was still considered crucial. But this was a kind of constructed surprise, not the kind of surprise one gets with true spontaneity. The person proposing therefore had to work hard to create a particular moment that could be experienced, or at least remembered and recounted, as a surprise. Kaitlyn, a twenty-nine-year-old woman who got together with her partner in 2005, told a story that reflects the work that proposals commonly entailed. She had started talking to her partner abstractly about marriage almost immediately after starting to date. They had talked theoretically about when the right time for marriage was (after finishing graduate school) and how couples should pay for it (with some parental help). They had been ring shopping together too, looking at the kinds of rings they might like *should* they get engaged. Thus, by the time they were ready to do it her partner "really knew it was coming, there was no question." This posed a challenge for Kaitlyn, as the one proposing. She said, "I remember feeling like 'God, now how am I going to surprise her? Crap!'" Nonetheless, in her more formal recounting of the proposal, Kaitlyn still felt comfortable presenting the proposal as a genuine surprise. She told an elaborate story of how she had tricked her partner into thinking they were doing something mundane and ended up on a beautiful roof deck terrace that she had set up with champagne as the sun was setting, concluding, "She was so surprised, and had *no idea* it was going to happen!" Like Kaitlyn, most identified no tension between expectation and surprise, so long as the person being proposed to could not have predicted exactly how it would occur.

GETTING THE DETAILS RIGHT

For Marriage Assumers it was not enough for there to be a formal, surprise proposal; certain details had to be included. The person proposing had to incorporate a given set of symbols and behaviors in the proposal so as to make the event easily recognizable and legitimate to their partner and others. The menu of common expected behaviors included proposing in specific locations or at special times (over fancy dinners, at special destinations such as on vacation or at locations that already had special meaning to them, on special dates such as anniversaries or New Year's Eve), asking parents' permission, involving close family and friends, getting down on one knee, offering rings or jewelry, and making speeches and other declarations of love. Some also referred to contemporary expectations that the proposal involve well-planned grand, public gestures and performances.

Examples in which key expected symbols and behaviors were missing demonstrated just how taken for granted and specific the proposal script was. For instance, Lizzie, who married her partner in 2005, told a story of her initial failure to recognize her partner's proposal:

> We go to the Cape and go out for a walk and we sit down and [my partner] starts saying these lovely things about us and our relationship and who I am and says "So, will you marry me?" and I said, "Someday. Someday we should do that." And she's looking at me like—as she tells the story, she's like, "Did she just say no?" But I didn't get it! Because there was no ring, there was no big thing. There wasn't a jumbotron! And so then she said, "No really, will you marry me?" and I was like, "Oh, shit! Like for real?"

Although some common elements of the script were present, such as being on vacation and declarations of love, others were missing, including not having a ring nor using any grand gesture like a jumbotron to pop the question.

By contrast, when proposals included an adequate combination of any of the expected details, LGBQ people referred to them as "traditional." Because it could be assumed that most people are familiar with the general expectations of what a proposal should include, describing a proposal as "traditional" was an efficient means through which LGBQ people conveyed details of their proposal experience to me, letting me know that they had adhered to specifics of the script without having to go into detail. For instance, Clara, a twenty-nine-year-old who got together with her partner in 2008, simply said, "You know, she did the whole traditional thing, talked to my parents, got us matching engagement rings, and proposed to me on a picnic." Additionally, these LGBQ people felt no need to explain why adhering to "traditional" behaviors was important to them. The importance of getting the details right was assumed to be shared, so that they could assume that I, like them, would agree that doing it "traditionally" was the "right" or "proper" thing to do and indicative of how "sweet" and "wonderful" their proposing partners were.

However, the way in which these Marriage Assumers connected adherence to specifics of the proposal script with "tradition" is somewhat misleading, since details they described are not "traditional" in terms of how proposals have historically occurred. Clara equated getting matching rings with tradition, but historically in heterosexual relationships only one partner—the woman—would receive an engagement ring or, more recently, each partner would have a different ring regarded as suitable for varying expectations of feminine and masculine jewelry wearing. To give another example, people who had proposals regularly described asking parents for their approval as a tradition they adhered to. But they often made clear that parental approval was not being sought in any formal sense and was not required for the proposal to happen. They were simply going through the motions of this traditional act out of a more abstract sense of respect for their partner and parents. Heather, a thirty-one-year-old woman who got together with her partner in 2010, said:

> [My partner] went and had dinner with my parents before she asked me to get married because that was something that was important; not to ask their permission—it's not that I wanted them to give permission for her to ask me—but it's that I wanted them to know from her why she wanted to do this. So she went and had dinner with them; she called them and made plans with them.

These references to untraditional elements under the general banner of "tradition" suggest that at its core what is deemed traditional is following *current* social and cultural expectations around how proposals should look, rather than the actual details of how proposals have looked historically.

Contemporary expectations for proposals have also grown over the past few decades, requiring increasingly elaborate performances and displays of effort. These grand gestures were not described as "traditional" but rather were used to connote the kind of romance expected from a proposal today. Truly romantic proposals were thought to involve substantial effort, planning, and creativity—just as when Lizzie had noted the absence of a "jumbotron." Marriage Assumers described elaborate scavenger hunts, games, flash mobs, songs, and other musical or theatrical performances that would have required greater creativity and planning than the more traditional short speeches expected to precede a proposal. Aptly, Kaitlyn described this as the "whole song and dance" that is now expected. In this way, innovation seems to have become a part of the contemporary proposal script. These LGBQ people expected the proposer to display creativity, not because they wanted to buck tradition, but rather because innovation is now more broadly part of the social expectations for what a proposal should look like.

These narratives show that Marriage Assumers understood the intricacies of existing cultural scripts for proposals and engaged in a lot of relational work to meet them—avoiding direct marriage talk, controlling their emotions to circumvent spontaneity, and creating the experience and impression of surprise. But they furthermore illuminate the extent to which younger LGBQ people, who started relationships after same-sex marriage was already legal, had internalized unspoken social expectations around getting engaged, which manifested in self-policing of "appropriate" engagement behavior. Their accounts therefore demonstrate that social norms continue to play a role in shaping relationship behaviors around marriage. Existing research on proposals highlights the ways in which heterosexual women engage in this work but positions it as a means to meet gendered expectations for behavior. However, both men and women in this study engaged in this relational work to achieve the desired proposal. Although beliefs about gender difference undergird existing heterosexual proposal scripts and norms, its core requirements for romance are so strongly internalized that these scripts and norms—and the work they necessitate—persist even without them.

But Which Partner Should Propose?

Despite very firmly internalized ideas among Marriage Assumers about how to get engaged, a centrally important detail of the existing script was unclear in the context of same-sex relationships: which partner should propose to whom, and why. In heterosexual relationships it is still almost always the case that the man proposes to the woman. But this heterosexual assumption is immediately questioned for same-sex couples, for whom there are either no males or two in a relationship. Even if we assume there are no sex differences between same-sex partners,[18] they can differ in terms of gender presentation, with one presenting as more masculine and the other as more feminine. However, relatively few LGBQ people in this study reported a clear gendered difference between themselves and their partners.[19] Only 30 percent of those who had been or were engaged reported that one partner was on the "masculine" end of a scale while the other was on the "feminine" end. Of these, only women reported such gender differences between partners. Further, the average point difference in gender presentation between partners was less than two (out of ten). Thus, there was a lack of gender difference as well as a lack of sex difference for most same-sex couples, at least in terms of self-reported gender presentation.

It is noteworthy that in the minority of cases in which there *was* a clear gender difference between partners, the more masculine presenting partner proposed in all but one couple. This suggests that when there are clear gendered differences, gender might continue to shape proposals along expected heteronormative lines (at least for women). But gender was very rarely brought up in the interviews as an underlying factor shaping their proposal decisions, and closer analysis reveals a more complex relationship between gender and who proposes than is typical for heterosexuals. For instance, Kaitlyn initially told me that gender was "an unspoken thing underlying all of this," meaning that although she and her partner did not directly discuss it, her more masculine identity and appearance made it clear to them that she would be the one to propose.

> It is a more masculine thing to do. I feel like I'm sort of the more masculine one, so, in the movies and everything I kind of always identified with the guy going down on his knee or whatever and popping the question or being like, oh yeah, that'd be so cool to do that to somebody. I think I'd feel weird if I was asked.

However, despite a seemingly easy identification with heteronormative norms, Kaitlyn was still open to doing things differently and may have done so if she had only known how. She reflected, "I didn't really have anyone to map onto, I had no example. I wouldn't have known any different. I think not having lesbian role models was why I was like, oh yeah, people like this [masculine] do that [propose], so I guess I would be the one to propose." Thus, script following requires both that your relationship fits easily into existing details of the script *and* that few alternative ways of doing things are readily available to you. As same-sex marriage becomes more common, younger LGBQ people in newer relationships, like Kaitlyn, could encounter a greater range of models for proposing, thereby further undermining the "unspoken" nature of gender in marriage practices in the future.

Overall, because few couples reported clear gender differences between partners, for the most part gender played little role in determining which partner proposed. Gender difference did not shape proposals because it was not a prominent feature of most relationships. Nonetheless, proposals did not occur in a social and cultural vacuum in which only individual personalities and desires shaped decision-making. As strongly as gender difference undergirds the existing heteronormative proposal script, it was not the only possible cultural basis LGBQ individuals had to draw on for making proposal decisions. As the cultural sociologist Swidler would put it, same-sex couples had a repertoire of cultural ideas in their "tool kit" that they drew on to inform proposal decisions.[20] Because LGBQ people are "dually socialized" in both heterosexual and LGBQ specific cultures and communities,[21] they drew on both heteronormative and LGBQ cultural scripts to shape decisions about who should propose. As I show next, heteronormative ideas about appropriate demonstrations of commitment led LGBQ people to make marginal adaptations to the existing script, while a strong commitment to equality in the LGBTQ+ community prompted them to develop more distinctively new ways of doing things.

DEMONSTRATING COMMITMENT

In the existing heterosexual script, the man is meant to propose to the woman in part because it is assumed he needs to demonstrate commitment. Many Marriage Assumers I spoke to subscribed to this heteronormative idea that the person who most needed to demonstrate commitment should be the one to propose. They could, therefore, fairly easily determine who proposes, even absent gender differences between partners. There were three broad reasons that typically explained why it was seen as necessary for one partner to demonstrate commitment by proposing, including that they had previously ended the relationship, had appeared more generally wary of long-term commitment, or had previously refused their partner's proposal for (a nonlegal) marriage.

Previously breaking up with a partner created a clear expectation regarding who should propose if they got back together. For Tina, a thirty-five-year-old woman and her partner of three years, the fact that she had previously ended the relationship was key to explaining why she later felt the need to propose. About a year into their relationship, when they had still been living long-distance, Tina had ended the relationship and briefly dated someone else. They got back together just four months later. By the time they felt ready to get engaged a couple of years later, it was clear that she would need to make up for that earlier decision:

> We started talking . . . more about our future. We didn't use the word "marriage," I think because it was just such a significant thing. But as I had been the one that balked before, and it was already clear that she wanted to be with me, in terms of who was going to propose it was kind of—I wanted to propose.

Tina did not consider proposing as something she felt she *had* to do, phrasing it instead as something she *wanted* to do. Yet she hesitated before framing it as a personal choice. Like most Marriage Assumers, Tina and her partner had not talked directly about marriage. Certainly, her partner had never explicitly stated that she expected her to propose. But she did not need to. Existing cultural ideas about commitment were internalized enough to make it clear.

For others, a more general sense that their partners were "commitment-phobes" who needed to prove readiness for marriage shaped ideas about who should propose. This ultimately put the more committed partner in the situation of "waiting to be asked," much like has been described of heterosexual women.[22] Most often the one waiting to be asked just silently bided their time until their partner figured it out, as if their proposing would not signal the same readiness or commitment unless they had truly decided to do it themselves. Josh was in his early thirties when he got engaged, but he had already been with his partner seven years because he was waiting for his less committed partner to be ready. He reasoned:

> I was ready before him. It was like a conscious decision on my end, which was when he's ready, he'll tell me. I'm waiting for that, because the last thing you ever want to do is be in a relationship and have somebody come back to you and say, "Well, I don't know if I was ready," so I waited.

It took several years for his partner to be ready.

Lastly, there were cases in which previous refusals to marry determined who needed to subsequently propose. These were not Marriage Assumers, but I include mention of them here because in the rare cases in which Marriage Embracers had a proposal, commitment concerns were an issue for them as well. Although proposals were rare outside the Assumer group, commitment issues between partners seemed to make a proposal feel more necessary for same-sex couples across the three groups. Tom, a fifty-seven-year-old who had been with his partner for fourteen years, told me how his partner had refused his proposals to have a (nonlegal) commitment ceremony and how, in large part because of this, he decided to end the relationship a year before same-sex marriage became legal. Having been together for almost a decade and owning a house together, this was no easy decision. When they got back together a couple years later, there was no question that his partner needed to be the one to propose. But when he finally did so, Tom did not immediately say yes. Stewing, he told me, "I still wish he'd just accepted [my proposals] before; it might have been simpler." In a classic display of power, Tom took several months to give a reply, during which his partner "was left just patiently waiting." Finally, at Christmas, he wrote, "My answer is yes" in a card, wrapped it up, and gave it to his partner as a present.

This shared expectation of the least committed needing to propose sometimes resulted in an insecure waiting game. Yet, if all went to plan, it could also lead to a more genuinely surprising, and therefore romantic, proposal. As already described, most proposals only had the veneer of surprise and were actually carefully constructed by couples. But when a partner's commitment was really doubted, the one being proposed to was more likely to be genuinely surprised. For example, Tina—who had previously broken up with her partner—said that she was able to pull off an "awesome" proposal because her partner did not think that she "was mentally ready yet." Looking back, any insecurity her partner may have felt while waiting could be minimized by Tina because it ultimately led to a more romantic proposal.

Drawing on ideas in the existing heteronormative proposal script around commitment to determine who should propose has complex and uneven consequences for power and inequality between same-sex partners. Without sex differences between partners, it is not always women "waiting to be asked," thereby reducing the kind of blanket inequality we see among heterosexuals. Nevertheless, adherence to the same overarching idea recreates a similar kind of power imbalance between partners, whereby the more committed in the relationship is kept waiting by the other. They have only the power to say yes or no, while the less committed controls the timing of relationship progression. On the other hand, in cases where one partner had previously broken up or refused nonlegal marriage proposals, needing to propose could become a means of re-equalizing power, helping to create a new equilibrium rather than heightening existing inequalities. As I show next, some Marriage Assumers were also creating a new proposal script based much more firmly on commitments to equality.

ENSURING EQUALITY

In deciding who should propose, Marriage Assumers also drew regularly on widely shared beliefs within the LGBTQ+ community about the importance of equality between partners.[23] Whereas for heterosexuals a proposal is typically only something the woman gets to experience, many LGBQ people made conscious efforts to ensure both partners were proposed to. Erin, who had been careful to create the "appropriate memory" of their getting engaged, proposed back to her partner shortly after she had been proposed to. She explained, "We felt like we needed to do a mutual proposal so there was mutuality. That is a critical part of the story." Closer attention to these proposal narratives reveals that efforts to achieve "mutuality" were based on two somewhat different cultural ideas: one centered on avoiding power differentials, the other on creating fairness.

Some couple's decisions to have both partners experience a proposal were purposeful attempts to avoid the kind of power imbalances they saw as typical of the heterosexual proposal script. They conceptualized heterosexual proposals as based on an unequal power dynamic, whereby the man proposing symbolized his ownership and control of the woman. Occasionally, these feelings emanated directly from their own previous heterosexual relationship experiences. For instance, Rachel, a thirty-year-old woman, knew that her partner would need to be the one to propose to help her overcome the sense of disempowerment she had experienced in a previous heterosexual proposal. When her partner had been only eighteen, her then-boyfriend had "pressured her into getting engaged by asking her in a very public way" and had then broken up with her just two months later. Proposing was therefore now her partner's opportunity to regain some feeling of power in the engagement process and overcome past negative experiences.

However, as most of the people getting engaged by means of a proposal were relatively young, few had experienced previous marriage proposals. Wanting to avoid disempowerment was therefore usually based more generally on cultural perceptions than personal experience. They observed flaws in the heterosexual proposal script as it was portrayed in popular culture and other people's relationships, and they were trying to avoid doing things the same way. Courtney, a thirty-seven-year-old woman, was initially on the receiving end of a marriage proposal. Her partner had first proposed to her while they were on vacation in Paris. Courtney then proposed back to her partner a couple of months later at home. She explained:

> I felt like it was important for us both to propose to each other as individuals—to put out our intent even though we knew what the answer was going to be, but to ask "Will you marry me?"—and it wasn't a one person taking ownership of the relationship in one way, that it was equal.

She even made sure to get "a similar ring" from the same jeweler for her partner, so that neither one had the sole financial burden of having to purchase a ring for the other, nor be the only one to wear one.

Heather, who had referred to her partner's initial proposal as "traditional," echoed similar sentiments about wanting to reciprocate, and proposed back just a few months later:

> I felt very strongly that regardless of the relationship that I was in, regardless of the sex or the gender of the person that I was with that I also wanted to do some sort of proposal. I don't really like a lot of the historical ideas about what women are supposed to do or not supposed to do, and one person wears a ring but the other person doesn't. I felt that if I was going to wear a ring then I wanted my partner to have one as well. . . . So, yeah, we both did a proposal; they were just a few months apart. I proposed to her on our anniversary. She knew it was coming. She just didn't know when or how.

As was typical for those attempting to achieve more equal proposal experiences, both Courtney and Heather said that their partners agreed with the need for equality and knew ahead of time that they would be getting a proposal too. Rather than one person waiting to be asked, these couples clearly established that both partners could expect a proposal.

Another version of the equality script was centered more on establishing fairness than avoiding the power imbalances perceived among heterosexuals. Here the focus was on ensuring that both partners got to experience being proposed to so that no one person had a special experience that the other did not. Both partners were seen as desiring and deserving of the romance and joy of being proposed to. For example, Maddy, a thirty-two-year-old, wanted to "re-propose" back to her partner after being proposed to because she "wanted her to experience something along the lines of a proposal too": "I wanted her to have a ring as well, and I didn't want to just say 'Oh, let's go get the ring together.' I think it really meant a lot to her [that I proposed too], and I knew it would." Maddy contrasted her "re-proposal" with the "unfairness" she saw in heterosexual proposals, saying, "It never felt right the idea of guy proposes to girl, she gets a beautiful three-year-salary ring and he gets nothing, some plain old stupid gold band a year later. I wanted her to have something just like me; it was only fair so far as I was concerned."

In these ways, while some people's initial decisions about who should propose was driven by a less gendered version of the existing commitment script that created an unequal and insecure waiting game, other people's efforts to create "mutual" proposal experiences served to equalize the same-sex proposal experience. However, efforts to create equality through mutual proposals were only mentioned by women. This might suggest that women have a stronger desire to create equal relationships. Alternatively, it might suggest that women have a stronger desire for romance and are thereby more committed to ensuring both partners experience it. It was also striking that many of those LGBQ people who proposed back to their partners often described their proposals as "less romantic" than the initial one. Hypothetically, LGBQ people could have conceived of their subsequent proposals as *more* romantic because they are premised on ideas about mutuality, equality, and care. The fact that they did not suggests that even when trying to introduce LGBTQ+ specific cultural norms into proposal practices, heteronormative norms still held sway. Because second proposals could not be so easily constructed as surprises, they felt less romantic to same-sex couples doing them. In this way, even LGBQ people attempting to do proposals differently interpreted their success through the lens of existing heteronormative scripts for romance.

Importantly, efforts to do proposals differently sometimes led to a messy mix of both (hetero)normative and LGBTQ+ cultural beliefs and practices in same-sex relationships. Ideas about showing commitment and ensuring equality in proposals were not mutually exclusive. In other words, it was not the case that some people used proposals to demonstrate commitment, while others used them to achieve equality. Instead, both sets of ideas existed in LGBQ people's cultural repertoires, and the same people utilized both to guide their behaviors. For example, Kimberly explained her desire for a mutual proposal as emanating from the fairness of both needing to demonstrate commitment:

> I'm definitely the more femme, but we've actually talked about it and I don't feel comfortable with just me having a ring, cause to me that feels like I will have committed and she hasn't. So, we are giving each other rings that we've actually talked about. And we don't know who will propose first but there will be two separate proposals.

Similarly, Vicky described her insistence on "re-proposing" to her partner as a sign of "balance" and "equality" and part of their continued practice of "sharing responsibilities" in their relationship, as well as an important "sign of commitment" back to her partner. In these ways, demonstrating commitment (a less gendered version of the existing heteronormative proposal script) and ensuring equality (a more LGBTQ+-specific script) merged in people's marital practices. Thinking about institutional change, we see that people tend to "layer on" new practices on top of old ones, or modify old ones with new versions, rather than completely remake institutional logics.[24]

Conclusion

One might think that being so new to the institution of marriage would make LGBQ people feel at liberty to make it their own and depart from existing heteronormative scripts for how to do it. And, for some, this was true. Having more secure relational commitment and a history of being excluded from, and critical of, the institution of marriage gave Marriage Embracers and Rejecters the freedom to ignore cultural expectations for getting engaged and do whatever felt right to them. But Marriage Assumers, who for the most part had started relationships only after marriage was already legal, had strongly internalized existing scripts about the right way to get engaged. The rules of engagement were clear. Of course, there is a certain freedom to being able to participate in a script that, until recently, LGBQ people were excluded from and could not see themselves in. Nonetheless, the engagement experiences of Marriage Assumers reveal a high level of constraint that Embracers and Rejecters were not subject to. Looking at the differences across the three broad groups of LGBQ people makes clear how much access to legal marriage has transformed same-sex relationships. Although getting engaged is a relatively short phase of the marriage experience, it creates a great deal of relational work and anxiety for new same-sex relationships. Contrary to existing theory, it was not unclear expectations for behavior that resulted in work and anxiety. On the contrary, it was overly prescribed and narrow rules for behavior and the effort involved in trying to adhere to them.

Nevertheless, there is no escaping the fact that a significant premise of the existing script—gender difference—provided insufficient guidance for same-sex couples' engagement decisions, for whom there tended to be little notable gender difference between partners. That gender played so little role in determining which partner should propose in same-sex relationships is a salient finding, one greatly at odds with existing research demonstrating the persistent and dominant role of gender in heterosexual proposals. But this gap in cultural guidance did not create panic. Nor did it provide space for same-sex couples to do engagements fundamentally differently. Marriage Assumers simply looked to other dominant cultural ideas to help them navigate proposal decisions. Gender difference was not the only cultural tool at their disposal. Heteronormative ideas about commitment and LGBTQ+ community ideas about equality merged to create a messy mix of proposal practices, some of which seemed to reinforce inequalities, even absent gender difference, while others allowed space for the creation of more egalitarian ways of getting engaged.

5

Fights and Finances

Raul, a Marriage Assumer, had always wanted to be married and had ended a previous relationship over the fact that his partner had not been willing or ready. By the time he met his now-husband, he was in his early forties and was very clear from the start about what he wanted. Things moved quickly and they were married in less than two years. But did being married change anything about his relationship? When I asked him that question, Raul said:

> After we got married? Yeah. Now if we have an argument I don't worry about it. He's stuck with me and I'm stuck with him. In the past if there was a conflict in the relationship, leaving was an option and a threat. Now I feel like we are beyond that, we can get over it, because we're married and committed. He's not going to get that mad that he's going to leave over the silly things. It's much more peaceful. We're just a married couple like any other married couple. You pick your fights, and you get through things, and I always know he's going to be there.

Raul was emotional as he spoke. That immense feeling of security, of being able to relax in marriage and not worry about his partner leaving, clearly meant a lot to him.

Harriet, a sixty-one-year-old Marriage Embracer, had "wanted to be married forever" and had "always fantasized about it." As soon as same-sex marriage became legal she wanted to do it, but her partner wasn't interested. As was true of several older same-sex couples, Harriet and her partner had different views on marriage. Harriet never thought of leaving her partner and respected her partner's lack of interest in marrying. But when Harriet changed her job and they had to be married for her partner to receive her health benefits, her partner finally agreed. Harriet was "ecstatic." After thirty years with her partner, Harriet finally got what she had always wanted. But did it change anything about their relationship? Harriet reflected:

> I didn't expect there to be this change however after the marriage ceremony I felt *really* strongly committed to making my life with her. And I thought I had felt that way all along but I—the feeling changed profoundly once we got married because I had said "for better or worse and richer or poorer," and that took a leap of faith on my part. And I thought, "Look, this is a serious relationship." [*laughs*] You're in it now. So yes, I felt this profound change, and she said she also felt a change.

Despite the big difference in premarital relationship durations, Raul and Harriet described similar transformations in their feelings of commitment and security after marrying. Nevertheless, there were some subtle differences between them: Raul, a Marriage Assumer, described the change more in terms of security, while Harriet, a Marriage Embracer, focused more on increased commitment. Moreover, Raul seemed to expect the change, while Harriet repeatedly described the transformation with amazement, as if she had not expected it at all.

Another postmarital shift that both Raul and Harriet experienced in their relationship were changes to their financial practices. In fact, both transitioned almost seamlessly from describing emotional shifts in the way they felt about their partners and relationships to divulging information about changes in financial practices. Raul told me:

> I feel our future is more secure because we're married. Like, I never had life insurance, but I got life insurance after we got married because I wanted him protected. I don't know what that means, but little things like that would come into my head, like I need to change my beneficiaries. I have a husband that I have to take care of now.

Similarly, within a minute or so of talking about the profound shifts in commitment she had experienced, Harriet pivoted to telling me how her wife, who was in property development, had always been reluctant to share finances before due to some bad experiences she had had with other people. But, much to her surprise, she had recently opened her bank account to discover a very large deposit from her wife, who had just sold one of her properties. At first Harriet had thought it must be a mistake, but after asking her wife about it, she was surprised to find out that her wife wanted to start combining their finances. Harriet confided, "She's also teaching me the ropes of being a property owner. I feel much more financially protected now. Like I'm more woven into the fabric of married life."

It is not a coincidence that the LGBQ people in this book described shifts in feelings and finances together. The findings in this chapter illustrate that feelings lie at the heart of how marriage shapes individual behaviors today—even behaviors as mundane as managing finances. More specifically, the cultural-cognitive pillar of the institution[1] provides widely shared scripts about what marriage means that individuals internalize and come to take for granted. These cultural beliefs then exert a powerful influence on how individuals feel about their partners and relationships once married. These altered feelings (of greater commitment and security) influence the kinds of behaviors they are willing to engage in. In this way, the institution of marriage continues to shape individual behaviors today not through rules or norms about what one should do, but less directly through taken-for-granted cultural scripts about what marriage means, which in turn changes the way people feel about their relationships. As such, most individuals feel unconstrained by marriage and free to practice it as they wish, but the reality is that the institution still influences personal details of their relationships, including, for example, how committed they are, how they argue, and how willing they are to pool their finances.

It's Not Like the Sky Opens

Most LGBQ people in this study did not experience being married as transforming the day-to-day functioning of their relationships. After they got legally married, their lives and relationships carried on much the same as they had before. They usually struggled to think of anything "tangible" that had changed about their relationships after getting married. This was because the routines of their daily lives and relationship patterns were already well established. As Steven, a thirty-six-year-old Marriage Embracer who had been with his partner seven years prior to getting married, put it, "The foundation had already been laid. So, I don't think it really impacted our relationship very much at all. I can't think of any ways that marriage changed the game for us."

Almost everyone was already living with their partner prior to getting married, and many had been living with them for several years. By the time they got legally married, Grace, a forty-eight-year-old Marriage Embracer, and her partner had been together for ten years. Reflecting on whether being married had changed their relationship, she said:

> I mean, we were living together already; we already wanted a kid. We didn't go on a big honeymoon because we were broke. No one had to get rid of dishes because we were combining households, none of that! And it wasn't like now

you have to pay more attention to my family, or show up more at family holidays, because we were already really integrated into each other's lives.

Among heterosexual couples in the United States, cohabitation tends to be unstable and short-lived. The average heterosexual cohabitation lasts only eighteen months, and less than 15 percent last more than five years.[2] In large part, this is because heterosexual relationships transition into marriage quickly. On average, married heterosexual couples lived together for only twenty-two months before getting married. When they get married, heterosexuals therefore tend to experience it as more of a life course and relational change. By contrast, the people in this study had been living with their partners for an average of six years before marrying them.

Given that Marriage Assumers were in newer relationships and viewed marriage as an important turning point, it was more surprising that they, too, said their relationships continued very much the same as they had before. Andy, a thirty-two-year-old Marriage Assumer, stated,

> The actual marriage didn't have much of an impact. It's not like the sky opens. Nothing changes. It was such a gradual transition from living together to being married that the transition from the day before we got married to the day after we got married felt like nothing.

Andy and her partner had been living together for four years prior to marriage. Although this was not as long as many of those in the Marriage Embracer group, she and her partner had not rushed into marriage either. Recall from chapter 3 that Marriage Assumers viewed marriage as a capstone, something to do only when they had already achieved the necessary prerequisites in their lives and relationships for it. They tended to believe that one's life should be very stable before marrying, and so it makes sense that they also experienced little need to change much about their relationships after marrying.

In fact, there was a feeling as well among some Marriage Assumers that getting married *should not* change anything practical about their relationships because couples should already have everything about the day-to-day aspects figured out before getting married. Andy explained,

> We had already worked out all the big stuff in our relationship: who was going to do the chores and how we were going to handle our money. We had already gone through those decisions. We didn't want there to be any big surprises afterwards where all of a sudden it's like "You want to do *what*?"

Jake, a thirty-four-year-old Marriage Assumer, agreed. "Marriage didn't really change our relationship, which I think is actually really good." He elucidated, "The fact that the dynamic and the way that we operate in our day-to-day life didn't change meant things were already good, and we just solidified it, or did something to lock it in." In terms of daily life and relationship practices, marriage was meant to adapt to them, not the other way around.

The Difference Marriage Makes

Yet despite this frequent insistence that nothing "tangible" about their relationships changed after marriage, the relationships of married LGBQ people appeared quantitatively and qualitatively different from those of unmarried LGBQ people in a couple key areas.[3] Examining these differences offers insight into how and why the institution of marriage continues to shape relationship behaviors today.

RELATIONSHIP RESILIENCE

First, married LGBQ people in this study were significantly less likely to report "seriously considering" ending their relationships than their unmarried counterparts. Among the married participants, 72 percent said that they had "never" seriously considered ending their relationships, compared to only 48 percent of unmarried participants. On the flip side, 36 percent of the unmarried said they had considered it more than twice, compared with just 12 percent of married participants. Overall, married participants were only about one-fifth as likely to seriously consider ending the relationship as their unmarried counterparts.[4] That is a substantial difference, and it's worth paying attention to.

It is possible that married individuals are different in some other way than unmarried individuals, and these other factors, rather than marriage per se, explain their greater commitment to sticking things out. Maybe married individuals are just better educated, older, wealthier, or more likely to have children, for example, and these things assist them in not giving up on their relationships. Remarkably, however, being married was the only factor that influenced how likely LGBQ individuals were to consider ending their relationships.[5] Moreover, relationship duration did not act as any kind of proxy for marriage. Individuals who were in long-term, unmarried relationships were not any less likely to consider ending their relationships than those in short-term relationships. Married LGBQ people were also not less likely to consider ending their relationships because they were more satisfied in them than unmarried individuals. They were simply more committed to staying in their relationships, regardless of personal satisfaction. Put simply, being married, and *only* being married, reduced the odds that LGBQ people would seriously consider ending their relationships.

SHARING RESOURCES

The second key way that being married shaped the relationship behaviors of LGBQ individuals was in relation to financial practices. Research with heterosexuals continues to show a strong connection between marriage and pooling money.[6] In the United States, 83 percent of heterosexual married couples still pool all of their money.[7] In general, couples tend to adopt an all-or-nothing approach to finances, either pooling all their accounts or keeping them all separate, and family scholars believe this reflects the extent to which they imagine their relationships as a shared, long-term enterprise. LGBQ individuals in this study followed a similar pattern, with over two-thirds having an all or nothing approach to financial management.[8] Within these all or nothing approaches, there were very clear differences in the way married and unmarried people managed their finances. Married LGBQ individuals were much more likely to pool all their money with their partners than unmarried LGBQ individuals: 59 percent of married individuals said they had both a joint checking and savings account, while only 20 percent said they had no joint accounts. These figures were almost opposite for unmarried individuals, with only 22 percent saying they had both joint checking and savings accounts and 51 percent saying they had no joint accounts. There was likely much variation in the particular ways of organizing their finances across both groups, but that married and unmarried participants had such broadly different arrangements suggests that they conceptualized their relationships differently. Married LGBQ individuals were also much more likely than their unmarried counterparts to own joint property with their partners and have the property be in both names. Among those who owned their own place of residence,[9] whether the property was in both partners' names was strongly linked to marital status: 79 percent of married people who owned their own property said that it was in both names, compared to just 39 percent of unmarried people.

Again, married and unmarried people often look different on a range of other variables, such as education, income, age, having children, and relationship duration, and these might help explain the link between marital status and financial arrangements. However, differences by marital status could not be attributed to these other factors. Even when other possibly relevant factors were considered, married LGBQ individuals in this study were over four times more likely to have joint accounts with partners than their unmarried counterparts and over ten times more likely to have a home in both names.[10]

Traditional Institutional Explanations for Behavioral Change in Marriage

Despite LGBQ individuals' frequent insistence that nothing "tangible" about their relationships changed after getting legally married, the data point to marriage shaping their relationships in important ways. But traditional sociological explanations for the way the institution of marriage shapes behavior, based on social norms and regulative incentives, provide inadequate insight in the case of same-sex marriage.

ENDURING SOCIAL NORMS?

Social norms offer a traditional sociological explanation for why married and unmarried individuals behave differently in their relationships. Informal norms are maintained through shared social expectations and pressures, or simply internalized as taken-for-granted practices of marriage. In general, family scholars agree that the norms governing social behavior in marriage are weakening, and individuals have much more latitude to behave as they wish once married than they did in the past.[11] But there may still be certain areas and relationship practices over which enduring social norms govern marital behaviors. Given the stark differences in behaviors around commitment and financial practices we see between married and unmarried LGBQ individuals, perhaps enduring social norms around marriage as a lifelong commitment and financial pooling have not completely disappeared. Yet the marriage narratives offered by LGBQ people in this book provide only limited support for norms as the primary mechanism through which marriage shaped their relationship behaviors.

There were no strongly shared norms about marriage as a lifetime commitment. Like heterosexuals,[12] most LGBQ individuals regarded divorce as a possible and reasonable option. Roughly equal proportions agreed and disagreed with the following statement: "Marriage is a lifetime commitment and should never be terminated except under extreme conditions" (42 percent disagreed, 38 percent agreed). There was clearly no internalized assumption that they had to stay with their partners simply because they were married.

Nonetheless, getting divorced can still feel socially stigmatizing and social norms against divorce can operate to hold people more accountable to the public promises they make in getting married. Marriage remains distinctive in this way, by producing "enforceable trust."[13] The idea of enforceable trust suggests that people are more committed to staying in their married than their unmarried relationships because other people—family members, friends, and people in the community—hold them accountable to the promises they made. However, Andrew Cherlin notes that "the difference in the amount of enforceable trust that marriage brings, compared with cohabitation, is eroding."[14] And, as cultural sociologist Ann Swidler argues, "the informal but once powerful sanctions that supported marriage as a set of enforceable social obligations have largely dissolved. Love relationships are increasingly matters of individual choice, and no authoritative power—kin group, community, or law—forces individuals to do what is right."[15] No married LGBQ individuals in this study talked about staying with their spouses out of any obligation to adhere to social expectations, or because they felt accountable to family, friends, or community members reminding them of the vows they had made.

A few people spoke about feeling some pressure not to fail in their marriages given how recently same-sex marriage had been legalized. They knew that same-sex marriage was not yet legal nationwide and perceived the eyes of the nation on them. To fail in their marriages, they felt, would be to let all LGBTQ+ individuals down and weaken the case for marriage equality. Interestingly, however, this social pressure was only brought up by unmarried individuals. Mikey, a thirty-eight-year-old unmarried Marriage Assumer, said, "I feel like there is a little bit more of this spotlight on our relationships, like if you get divorced people will use it, like 'See, they want to get married, but look what happens.'" Dennis, a fifty-three-year-old unmarried Rejecter, likewise said, "I really hope we can keep the divorce rate lower than heterosexuals, because I feel like we have to prove ourselves, be beyond reproach."[16] But as it was not something married individuals mentioned, it cannot explain the differences between married and unmarried relationships observed. Further, this kind of social pressure is different from the kind of enforceable trust marriage scholars typically refer to, and it is likely to be short-lived as same-sex marriage rights become more secure.

Social norms have always shaped the management of money in marriage. In the mid-twentieth century, money pooling became popular as a response to an ideology of companionate marriage.[17] Two people were supposed to become "one" with marriage, and having joint finances symbolized the idea that the activities of both spouses were of the same value irrespective of their financial contributions. The greater the relationship investment, the more couples are expected to prioritize family unity over economic autonomy and adopt collectivist money arrangements. In their classic study of American couples in the 1980s, Philip Blumstein and Pepper Schwartz found that financial pooling seemed like "such a natural part of marriage" to their participants that they "could hardly imagine living any other way"; it was "unconsciously assumed."[18]

Today marriage is thought to be in a new, increasingly "individualized" institutional stage.[19] Spouses are less likely to sacrifice their own individuality for socially defined roles within marriage. As such, shared social expectations and norms around financial pooling in marriage are likely to have lost some of their weight. Nonetheless, most Americans continue to favor married couples fully sharing their income, and preferences for financial pooling remain stronger in relation to marriage than to unmarried cohabiting or parenting status.[20] At least for heterosexuals then, financial pooling appears to be an enduring social expectation for marriage.

Yet, as was true about attitudes toward divorce, only a minority of LGBQ individuals (42 percent) in this study agreed with the following statement: "Married couples should pool all their property and financial assets." Financial pooling was far from an internalized assumption of marriage. Moreover, in the interviews, only a handful of people described their marital decision to pool finances as a result of adherence to social norms or taken-for-granted assumptions about marital behavior. And, notably, only Marriage Assumers described decisions to pool this way. Recall from chapters 3 and 4 that Marriage Assumers are those who are most concerned with doing marriage the "right way" and who tend to follow (hetero)normative expectations for marriage. Rather than treating marriage as more of an "individualized" enterprise, for these younger individuals in newer relationships, social norms and expectations held considerable sway. Older LGBQ people in longer-term relationships that predated marriage legalization cared much less about adhering to social norms about how one "should" do marriage.

Among some Marriage Assumers, financial pooling was described as a norm both in the sense of a behavior they assumed all, or at least most, other married couples do and as an expected behavior—something they felt they *should* do as a married couple. Chris, a thirty-two-year-old Marriage Assumer, who was with his partner five years before marriage, said that how he and his partner managed their finances was the "one practical thing that changed after we got married." They had always had separate bank accounts but then decided to merge their finances and open joint accounts after they got married. When I asked him why, he responded, "I guess because we said 'We're officially one now.' [*laughs*] It just seemed like a natural step once you're married to do that. I mean, we don't know any married couples who have separate finances." Merging finances both seemed like what they were meant to do as a married couple and what they observed other couples doing.

Rachel, a thirty-year-old Marriage Assumer who had been with her partner four years before getting married, told me that the "only day-to-day thing" she thought being married had changed was that they had "talked more about sharing bank accounts." She described this as a kind of social obligation: "We're just like, 'Yeah, we should probably do that at some point.'" When I asked her why, she could give no other reason than "I guess it just sort of seems like the thing to do." She admitted that they had not actually got around to merging their finances yet, but it was on their list of things they thought they "should" be doing now they were married, and she was almost apologetic that they hadn't done it yet—as if it indicated something negative about their marriage.

The greater prevalence of pooled financial practices among married LGBQ individuals results, at least in part, from institutional pressures based on social norms and taken-for-granted assumptions regarding how to behave in marriage. Social norms are enduring for some Marriage Assumers. This suggests that these norms are still being adhered to today as the best way to enact marriage and are not some outdated holdover only present in older marital relationships. Nonetheless, norm-based explanations for changes in marital behaviors were not frequently discussed. Even if norms continue to play some institutional role through which marriage shapes relationship behaviors, they could not fully explain the impact that being married has on commitment and financial practices.

LEGAL BARRIERS AND INCENTIVES

Marriage can also shape behavior through what the institutional scholar Richard Scott refers to as the "regulative pillar" of the institution—formal rules that constrain and enable behavior.[21] If we consider why married LGBQ individuals are less likely to seriously consider ending their relationships than unmarried LGBQ individuals, the formal legal structure of marriage might help explain the difference. When any relationship ends there are practical decisions to make regarding how to separate, but legal marriage introduces another layer of institutional complexity to the process, creating new barriers to ending one's relationship. As Lizzie, a forty-eight-year-old Marriage Assumer, who had been with her partner four years prior to getting legally married, put it: "Being married complicates things legally and financially." Lizzie was not considering ending her relationship, but she admitted that in those times when things felt tough or she even gave it a passing thought her mind would go to the practical and financial difficulties of divorce: "You know, I start to think about money and I think about 'Wait a minute, what if we were to get divorced, does she get access to half my money just because we've been married?' and so on, and so on."

For Josh, a forty-year-old Marriage Assumer who had been with his partner seven years prior to marriage, this kind of legal barrier to ending things was a good thing: "I think it is harder to have a substantial relationship that lasts when you know that if things don't work out, you can just leave. Being legally and financially intertwined with someone means that even when you have hard times, you're bound to them." In Josh's mind, because separating would be a difficult legal process, it makes seriously considering ending the relationship a much weightier psychological and financial process that could put people off doing it too hastily. However, although the legal structure of marriage may introduce additional barriers to separating, there is little empirical evidence that it ultimately stops people seriously considering ending their relationships.[22]

In fact, some people regarded having the legal structure of divorce as helping people to separate. Although the process might be more difficult, the law offers married couples protections that unmarried partners do not have access to when separating. The legal structure of marriage offers a safety net that has the potential to help protect people in times of crisis and help them reach fair resolutions to problems. Lizzie recognized this when she said, "I mean, the bad news is that our lives are more enmeshed and interconnected, but the good news is that in some ways legal marriage helps me to protect myself if we did ever get divorced." Evan, a forty-seven-year-old unmarried man agreed that the legal structure actually made getting divorced easier.[23] Having divorced his previous same-sex partner, he was grateful for the protections that legal marriage had offered him.

> At least because we were married we had a structure imposed on us, which is why I think we're in better shape than some of my friends who never got married and then separated with children. If we had not been married, then other than custody of the children, everything else would've been a grab-as-fast-as-you-can kind of situation. So, there was discussion on all of our assets, everything. If we didn't have the divorce structure thrust upon us it could have got very ugly.

As far as offering a compelling explanation for married couples being less likely to seriously consider ending their relationships, the additional legal structure that marriage offers appears to be as much a possible support as it is a barrier to exiting a relationship.

Many family scholars have argued that it is the legal protection of marriage that explains the greater financial pooling as compared to unmarried relationships.[24] Conversely, unmarried cohabiters' propensity toward independent money management can be attributed to the lack of legal protection for joint investments. However, at the time of this study, there was no federal recognition for same-sex marriage, so LGBQ individuals still lacked many of the federal financial benefits and protections of marriage. Even though they were legally married in their state, they still had to file federal tax returns as single individuals,[25] could not transfer assets without paying a federal gift tax,[26] could not receive a spouse's Social Security benefits on their death,[27] and paid what became known as the "gay tax" on health insurance.[28] As such, there was actually little financial benefit to married LGBQ spouses pooling their financial assets, and the complex and unresolved legal landscape surrounding same-sex marriage at the time offered little security to same-sex spouses. Legal protections from marriage were therefore unlikely to offer a compelling explanation for the much greater financial pooling among married LGBQ individuals observed in the data. To the contrary, observing stark differences in financial pooling by marital status despite a lack of legal protections alerts us to the fact that other institutional mechanisms must be at play in shaping relationship behaviors.

Making Sense of Feeling Different

Despite the regularity and consistency with which married people insisted little that was tangible had changed about their relationships, 87 percent still reported that marriage had made their relationship "better." And, in the interviews, the one thing that LGBQ individuals routinely said was different about marriage was the way it made them *feel* about their relationship. Language like an extra "weight," "cover," "cement," or "solidity" were commonly used to describe this sense that being married felt different. These terms indicate that marriage had added onto or deepened something that was already preexisting in some way. Gail, a fifty-six-year-old Embracer, who had been with her partner twenty-four years before marriage, reflected, "Nothing changes in your day-to-day life. I mean, after twenty-four years and a kid, it's hard to know what difference it's made! But there is some kind of intangible way in which I feel it has made us more solid." Hannah, a thirty-nine-year-old Embracer, who had been with her partner seven years before marriage, concurred: "I mean, it did and it didn't, right? I mean, on a day-to-day I don't think it really changes it much. But it does give this sort of weight to it at times, right?"

Although married LGBQ people often initially described the shifts in feelings they experienced as "intangible" or by drawing on fairly abstract language centering on weight and solidity, their responses also made clear that shifts in feelings emanated from deeply internalized dominant cultural scripts about marriage and what it means. Across all the marriage stories, two cultural scripts dominated explanations of shifts in feelings post-marriage: that married relationships are more committed and that they are more secure. Commitment and security are obviously interconnected—you could even think of them as two sides of the same coin. After marrying, LGBQ people felt more committed to making their relationships work, and they trusted that their relationships would work out more as well. Yet the two sides reflect the experiences of different marriage groups. Marriage Embracers mostly occupied the commitment side of the coin. They described being married as deepening the commitment they felt to their partners and their relationships. Because they had typically been together for a long time prior to the availability of legal marriage, they did not need to be married to feel committed, but instead experienced marriage as deepening and strengthening the commitment they had already created. They often experienced this as a surprising and profound feeling precisely because they had not expected marriage to make much difference. By contrast, Marriage Assumers mostly occupied the security side of the coin. They almost all spoke about feeling more secure in their relationships after getting married and described being married as a relief. They needed marriage to feel completely secure and trusting in their relationships.

It is noteworthy that most Marriage Rejecters did not experience being married as significantly altering either their feelings of commitment or security. That is because they did not enter the institution of marriage subscribing to the same cultural beliefs as Marriage Embracers and Assumers. They did not believe that legal marriage was necessary for demonstrating commitment, nor that it is better than the forms of commitment they had already sustained. As such, they did not experience the same kind of transformation in the way they felt about their partners and relationships after getting married. The differences across the three groups of LGBQ people make clear that the impact marriage has on behaviors within couple relationships is not uniform but depends on the particular cultural scripts one subscribes to.

MARRIAGE EMBRACERS FEELING MORE COMMITTED

Marriage Embracers subscribed to dominant cultural scripts that marriage is how to demonstrate love and commitment. But, having been excluded from legal marriage, they had sustained commitment without it and found ways to participate in other marriage-like commitments instead. When legal marriage became available, they saw it as an opportunity to publicly demonstrate and celebrate the marriage-like commitments they had already made (chapter 1). Having often been in very long-term relationships and because they were already so committed to their partners, most did not expect being legally married to feel very different to them and were therefore surprised and caught off guard by the strength of the change they experienced. Ricardo, a fifty-two-year-old Marriage Embracer who had been with his partner for twenty-four years before marrying him, explained, "Marriage is an experience you've got to have for yourself." He remembered that some of his "straight friends" had told him marriage "feels different" but he hadn't believed them until after he got married himself. Trying to explain the change, Ricardo said, "There's no way to describe that feeling other than there's really sort of like a spiritual bond that sort of cements the two of you. We were surprised and we couldn't describe it. We just knew that something had changed."

Despite the strength of their preexisting commitments, Marriage Embracers had internalized the cultural belief that legal marriage is distinct—they recognized that it is the dominant social and cultural gold standard for relationships. Acutely aware of the legal, social, and cultural dimensions of marriage, they understood that, without marriage, they had not been able to demonstrate their commitment to their partners in the way society deems most valid. Robert, a fifty-one-year-old Marriage Embracer, explained that, for better or worse, when it comes to commitment there is no real substitute for getting legally married:

> In our society, the only way to show commitment really is through marriage. No matter how long you've been with someone before you get married, when you're dating someone, that's all you're doing is dating. You can *say* you're committed as much as you want but still there is nothing that really binds you to each other that shows that you're committed. There's no real commitment. But when you're married, you know it.

Despite the fact that he and his partner had been together for several years before they were legally married, had already purchased joint property, and had a child together, they still experienced legal marriage as deepening their commitment. He said, "Now I look at my ring all the time and I'm proud of our commitment. Nothing dramatically changed between us, but we are more spiritually connected to each other." Other Marriage Embracers similarly described feeling "proud" of their commitment, knowing that they had finally been able to achieve the highest form of commitment socially available.

Like so many others, Tom, a fifty-seven-year-old Marriage Embracer who had been with his partner for fourteen years prior to getting married, initially struggled to define what marriage had changed about his relationship, stating, "It's very hard to put it in any kind of tangible, concrete ways because we didn't change kind of who does what or anything." But he went on to describe marriage as feeling "completely different than not being married." And when I probed him to explain what exactly felt different, he focused on the distinctive commitment that it represents:

> Well, it's a huge step to be married; it's a huge step to have a husband or a wife. It's about commitment. Even though people can get divorced, but you don't go into it with that in mind. So, it's saying, "We want to be together forever, and we've made this choice, and had this public ceremony." And the moment it happened, we felt different. You know, one day you are two people who are living together and the next you're a married couple. It's really different.

Marriage provided Tom, and others like him, the institutional context in which his internalized cultural beliefs about the distinctive nature of marital commitment could be enacted and achieved, resulting in a profound transformation in the way he felt about his relationship.

Grace, a forty-eight-year-old Marriage Embracer, had been with her partner ten years before marrying her and had adopted a child with her two years after legally marrying. She told me:

> There are times when the parenting is so hard and it just takes such a toll on us and I just want to pack up and not leave a forwarding address, and then I remember that we have made this huge commitment to each other. And I don't know if I would feel differently if we weren't married, but we are married and that means something to us.... So, I don't experience on a day-to-day this tremendous benefit [from marriage], it's just deep in my heart.

Becoming parents had changed their relationship dynamic much more than getting married, but it was being married—not having a child together—that made Grace feel more committed to staying together.

After getting married, Marriage Embracers found themselves being able to tap into deeper feelings of commitment to their partners because they were able to enact a cultural script they had internalized but had been denied full participation in. No matter how committed they already were to their partners, they also believed that legal marriage is a distinct form of social and cultural commitment, and being able to achieve that with their partners released new and deeper feelings of commitment that were experienced as profound, even if unexpected.

MARRIAGE ASSUMERS FEELING MORE SECURE

Whereas Marriage Embracers referred to feelings of deepened commitment to one another and the relationship post-marriage, Marriage Assumers much

FIGHTS AND FINANCES 151

more often described feeling more secure in their relationships after getting married. Being legally married demonstrated that their partners were "not going anywhere" in a way that nothing prior to legal marriage could have. And whereas feelings of deepened commitment were surprising to Embracers, feelings of extra security seemed to come as a relief for Assumers, as if they had been waiting desperately to be able to feel that way.

Even if they knew rationally that their premarital relationships were stable and secure, Marriage Assumers admitted to never feeling quite safe in that knowledge. Being married immediately allowed them to stop doubting their partner's commitment. Eva, a thirty-eight-year-old who had dated her partner for two years prior to marriage, admitted that before they were married, she could not help worrying about "what would happen if she meets somebody else." Now, she said, "I never worry about that anymore." Eva acknowledged that "marriage is not a guarantee that we're going to make it," but she nevertheless relaxed into the knowledge that she had committed to her. Similarly, Vanessa, a thirty-seven-year-old who had been with her partner four years prior to marriage, told me that the only thing that really changed about their relationship was that she "felt more secure." She confessed:

> Before I did feel less secure about our relationship in that there wasn't this bigger thing tying us together. I think that I always had in the back of my head when we were just dating that she might just change her mind and leave. I don't have that at all now.

Vanessa added that with more security, there was more space to focus on other things: "Now I have more like 'What are we going to do about this issue?' or 'How are we going to address that or work on these things together?'"

It was not that their married partners could not or would not ever leave them, but it was not something they had to think about anymore because they trusted that it would take something much more than an argument or problem, even a big one. LGBQ individuals in this study were well aware of high divorce rates, and most saw divorce as a possible option. Yet this did not make marriage flimsy or weak in their minds. They still fundamentally subscribed to the cultural belief that marriage is the ultimate demonstration of commitment, something to be worked hard at and not to be ended easily or casually. Marriage was, by nature, a commitment to work things out together.

In part, being married created feelings of greater security because married LGBQ individuals knew that the legal and institutional structure of marriage made it more difficult for their partners to leave them. Referencing the common idiom about heterosexual marriage being a "ball and chain," participants sometimes joked that the added security they felt came from the knowledge that it would be harder for their partners to leave them, "even if they wanted to," and that they had successfully "trapped" their partners now. For example, Sophie, a twenty-seven-year-old Marriage Assumer who had been with her partner three years prior to marriage, joked, "She can't just up and leave me now. [*laughs*] She's tied to me in multiple ways."

But Marriage Assumers mostly understood marriage as a meaningful personal choice. They did not feel more secure only because the legal structure of marriage made it more difficult for partners to leave them. To the contrary, it was because partners had freely chosen to legally marry them that they could trust they had no desire to leave them. Nate, a forty-year-old who had been with his partner five years before marriage, explained it as "being willing to make that legal jump." He recognized that his partner's choice to marry him entailed publicly stating that the relationship was "not some throw away, disposable thing." In this way, although it was the legal structure that "made it difficult to separate," it was also knowing that one's partner had been willing to enter it that made Marriage Assumers feel more secure. The legal structure of marriage cannot exist without people willing to enter it. Nate got choked up and teary-eyed as he played with the ring on his finger. He added, "It changed things almost immediately. I felt protected and secure, justified, loved."

Heather, a thirty-one-year-old Marriage Assumer who had been with her partner two years before marrying her, clearly articulated this idea that it is both the legal structure and one's personal willingness to enter it that creates the additional security of marriage. She started crying as she told me how before she got married she "didn't feel there was that level of commitment" and was always doubting the relationship. By contrast, now she can always "fall back on" the knowledge that in "getting married [my partner] was saying to me, 'I want to make that commitment.'" Now whenever she worries about her partner or they have an argument, she draws on two pieces of knowledge: "One, I know it wouldn't be easy for her to leave me even if she wanted to, [*laughs*] and two, I know she wants to be with me—she was willing to sign a legal document saying that she wanted to marry me, it's a huge commitment." Heather astutely described these two components as "the combination of the legal piece with the love piece" and explained how once she was married, they felt "one and the same" to her. In these examples, we see the regulative pillar of marriage (see introduction) playing a supporting role in providing the necessary structure for cultural beliefs about marriage to be enacted.

Swidler, who studied what love means to middle-class Americans, argues that, despite its fragility, the instituion of marriage makes plausible perhaps the most implausible aspect of the "mythic love myth": that true love lasts forever. When marriages end, people simply reevaluate them as not having been based on "true love" after all.[29] Yet the marriage accounts from this study suggest something different. They suggest that, as a show of commitment, marriage is simply the best we have available. Marriage Assumers had not bought into some mythic version of love—that it would last forever, even within marriage. Instead they had internalized the cultural script that, by marrying, their partners were offering them the best demonstration of commitment socially available: they were publicly saying that they were willing to work hard at their relationships and stick it out, even when things got tough. They had internalized the cultural belief that marriage is a unique form of commitment, not the mythic idea that marriage is a lifelong commitment. As soon as their partners were willing to "take that step" to enter the institution of marriage with them, they could relax into a shared understanding that this was a long-term, serious commitment that would not be ended casually.

Feelings and Behavioral Change

Both of the major areas of difference between unmarried and married LGBQ individuals—reducing the odds of seriously considering ending one's relationships and increasing the odds of pooling finances—are best explained by the shifts in feelings of commitment and security individuals experienced after getting married. Being married changed the way they *felt* about their relationships, and these affective changes then impacted the ways they *behaved* in marriage. Put simply, married LGBQ individuals not only *felt* more committed but also *behaved* as if they were more committed. Hannah instinctively understood this when she said, "I mean, I think it has to be more than just a feeling, right? I think that it probably trickles into some of how we interact too."

Married LGBQ individuals regularly spoke about how being married had changed the way they reacted when they were experiencing a difficult time with their partners. Liam, a thirty-three-year-old Marriage Assumer who had been with his partner for two years before marrying him, articulated the difference he thought marriage made this way:

> Like any couple, there are periods of ebb and flow in how you feel about a person, and marriage for me has provided a certain level of stability that I'm thankful for because when maybe there's been some sort of a valley moment when I question things, you know we've had a fight or things are not quite as good as they are sometimes, I do think "But we're married." And when you're married you get through these periods and remind yourself that it hasn't always been this way and it won't feel this way again before long.

Being married gave Liam pause and helped him adopt a broader perspective on his relationship so that he did not give up in those moments when things seemed too difficult.

Several people gave specific examples of drawing on the feelings of extra commitment in efforts to stay together. Art, a forty-four-year-old[30] who had been with his partner for six years before getting married, told me that they had a "major relationship crisis" about five years after they got married and "came very close to getting divorced." He thought that "the fact that we were legally married probably made the difference between our separating and not" because "it meant that the glue there was a bit stronger."

> Obviously [being married] wasn't the only reason we stayed together—that would be crazy—but still in those moments when we were very close to splitting there was a bit more of a bond between the two of us. Plus, there would have been a lot more to go through to actually divorce one another. You know, if there was no legal structure to it, we could have just separated and that would be that.

For Art, the added "glue" and "bond" combined with the legal and practical difficulties of divorce to help them work through their problems and stay together. The cultural and legal components of marriage worked in tandem to help them stick things out.

Survey data from this study shows that being married did not change *how much* LGBQ individuals argued with their partners. However, married individuals regularly reported that it had changed *how* they argued with them. During their first big fight after getting married, Brianna, a thirty-one-year-old Marriage Assumer who was with her partner for eight years before marrying her, explained that leaving was not something they threatened lightly anymore: "I feel like before when we would fight, we would just threaten each other to break up. It was like, 'Fine, leave me, whatever, I don't care!' We felt like it was more expendable as a relationship." But, Brianna said, "Now we sit down and talk about things more, and leaving isn't even a threat anymore." Of course, marriage was not a panacea for their relationship problems, and "every once in a while, those threats still come out," but she said that it was "not like it used to be."

Relationships did not become easier when LGBQ people got married. Married couples experienced relationship problems and fought just as much as unmarried couples. But the way they handled fights changed. Married LGBQ individuals did not stick it out with their partners out of some sense of societal obligation, or only because the legal process of divorce made it too difficult to leave. Instead, even when things were tough, they had a reserve of energy for their relationships that their unmarried counterparts did not: they had heightened feelings of commitment to their partners and relationships, as well as greater feelings of security and trust. And they drew on these feelings to keep working on their relationships.

With regard to pooling finances, feelings of greater commitment and security impacted how married LGBQ individuals made financial decisions in two main ways. First, feeling more committed helped same-sex couples imagine the future differently and make more concrete financial plans together. Jo, a thirty-two-year-old Marriage Assumer, expressed very firm views on the matter. Before she and her partner of ten years were married, they had essentially "lived together as roommates" with all their finances "completely separate." But since getting married they were engaging in "joint financial planning" together and having lots of conversations about what they wanted to do with their money. When I asked her why she thought they had not done that before getting married, she seemed surprised and replied, laughing, "Because I would never do that before getting married! I mean, like, how many people end up breaking up or somebody cleans out an account and walks out. I just think it's stupid. You're setting yourself up for a bad situation!" Jo had not been able to trust the longevity and security of their relationship without marriage, and it seemed obvious to her that merging finances without the commitment of marriage was a bad idea.

For most, being married resulted in more subtle shifts in their feelings of commitment that then resulted in greater financial planning and pooling. Clara, a twenty-nine-year-old Marriage Assumer, and her partner were together for two years before getting married. When they had first moved in together they had "established one joint bank account" that they "both put money into every so often" so that they could pay for house expenses and groceries together, but they did not "really combine" their money until after they got married. When I asked Clara why they waited until after marriage to combine their finances, she explained:

> Well, knowing that we've committed to planning our lives together changed the way we looked at the future, obviously. At that point we made a plan in terms of saving to buy a place to live, and when we would have kids and how much that would cost and saving for that. With financial planning, that makes a big difference knowing that you're committed to doing it all together. Now any decisions we make together. We have a condo fund and a family fund that we're trying to build up, for saving money to have babies and vacations and that sort of stuff.

Similarly, Esteban, a thirty-four-year-old Marriage Assumer who had been with his partner four years before marriage, described joining finances after marriage as one part of a larger pattern of "planning and investing together." He explained, "We are definitely more unified financially now. We have a joint savings account. He gets health insurance through my work. We're talking about kids, where to live, retirement, you know, the rest of our lives." When I asked Esteban what about being married allowed them to do that, he responded, "It's like there's no foot out the door, it's just not an option now. Being married solidifies things."

The second way that married LGBQ individuals described postmarital feelings of added commitment and security impacting their financial practices was in becoming more relaxed about individual financial contributions. Before getting married, many individuals in same-sex relationships worked hard to ensure they contributed equally or fairly to the relationship. It was common for couples to keep strict accounts or have systems to make sure each partner's financial contribution to the relationship was fair or equitable. However, after getting married, feeling more committed and secure often translated into a sense of becoming one family that did not require such strict equality or accounting.

Brianna told me that, before getting married, even though she and her partner had already bought a house together, they had otherwise kept their finances separate. After they got married, they combined their money into one joint account. When I asked her why they had previously kept their finances separate, she initially responded, "Because you never know what will happen, and so we were both a bit cautious before." But she went on to explain that because she had earned more money than her partner, having separate accounts had made sense as a way to keep their financial contributions proportionally equitable. Also, she said, they had each purchased "random crap" and refused to contribute to one another's purchases. But after they were married, keeping separate accounts became "annoying" and the hassle of having to figure out which accounts to pay what out of started to feel "silly" to them. Being married translated into greater trust regarding the other person's intentions and a sense that both partners were working toward the same family goals.

Vanessa similarly described their premarital system as now seeming "idiotic." Like Brianna, before getting married she and her partner had had a "house account" that they both contributed to and out of which they paid house-related expenses. Both also had had "separate money" for "blowing on nonsense." Now they were married they were combining all their money into one account. Explaining what had changed, she said, "Before [my partner] was more psycho about everything having to be equal and now that we're married it's more like 'whatever.' I mean, we still try to make things relatively even, but it was idiotic before." This perception that premarital financial systems to keep things separate and equitable were "silly" and "idiotic" in the context of marriage was commonly articulated among Marriage Assumers. If one subscribed to cultural beliefs that marriage was the ultimate demonstration of commitment and trust, then it started to feel petty and unnecessarily distrusting to quibble over who was contributing what financially once married.

DIFFERING DEGREES OF CHANGE

Changes to relationship behaviors post-marriage differed across the three groups. LGBQ individuals in both the Assumer and Embracer groups described feeling more committed and secure post-marriage. They also described these feelings as translating into being more committed to the relationship post-marriage, including handling problems with partners differently and not wanting to give up when things got tough. Marriage Rejecters very rarely described feeling this way. Marriage Assumers very commonly experienced the feelings of greater commitment and security impacting their financial practices in marriage, but the effect of marriage on finances was less pronounced for Marriage Embracers and Rejecters. The typical Marriage Embracer and Rejecter had already pooled finances *before* marrying, whereas the typical Marriage Assumer typically did so only after marrying.

Many Marriage Embracers and Rejecters had already sustained long-term committed relationships while being excluded from the institution of marriage. They had therefore already made decisions to combine finances, not believing they would ever gain access to marriage or not deeming it important. As such, any feelings of extra commitment and security they felt after getting married did not translate into changes to their financial practices. By contrast, Marriage Assumers had never had to sustain commitment without access to the institution of marriage. They therefore regarded decisions to combine finances without marrying as risky and irresponsible, and they did not combine finances prior to legally marrying.[31] As such, the feelings of extra commitment and security they experienced after getting married also translated into meaningful behavioral changes to their financial practices.

Same-sex couples had not put their lives on hold in the absence of access to legal marriage. Without access to legal marriage, relationship duration became a measure of commitment instead, and the longer participants had been together the more likely they were to have joint accounts and property in both names.[32] Moreover, the longer LGBQ individuals had already been living with their partners before marrying, the less likely they were to think that getting married had made any difference to their finances.

Whereas Marriage Assumers only started to feel that keeping strict accounting of who was contributing what was burdensome or "stupid" after being married, some Marriage Rejecters described starting to feel this naturally with growing commitment in their unmarried relationships. For example, when Daniel, a thirty-five-year-old unmarried Marriage Rejecter, was thinking about "milestones" over his five-year relationship with his partner, he said:

> I've got a milestone for you—splitting expenses. It got to a point where it was frustrating and we just didn't want to do it. We had agreed to keep track of it, and then receipts would pile up that we would need to go through, and I think we had like a year of receipts! So, we decided to get a joint account, and that was much easier. We never did end up going through those receipts! I guess we just decided that it had worked itself out somehow. I guess that's a milestone because we've grown closer. Our finances and our lives have grown more intertwined.

Reflecting on this financial decision, Daniel realized that he had not recognized it as a significant milestone at the time. Instead, it had felt like a "natural progression" in their relationship, just like other financial decisions had been, "like adding each other as beneficiaries on our retirement plans and stuff like that."

Whether Marriage Rejecters had no plan to marry or had already legally married, they usually described combining their finances as signifying a meaningful commitment that was not dependent on marriage. Zoe, a thirty-five-year-old unmarried Marriage Rejecter who had been with her partner for nine years and had no intention to marry her, put it this way:

> Marriage doesn't signify that much to us. Truthfully, the commitment was when we purchased property together, had credit cards, bank statements, that was for both of us melding our two existences together. I've always been very sensitive about separating with previous partners, you know we pay half and half so it's very equitable, so I think taking that next plunge and being "This is ours now" was a big plunge.

Dianne, a fifty-two-year-old Marriage Rejecter who was now legally married, answered somewhat sarcastically when I asked her if she and her partner had ever made any explicit commitments to one another during their fourteen years together prior to getting married. She responded, "No, we didn't do anything to express commitment except plan our entire lives together!" Dianne went on to tell me that as soon as they had gotten together and started making enough money, they opened joint accounts and had bought cars and property together.

In addition to sharing income and assets as a way of demonstrating commitment without marriage, Marriage Rejecters also conceptualized a willingness to share debt and financial troubles as doing the same thing. Whereas Marriage Assumers were reluctant to combine finances prior to marriage precisely because they did not want to take on financial risk without the commitment and security of marriage, some Marriage Rejecters were willing to take on financial risks without marriage precisely because it was a way of demonstrating commitment. For example, Larry, a forty-two-year-old unmarried Marriage Rejecter who had been with his partner for fourteen years, told me how he and his partner had to "drain" their "shared savings" to pay for a surgery he had to have (because he had a preexisting condition that his health insurance would not pay for, and he could not get the surgery on his partner's coverage).[33] Larry interpreted his partner's willingness to spend the money as a clear signal of commitment: "He proved to me—because we had almost a decade worth of savings, and without a heartbeat, went in and paid off all that debt. And he didn't see it as my debt; he saw it as our debt."

Here we can see Marriage Assumers and Rejecters utilizing two very different cultural scripts regarding the meaning of finances for commitment. Because Rejecters deemed legal marriage unnecessary for their relationships, they used merging finances as an alternative means of demonstrating commitment. Because Assumers had internalized ideas about the importance of marriage for relationships, merging finances was a practice that only flowed out of marital commitment.

Marriage Embracers fell somewhere in the middle, having been excluded from the institution of marriage for a substantial portion of their relationships and not having relied on marriage to be committed, but nevertheless still imbuing legal marriage with distinctive social and cultural power for demonstrating commitment. They therefore exhibited messier, mixed kinds of pre- and postmarital financial practices. Because they sustained relationships for decades without the hope of ever gaining access to legal marriage, they did not hold back from pooling some of their finances with their partners prior to marrying. But because they also experienced deepening feelings of commitment post-marriage, they also engaged in new financial practices post-marriage too. Talia, a forty-seven-year-old Marriage Embracer who was with her partner eight years before marrying her, represents this kind of more limited change: not being reliant on marriage to engage in any financial pooling, but marriage nevertheless having a significant impact. Prior to marriage, she and her partner took some leaps of faith and financial risks in their relationship and used financial pooling as a means of demonstrating commitment to one another. Talia earned a lot less than her partner and was not expected to contribute to the rent or mortgages of homes they had shared together. Without access to marriage, they had trusted the other person's commitment enough to say that it did not matter. But Talia also described their premarital relationship as "somewhat of a balancing act" when it came to "trying to keep things equal." There was a careful system of "tallying up" regarding who should do what in the relationship, and because she couldn't contribute financially, Talia was expected to pick up the slack in other ways. After getting married, deepened feelings of commitment resulted in some significant changes to their financial behaviors. Most importantly, her partner added her to the deed of the house. And it was only after they legally married that they stopped caring about keeping track of who was contributing what. Talia recognized the difference being married made: "There's a sense of a real partnership now. Now it feels like we're in this together and we make sure that we have an equal interest and an equal level of investment, I guess. It doesn't matter anymore."

Attending to the different experiences of LGBQ people across the three groups in this book highlights how the impact of marriage on relationship behaviors is uneven. The magnitude with which marriage changes individual same-sex relationship practices varies across the groups, depending on both prior experiences of institutional exclusion, the length of premarital relationship durations, and the internalized cultural beliefs one enters marriage with.

However, there is good reason to believe that LGBQ individuals will increasingly come to converge around the kind of marital experiences Marriage Assumers have. Now that legal marriage is available from the start of all same-sex relationships, getting legally married will come to have a more transformative impact on a growing number of LGBQ individuals' relationship practices. We can already see that with the availability of legal marriage, relationship duration now plays much less of a role in same-sex couples' decisions about financial pooling, with couples waiting until marriage to feel committed and pool their finances.[34]

Conclusion

In their classic study of American couples in the early 1980s, Blumstein and Schwartz found that same-sex and heterosexual couples differed with regard to financial practices because whereas for heterosexual couples the kind of trust necessary for financial pooling was produced automatically on getting married, for same-sex couples without access to marriage it took many years of a relationship to build a similar kind of trust.[35] Interestingly, not being able to imagine the legalization of same-sex marriage in the future, they predicted that same-sex couples "offered a glimpse of what the future may hold for all married couples." They thought that heterosexual married couples would come to realize that the impermanence of "couple life" also applies to them and would come to increasingly question the "traditional concept of putting all their resources together."[36] In fact, the findings in this book suggest that heterosexual married couples in the 1980s actually offered a glimpse of what the future held for same-sex couples. Even though many individuals have come to accept the impermanence of marriage as an institution, this has not diminished its power in producing the kind of trust and security necessary for behaviors such as financial pooling. Being married still has a unique power in the way it makes people feel automatically more committed and secure. Now that same-sex couples have gained access to marriage, this power applies to them as well.

If marriage were truly losing its institutional power, married people would behave in a myriad of unpatterned ways and there would not be significant differences between married and unmarried people. Clearly though, this has not happened. Married individuals continue to behave in ways that are distinct from unmarried individuals. But they do not do so because of adherence to social rules and norms that constrain their behavior and tell them how to behave. The institutional mechanisms that shape marital behavior today are subtler and more complex. What has endured are taken-for-granted cultural beliefs about what marriage means, particularly the belief that marriage represents a distinct and unique form of commitment. When individuals internalize these beliefs, they have the power to change the way people feel about their partners and relationships once married, even after many years and acts of previous commitment. These new feelings subsequently impact the kinds of behaviors married people are willing to engage in. The declining salience of social norms governing individual behavior does not signal the weakening of marriage as an institution if what is shaping behavior is less visible and more deeply internalized at the cultural-cognitive level. In fact, when marriage can shape behavior without reliance on external rules and social pressure, and individuals act as if they are only responding to their own personal, internal feelings, this points to a stronger, more firmly institutionalized governing structure.

While the institutional process is different, the end result, however, is the same. Behaviors that were previously compulsory in marriage, such as not walking out on one's partner and financial pooling, have been re-invoked through a process that on the surface appears to be more personal and individual. Today's feelings may simply be yesterday's norms rebranded. This is the power of institutions. They endure by recreating themselves, and they do not depend on only one mechanism to shape behavior. As one mechanism diminishes in strength, another is already there to take its place.

6

Marital (Non)Monogamy

Liam, a married thirty-three-year-old gay man, was a big talker and had no problem sharing his views on any number of topics. But when I asked him what he thought about monogamy (being sexually exclusive), he was unsure what to say. He hesitated for a long time before sighing deeply and responding, "I—I'm very—I'm very conflicted about it." He thought that "his generation" had witnessed "way too many STDs" and that should definitely be cause for concern for anyone engaging in anything other than monogamy. But he did not think monogamy was necessary for a successful marriage: "I think it's possible for two people to have a committed, loving, rewarding relationship and not be monogamous." He also believed that it was "important not to immediately just assume that anything other than monogamy is less than ideal."

Liam credited same-sex couples with being capable of thinking about nonmonogamy in ways that most heterosexuals were not. In part, this was because same-sex marriages were new enough that they did not yet impose institutional expectations in the same way that heterosexual marriages did:

> I think that gay relationships and gay marriages are so novel that a level of hardening that might have happened in straight relationships over millennia hasn't set in yet. So, it's a new thing, we're still figuring this out, so we still have some latitude to decide what it is and what it has to be.

He understood this openness to nonmonogamy as coming from sexual orientation more generally as well. He regarded gay men (and possibly other LGBTQ+ individuals) as having a "different view of sexuality" and as being "more sexually aware" than heterosexuals. This was because "accepting gay identities requires getting past sexual stigma." To him, having a minority sexual identity already required "questioning other social stigmas around sexuality," and this made LGBTQ+ people "much more willing to examine the stigma around nonmonogamy too."

Liam's openness to nonmonogamy was more than just theoretical. Although he and his husband were currently monogamous, they had experimented with nonmonogamy. The previous year they had been celebrating their five-year wedding anniversary and had both started to feel a desire to explore nonmonogamy:

> We were starting to realize that I could blink and next thing you know we'll be married for thirty years and your options to be with someone else sort of might narrow once your youth is gone and what level of physical attractiveness you think you have has faded! So, it was like "Oh, if I wanna sow some oats, now's the time!"

They "gave one another permission" to engage in sex outside the marriage, with clear rules in place regarding safety and protection, and for keeping it private between the two of them. They were both very happy in their marriage and had no desire to end it. To the contrary, Liam believed that "too often really good relationships end because there's just no latitude to let people work things out of their systems." However, in the end, neither Liam nor his husband could bring themselves to engage in sex with anyone else, and they called the "experiment" off. Liam laughed but also sounded woeful as he said, "I just found out that I'm not much of an oat sower!" Several factors got in the way of Liam acting on his desire to experiment with nonmonogamy: concerns about STDs, worries about undermining their marriage, and the social stigma of enacting nonmonogamy in the context of legal marriage. Yet Liam remained open to trying again in the future and was confident that he and his husband would "be willing to work on it together" if that was what they both wanted.

Liam is one of the Marriage Assumers featured in chapter 3. Being relatively young and having only started to date same-sex partners after marriage was already legal, Liam always assumed that he would get legally married. There was a lot he took for granted about marriage but, surprisingly, monogamy was not one of them. Like many of the LGBQ individuals in this study, Liam exhibited a remarkable capacity to challenge institutional norms and expectations regarding marital monogamy. He was dogmatically nonjudgmental about nonmonogamy, communicated openly with his partner about shifting sexual needs and desires, and was even brave enough to attempt a nonmonogamous experiment in his own marriage. At the same time, however, he was hesitant to share his views and decisions with others, especially heterosexuals, acutely aware of social stigma surrounding nonmonogamy, and ultimately struggled to act on his desire to enact nonmonogamy in his marriage.

This chapter tells a story of both sexual freedom and constraint in same-sex marriages. On the one hand, LGBQ marriages exhibit an extraordinary departure from norms about marital monogamy. Unlike heterosexual marriages, the vast majority of which remain premised on the assumption of monogamy, a quarter of same-sex marriages in this study were nonmonogamous. But challenges to marital monogamy extended beyond simply practicing nonmonogamy and existed on a spectrum. Monogamous LGBQ individuals demonstrated respect for nonmonogamous practices. Many also displayed an openness to nonmonogamy as a future relationship form and are therefore more accurately defined as sexually fluid than monogamous, with flexible notions of sexual desires and behaviors that they expected to shift over the course of their relationships. They refused to adopt a strictly monogamous framework for their marriages and were consciously attempting to question and rethink the marital monogamy norm. They had internalized different cultural beliefs, which gave them alternative scripts for behavior within marriage.

However, despite attempts to think about and practice marital monogamy differently, LGBQ individuals found themselves struggling to navigate between two sets of powerful but competing cultural beliefs: a commitment to sexual freedom and equality dominant within the LGBTQ+ community, and ideas about sexual ownership and respectability dominant within heteronormative culture. Additionally, LGBQ individuals were not free from other people's expectations about marital monogamy. Taken together, these tensions resulted in a notable disconnect between attitudes and practices, with practicing nonmonogamy remaining much harder than expressing openness to it. With three-quarters of participants currently practicing monogamy, monogamy clearly remained the dominant sexual practice among same-sex couples. Nonmonogamous individuals were also reluctant to openly discuss their nonmonogamy and allowed social stigma to limit their sexual opportunities. Moreover, in spite of attempts to be open-minded, attitudes toward nonmonogamy were more complex than they first appeared, with LGBQ individuals regularly expressing subtle forms of normative judgment against nonmonogamy. Overall, LGBQ individuals face institutional, social, and cultural barriers to doing marriage differently when it comes to monogamy. Nonetheless, it is in the case of monogamy that we see the most deliberate challenge to the institution of marriage.

Marriage and Monogamy

In questioning the need for marital monogamy, Liam and others were countering legal, social, and cultural precedent. In Western societies, legal marriage has been inextricably linked with monogamy.[1] For centuries, marital monogamy was legally enshrined through the system of coverture, which established that a husband owns all forms of property emerging from the marriage, including sexual property and the expectation of a wife's sexual obedience and fidelity.[2] Although the laws upholding sexual monogamy in marriage are now a historical remnant, monogamy is still maintained by social and religious institutions as the "natural and/or morally correct form" of romantic coupledom.[3] When Justice Kennedy issued the majority opinion making same-sex marriage legal nationwide in 2015, he reiterated this dominant cultural belief: "No union is more profound than marriage, for it embodies the highest ideals of love, *fidelity*, devotion, sacrifice, and family. In forming a marital union, two people become something greater than once they were" (emphasis added). Marriage is elevated to the status of a "profound union" because it entails fidelity between only two people.

When marriage scholars look for evidence of the institution of marriage becoming "deinstitutionalized"[4]—with a weakening of the informal rules for how to behave in marriage—one of the key areas they look at is monogamy. Because monogamy is such a central marital norm, if marriage really were becoming deinstitutionalized, norms around marital monogamy should have significantly weakened.[5] But this has not occurred. National surveys show that 89 percent of US adults in romantic relationships report being monogamous.[6] Of course, many heterosexual relationships are monogamous in name only, with rates of infidelity in marriage estimated at up to 60 or 70 percent.[7] Nonmonogamy (honestly communicated sexual relationships outside the marriage) is rare for heterosexuals, but sexual infidelity (dishonest and hidden sexual relationships outside the marriage) is not. Monogamy then refers to the agreement, understanding, or assumption of fidelity within marriage, not the actual practice of it.

By contrast, researchers have consistently found that same-sex couples often maintain openly agreed upon nonmonogamous relationships, although there is some debate about whether rates of nonmonogamy in same-sex relationships are declining over time.[8] Male couples appear more likely than female couples to openly discuss nonmonogamy and to agree to allow sex outside the relationship.[9] But lesbians and bisexual women do not hold the same expectations of monogamy as heterosexual couples, suggesting that sexuality matters as well as gender.[10] Not having access to legal marriage may have allowed for and encouraged greater nonmonogamy among same-sex couples. Already existing outside heteronormativity, and without clear legal and social norms guiding their relationships, same-sex couples had the freedom to construct their relationships differently. Excluded from legal marriage, alternative sexual cultures developed within the LGBTQ+ community in its place, with the freedom to question and challenge what they saw as the worst parts of heterosexual relationships: sexual ownership, distrust, and a lack of communication and negotiation. Indeed, many queer and feminist authors and activists have presented nonmonogamies as potentially liberating, cooperative, and empowering alternatives to the ownership, possession, and even violence located within traditional monogamy; nonmonogamies become a place where celebratory pride in sexuality can be embraced.[11]

What then does same-sex marriage mean for nonmonogamy? Although the fight for marriage equality brought issues of *sexual identity* to the fore, *sexual practices* have never had a clear place in the movement. Becoming sexual subjects entails a heightened focus on sexual identity as the key to rights and belonging,[12] but this has not always existed comfortably with discussions of actual sex, especially when accessing institutions as (hetero)normative as marriage and when the group seeking access has historically not conformed to the sexual standards established for the institution. Conservative opposition to same-sex marriage has been driven in part by mental associations between homosexuality and promiscuity: the idea that married same-sex couples would be openly promiscuous and set a bad marital example.[13] At the same time, queer opponents to marriage have worried that same-sex couples would experience a pressure to conform to heteronormative standards for marriage, including monogamy.[14]

Defining Key Terms:
Monogamous, Nonmonogamous, and Monogamish

It is necessary to briefly introduce and explore definitions and variations in monogamous and nonmonogamous practices. Monogamy is the most straightforward, defined simply as sexual exclusivity. Monogamous partners agree to only engage in sexual activity with one another. By contrast, nonmonogamy is sexual nonexclusivity. Nonmonogamous couples have open relationships, in which both partners are allowed to engage in sexual activity with people outside the dyad. The key to nonmonogamy is openness and honesty, for it is not the same as adultery. Stephen Haas and Pamela Lannutti use the term "consensual non-monogamy agreements" in order to emphasize this point. Another important aspect of nonmonogamy is that open sexual relationships do not usually include developing emotionally close relationships with other people. Same-sex couples often distinguish between sex as "just sex" and the emotional commitment that is their relationship.[15] In this way, nonmonogamous relationships are distinct from polyamorous relationships, which involve emotional and familial bonds as well as sexual ones.[16]

Although honest communication and emotional exclusivity are typical for nonmonogamous relationships, there remains a great deal of variation within them. One form of variation is in how much partners discuss outside sexual experiences with one another. Some partners share details about outside sexual encounters with one another. Other nonmonogamous couples have more of a "don't ask, don't tell" approach, having agreed for it to occur but preferring not to know any more beyond that. Another point of variation is how much outside sexual activity partners actually engage in. Some engage in very regular outside sexual activity. Others define themselves as nonmonogamous but rarely actually engage in outside sexual activity. How much outside sexual activity couples engage in is also not static. Sexual drives and behaviors ebb and flow over the course of nonmonogamous relationships, with outside sexual activity shaped by a range of external factors, such as paid and unpaid work and parenting demands, just as is true for heterosexual monogamous couples.[17]

In monogamish arrangements, sex outside the relationship is only allowed when both partners participate in it together with a third person.[18] These couples regard themselves as partially monogamous—"monogamish"—because they do engage in sex with other people, but only ever at the same time, together, as part of a shared couple experience. Some LGBQ individuals knew and used the term "monogamish" to describe this arrangement, while others described the arrangement without using the term. Monogamish arrangements were a way for couples to avoid feeling as if they had to enter an "either/or" situation. This was a middle-ground position that allowed them to explore shifting sexual needs and desires together within the framework of their relationships.

What Matters for Nonmonogamy? Gender and Marital Status

In line with existing research, men in this study were much more likely to practice nonmonogamy than women. Whereas 96 percent of the women in this study were monogamous, by contrast, only slightly over half of men were monogamous (56 percent), while 24 percent were nonmonogamous and 20 percent were monogamish. At first glance, gender matters a great deal for monogamy. Yet women exhibited much greater openness to nonmonogamy than this basic data suggests. There were no significant differences by gender in attitudes toward monogamy: the majority of both women and men disagreed with the statement that "couples should always be monogamous." Moreover, as I will show, women displayed a remarkable fluidity in their own relationships regarding sexual exclusivity, even if they did not currently participate in nonmonogamy. As such, although current sexual practices differ significantly by gender, sexual attitudes do not, and attention to sexual fluidity in addition to rates of nonmonogamy among women reveals a much more complex gendered picture. In the usual narrow focus on behavior, women's contributions to change are typically overlooked, but if we consider there to be a spectrum of challenges to marital nonmonogamy, we see that both women and men have roles to play in shifting marital norms.

The survey data suggest that marital status does not appear to make much difference to nonmonogamy. Of the married participants, 74 percent were monogamous, 16 percent were nonmonogamous, and 10 percent were monogamish. Of the unmarried participants, 85 percent were monogamous, 10 percent nonmonogamous, and 5 percent were monogamish. In other words, similar proportions were monogamous and nonmonogamous across marital status. This fits with existing survey research on rates of nonmonogamy by marital status among same-sex couples.[19] When I asked married participants in the survey whether they thought being legally married had changed how monogamous they were with their partner, very few thought that marriage had made any difference.[20] When it came to attitudes toward monogamy, there were also no significant differences by marital status. However, survey data can only tell us so much here. Interview data helps illuminate how being married shapes the lived experience of practicing nonmonogamy, making it feel more socially awkward and stigmatizing to discuss and enact, and harder to find sexual partners.

Embracing, Rejecting, or Assuming Marital Monogamy?

Surprisingly, in contrast to other areas of married life, the three marriage groups I outlined in part I of the book—Marriage Embracers, Rejecters, and Assumers—matter little for the practice of marital monogamy. With such fundamentally different beliefs and feelings about marriage, one would imagine that each marriage group also approached the issue of monogamy in very different ways. We might expect to see one group embracing marital monogamy, another rejecting it, and another simply assuming it. However, they did not. This is important because it shows that when it comes to monogamy there are no simple "types" of married LGBQ people, likely to behave in one way or another. Monogamous attitudes and behaviors do not map neatly onto other marital orientations or trajectories.

Let us look only at the Rejecters for a moment. Seventy-two percent of

Rejecters were monogamous, compared to 80 percent of Embracers and 83 percent of Assumers. Slightly fewer Rejecters practiced monogamy than those in the other groups, but this is not a large difference. The vast majority of Rejecters, who rejected the need for marriage and were highly critical of marriage as an institution, still practiced monogamy. For contrast, let us take a look at the Assumers. Seventeen percent of this otherwise very heteronormatively conforming group practiced nonmonogamy. Perhaps even more important, most Assumers did not assume that their marriages should be monogamous. They were just as likely to reach the decision to be monogamous through negotiation and discussion with their partners as their peers in the Embracer and Rejecter groups.

On the one hand, if we focus on rates of monogamy, we see that monogamy reigns supreme across the groups as the dominant relationship form. Monogamy is such a culturally strong normative ideal that perhaps it united groups who are otherwise very different given their varying life-course trajectories and ideological positions on marriage. On the other hand, focusing instead on nonmonogamy, one can interpret the lack of difference in nonmonogamy rates across these groups as evidence that the institution of marriage has *not*, thus far, been powerful enough to supersede cultural beliefs and norms emerging from the LGBTQ+ community, which continue to be endorsed and practiced by a wide variety of individuals even in the post–legal marriage era. What we are left with is the dominance of monogamy as a sexual practice alongside a remarkable openness to nonmonogamy. Rather than very clear differences across the three groups outlined in this book, a complex mix of beliefs around sex combine to create a much messier variety of attitudes and practices in the case of monogamy. In this chapter, I therefore discuss the three groups together while highlighting any notable differences between them, when relevant.

Challenging Marital Monogamy Norms

Below, I outline several kinds of potential challenges the LGBQ individuals in this book made to the (hetero)normative practice of marital monogamy. These challenges exist along a spectrum, ranging from shifting attitudes to engaging in nonmonogamy within marriage and are therefore engaged in by LGBQ individuals who are both monogamous and nonmonogamous.

REFLEXIVE VIEWS OF NONMONOGAMY

In the United States, the vast majority of heterosexuals continue to hold a normative view of marital monogamy.[21] A "normative view" holds that marriage and monogamy are inextricably linked and that alternative arrangements are a violation of the foundation of a marital relationship.[22] Yet only 27 percent of LGBQ individuals in this research agreed that couples should "always be monogamous." The rest either disagreed (37 percent) or did not have a view one way or another (36 percent).[23] Most importantly, attitudes did not correspond neatly with behaviors, so that those who practiced monogamy were, for the most part, not morally opposed to nonmonogamy. Instead, they held "reflexive views" of marriage, rejecting any universal opposition to nonmonogamous marriage and understanding marital monogamy as a choice best left to each couple to negotiate.

It was very common for married monogamous individuals to quickly and forcefully assert nonjudgment of other LGBQ people who were nonmonogamous.[24] They wanted to make it very clear that their own choices did not reflect any negative judgment regarding other people's choices. Monogamous individuals therefore often told me, as part of the same answer, that they were monogamous and that they did not judge those who were not. For example, Robert, a fifty-one-year-old monogamous married Embracer, said:

> For us, monogamy works. Neither one of us would want it any other way, but if other people like that [nonmonogamy], that doesn't bother me. That's their business, and if it works for them then it's fine. I'm not going to put anybody down. Just because it doesn't work for us doesn't mean it's not OK for somebody else.

In addition to articulating general reflexive statements such as this, LGBQ individuals employed two discursive strategies for expressing nonjudgment of their nonmonogamous peers. The first strategy was to assert that nonmonogamous individuals had skills that they personally lacked. They were not morally opposed to nonmonogamy; they just did not believe they were capable of it. For example, Grace, a forty-eight-year-old monogamous married Embracer, believed she and her partner were not good enough "planners" to be capable of enacting nonmonogamy without hurting one another:

> I mean, we both made a commitment to be monogamous with each other, always, from the beginning. But it's not that either of us feel that a relationship has to be monogamous, we certainly don't judge people that are nonmonogamous. I think it's really hard to do that. We're not great planners together. And at this point I wouldn't feel very confident that we'd be able to work it out in a way that wouldn't end up hurting us. But it's not because I'm opposed to it or because she's opposed to it.

Raul, a forty-eight-year-old monogamous married Assumer, similarly said that he would not be capable of "keeping track" of multiple sexual partners and that nonmonogamy always sounded "too complicated" for him. But he was sure to make clear that "I think every couple is different and people make the compromises that they want to. Even if I sometimes can't wrap myself around it all, I respect it and I don't judge it, it's just not for me." If it was hard for him to imagine or understand, that was his limitation and not a problem with the practice of nonmonogamy itself.

Dennis, a fifty-three-year-old monogamous unmarried Rejecter, told me that when a prior partner of his had wanted an open relationship he had been unable "to handle it" and they had split up. When his subsequent partner then also decided that he wanted an open relationship, rather than "freaking out about it," Dennis introduced the two of them and they fell in love! His two exes stayed together for many years until one of them passed away, and Dennis remained good friends with them both. Looking back, Dennis said, "They just had different ideas about what they wanted in the relationship than I did. I didn't feel secure enough for it." In his mind, the failing was his, and he did not judge them for wanting something different. Laughing, he joked, "So, I didn't come to the conclusion [to be monogamous] by just saying 'This is my moral stand on it!'" Instead, his personal experiences had shown him that he was not personally capable of it.

A second common way of asserting nonjudgment and support for LGBQ peers who were nonmonogamous was by connecting it to what is "natural" for humans as a species. This argument was most commonly made among Marriage Rejecters (chapter 3), who tended to reject dominant cultural beliefs about what is "natural" for marriage. In contrast to dominant cultural ideas, they claimed that nonmonogamy was actually the "natural" way for humans to behave.[25] Linda, a fifty-four-year-old monogamous married Rejecter, said:

> It's [nonmonogamy's] not right for me. But I do understand that it is the human condition. And I know that a lot of married people, gay and straight, don't have monogamous relationships. I don't understand some of the things that people tell me, [*laughs*] but it's their personal decision.

Linda personally did not feel any desire to be nonmonogamous, nor did she comprehend all of her nonmonogamous friends' sexual experiences, but she understood them as natural based on "the human condition" and respected others' personal choices.

Some Marriage Rejecters went even further, arguing that they were monogamous only because they could not escape their social conditioning to be so. For example, Chelsie, a twenty-eight-year-old monogamous unmarried woman said, "We are in a monogamous relationship, but we don't really think humans are necessarily meant to be in monogamous relationships. It's just that we have been so socialized this way that now there is no way we personally couldn't be." Likewise, Alisa, a twenty-seven-year-old unmarried Rejecter, somewhat mournfully said, "Because our society has trained us that this is the way to do it, that's all I know. I can't even explain it. But I respect the fact it can work for other people." These kinds of "to each their own" reflexive attitudes about nonmonogamy were common and clearly articulated by married and unmarried LGBQ individuals alike, and across the marriage groups. However, Marriage Rejecters were more likely to express them as part of a broader rejection of ideas about what is "natural" for sexuality.

DIY MARRIAGES

Moving beyond attitudes about nonmonogamy, many nonmonogamous LGBQ individuals also presumed that they could integrate nonmonogamy into their marriages. Although the institution of marriage is still culturally very much associated with monogamy, they felt that marriage was adaptable enough that they could create their own unique relationships within it. Nonmonogamous individuals were simply careful to avoid the parts of marriage that they did not plan on adhering to. They did not want to promise something they could not commit to. In this way, they perceived marriage as a kind of DIY institution that could be designed and adapted to suit their own individual needs. Patrick, a fifty-year-old married Embracer, said that he and his partner had thought "very carefully" about the wording of their vows in order to avoid committing to monogamy.[26] He explained, "In the standard book or prayer that is usually used—the one you always see in movies—it does include something about monogamy. So, we were careful not to include that."[27] Rachel, a thirty-year-old Marriage Assumer, and her wife never felt any pressure to become monogamous after they got married. She knew that other people probably assumed that she and her wife were, but she did not think it mattered, explaining, "We've made the space for our unique relationship inside of the marriage concept. I think most people still have an idea that marriage fundamentally means this monogamous dyad lifetime commitment, but the reality is that everybody brings their own flavors to that."

Some LGBQ individuals found that being married made practicing nonmonogamy easier. Most often, this was because they drew on other widely shared cultural beliefs about marital commitment to define the parameters of outside sexual activity and feel more secure doing it. Heather, a thirty-one-year-old Assumer, and her wife occasionally allowed one another to engage in outside sexual activity with strangers, so long as they always discussed it openly with one another. Heather found that being married made the distinction between sex and their emotional and relational commitment to one another all the clearer: "You have a couple of drinks and start kissing someone. Some people think, 'Oh my gosh, they cheated on you!' But she's married to me and responsible for coming home to me. Sex is sex but being married to each other is a lifelong commitment that we made." Being married defined their relationship as a "lifelong commitment" so she could feel secure knowing that momentary attractions or brief sexual activities with other people would not change the commitments and responsibilities they had with one another. Being married also helped them to more clearly define their relationship with another married couple that they occasionally engaged in sexual relations with. She explained:

> After we got married it was a discussion we had. It came up as a joke, but then we actually started talking about it. "Well, what would that mean? How would that work?" And then everyone was like, "Well, actually, we're kind of more comfortable with the idea now because we are both married."

Getting married opened up an opportunity to have a deeper discussion about the meaning of what they were doing and to more clearly establish boundaries around their relationship. In this way, being married helped Heather better define and conceptualize nonmonogamy both internally and interactionally.

In a study with gay men in Canada, Adam Green found that marriage gave some gay men the extra security and confidence to be nonmonogamous. No one in this study started being nonmonogamous *after* they married, but some reported that being married made them feel more secure and confident in their nonmonogamous relationships. Bill, a sixty-one-year-old married Embracer, and his partner of seventeen years had always been nonmonogamous, but Bill admitted that, if it were up to him, he would "prefer to be monogamous." Over the years they had both engaged in sex outside the relationship, together and separately—what Bill described as various forms of "sex without commitment," including with friends and strangers. That arrangement did not change when they got married, but how Bill felt about it did. When I asked Bill what exactly marriage had changed, he emphatically replied:

> The security. Just the fact that you're not so worried anymore about fooling around on one another. I think both of us understood that what we were doing was still pretty much the same thing, but now the commitment between us was stronger. [Now] playing outside was only that; it wasn't going to be anything disruptive.

Bill had always worried that his partner would leave him for someone else. Outside sex did not bother him, but he had always felt nervous that it might become something more. He confided, "I feel silly for even having those thoughts. But you hear about people, after twenty or twenty-five years, their relationship just gets stale. I don't want to all of a sudden realize that he's now found someone else." They had always had a rule that they were not allowed to have "repeats"—that is, engage in outside sex with the same person more than once—in order to try to prevent that from happening, but getting married had really helped to relieve those ongoing concerns. "I feel better now. I think the fact that we're married makes us stronger. I'm loved by all his family. He'd get in trouble if he ever tried to break up with me! His family would divorce him. [*laughs*] It feels really good to be married."

Marriage offered LGBQ people the shared cultural understanding of commitment, which helped them to better define outside boundaries and feel more secure in their relationships, aiding in the practice of nonmonogamy. In this sense, although they were challenging institutional norms of marriage by being nonmonogamous, they were also still very much drawing on widely shared cultural beliefs about what marriage means to make sense of their nonmonogamous practices. And being legally married was changing the meaning-making associated with nonmonogamy in same-sex relationships.

SEXUAL FLUIDITY

To gain a full picture of the challenges LGBQ individuals pose to norms of marital monogamy, it is necessary to pay closer attention to *monogamous* same-sex couples. This is because it was common for currently monogamous LGBQ individuals to hold a fluid, flexible notion of sexual desire and behavior. Many of those who were currently monogamous had not been in the past nor necessarily expected to be in the future. They were open to their sexual desires and practices shifting over the course of their relationships. Sexual fluidity among LGBQ individuals is a useful reminder that one's current monogamy status is a somewhat misleading piece of information. In this way, although only a minority of individuals were currently married and nonmonogamous, a much greater number of same-sex couples refused to adopt a strictly monogamous framework for their marriages. Rather than conceptualizing same-sex marriages as either monogamous or nonmonogamous, the data shows that it is more accurate to view same-sex marriages as either sexually fluid or not. And it is through openness to sexual fluidity that many LGBQ individuals challenge marital monogamy norms.[28] Sexual fluidity was not distinct to marriage. In what follows, you will notice that married and unmarried LGBQ individuals alike described a very similar sexual fluidity. The data makes clear that participating in marriage did not constrain the ability of LGBQ people to conceptualize or enact sexual fluidity.

Sexual fluidity entailed conceptualizing their relationships as fluid—as open to change, likely to change, and as requiring honest communication and negotiation about changing sexual needs. Green et al.'s study of married Canadian couples in the mid-2000s similarly identified a flexible approach to marriage, with monogamy as something that could be negotiated over the course of a marriage: "as tentative lines of action that require ongoing discussion and room for future adaptation."[29] For Green et al., this flexibility reflected Anthony Giddens's "plastic sexuality"—the late modern form of intimate relations, marked by sexual malleability and the fulfillment of individual needs. However, for the LGBQ people in this study, sexual fluidity was about prioritizing relationships and one's partner above oneself. Rather than only about the pursuit of individual needs, sexual fluidity was very much relational. It was a dedication to maintaining open communication, support, adaptation, and commitment to one another even as individual sexual desires change.

Just because someone is currently monogamous does not mean that they always have been, or always will be. Take Andy, a thirty-two-year-old married monogamous Assumer, as an example. Before she and her wife married, they had lived long distance, and in "coming up with rules about how to make it manageable," they had decided not to be monogamous. Only able to see one another every few months, they were open to the fact that they had sexual desires and needs that they could not meet for each other. Andy said, "We wanted one another to both really live our lives" and not just be "home never going out and feeling sad." Looking back, Andy laughed as she recalled how they had shared "funny stories" of their outside sexual experiences. But once they were living in the same place, nonmonogamy no longer felt necessary to them and they transitioned to a monogamous relationship. Nevertheless, even now they were married they maintained that there was "always the option for them to not be monogamous" again in the future. Andy could not imagine ever opening up their marriage to include multiple partners, but she could imagine being open to occasional exploration, perhaps if they were "out dancing and someone hit on us." She had no idea if they would "ever put it into practice," but having that openness helped her to feel like there was "a little bit more space" in marriage.

Sexual fluidity required LGBQ individuals to talk openly with their partners about changing sexual needs and desires. Same-sex couples were committed to sexual honesty, openness, and authenticity. They never wanted to go behind their partner's backs and engage in sex that they were not aware of. But these conversations and changes weren't always easy. Greg, a twenty-nine-year-old unmarried Rejecter, had been "totally monogamous" all his life but had recently found himself wanting to engage in nonmonogamy with his partner of three years. He explained that his partner was "a total bottom" and although he had not minded always being a top in the past, over time his sexual needs had changed. Greg had been "really scared to talk to [his partner] about it, and it took a long time" for him to have the courage to bring it up. He had no desire to end the relationship and was scared to lose his partner, but he also wanted to be honest about his sexual needs. His partner agreed to experimenting with nonmonogamy as a way to meet their sexual needs. They had "given each other permission to have a fling every now and then," so long as they did so safely, and abided by a "don't ask, don't tell policy." Greg had to "trust that [his partner] was OK with it" and wanted to take his time to work on it with his partner, and so he had not actually engaged in any outside sexual activity yet. Transitioning from monogamy to nonmonogamy was not always easy or fast, and it required a lot of discussion, but many same-sex couples were willing to put in that kind of work to sustain their committed relationships.

Even if they were not currently transitioning their monogamy status, or had not done so in the past, it was common for couples to discuss nonmonogamy as a future possibility. Same-sex couples were careful not to box themselves into monogamy and to remain open to exploring new sexual opportunities in the future, if that was what was needed for the relationship to last. Just as Greg had sexual needs that could not be met in his current relationship, Megan, a thirty-one-year-old unmarried Rejecter, understood that her partner had a very specific sexual desire that she could not accommodate: to "be with a guy." Megan had already been with men before, but her partner had not, and Megan wanted to support her in having that sexual experience. The way Megan described it, her partner "just wants dick! In and out! A one-night stand." Megan suspected "there's going to be a lot more emotionally to it than she thinks," but nevertheless she wanted to support her partner in exploring her sexual desires. They had "talked about it a lot" and agreed to have a "threesome" in the future. To Megan, being able to talk about their needs was what mattered, and she assumed that this was typical for lesbian relationships: "You know, we're total lesbians, talking about it! [*laughs*] That's what works for us is having that kind of communication and figuring it all out."

Others did not have specific sexual desires or needs that needed meeting but rather more generally presumed that new needs would arise over the course of a long-term relationship or marriage. Someone might develop an "interest in something or someone" or decide that they "would like something casual" with someone else. Just as nonmonogamous individuals avoided promising monogamy in their wedding vows, so too did monogamous individuals because they were not willing to commit to a lifetime of monogamy. Jo, a thirty-two-year-old married Assumer, told me that she and her wife had specifically "not included the forsaking all others vow" when they got married because it wasn't a promise either of them felt able to make. She explained, "We don't have an open relationship, but looking at a lifetime together, we can imagine that there might be the possibility where one or both of us would like something casual with somebody else, and maybe that could be negotiated." Jo believed that although "sex can be incredibly meaningful, it can also just be fun." That view of sex allowed her to see that there might be future potential to negotiate opening up their marriage, although she stressed that it would have to be "explicitly negotiated" at that time and not something "someone just went out and did without discussion."

Hannah, a thirty-nine-year-old married Embracer, described being monogamous as something she just "happened" to currently be. Her current monogamy status was not a significant indicator of her inner sexual desires or needs, which she expected to change over time. Monogamy was a current practice, not an identity or lifelong commitment:

> We happen to be monogamous, but we've had conversations. We've known lots of friends who are nonmonogamous in various forms. And we've talked about the possibility that if one of us had something or someone that they were interested in that we would be open to that discussion.

Hannah also said that she experienced it as "freeing" to establish openness to change as a key value in their marriage.

In addition to many currently monogamous relationships and marriages being more accurately described as sexually fluid, many same-sex couples refused to allow nonmonogamy to become a deal-breaker for their relationships. To be clear, this is not exactly the same as sexual fluidity. These LGBQ individuals would rather keep their relationships monogamous and did not have any real desire to explore nonmonogamy in the future. However, they believed that they could make it work, if they had to. They stated that they would "find a way" to adapt to nonmonogamy or "figure it out" rather than lose their partners, should one partner really desire it in the future. In this way, they exhibited a kind of relational malleability not typically present in heterosexual marriages.

This is particularly remarkable for those in the Marriage Assumer group, who were completely unwilling to compromise at all around getting married (see chapter 3): recall that having partners who were disinterested in marriage was a complete "deal-breaker" for Marriage Assumers. Yet, once married, many of them were willing to compromise on the details of how to do marriage in order to keep those marriages intact. We also see a similar approach among Marriage Embracers, who embraced heteronormative marriage rituals even before marriage was legal (see chapter 1) but refused to embrace the heteronormative idea that nonmonogamy should end their relationships. Again, the LGBQ people in this book engaged in a kind of DIY approach to marriage, valuing some parts of marriage but feeling free to ignore others.

Clara, a twenty-nine-year-old married Assumer, described herself and her wife as "both really monogamous-type people," and nonmonogamy as something she had "never wanted at all." Nonetheless she said that she had always entered her relationships "feeling flexible" on the subject. She explained:

> It's not something I want, but I don't feel like it's a deal-breaker. [My wife] and I both happen to be very monogamously minded. But it's not out of the question. I think there would have been a lot of discussion about details of how it would work or whatever, but if everything else was awesome, it wouldn't ruin it for me.

Another Marriage Assumer, Sophie, (age twenty-seven) already knew that her wife felt differently about monogamy than she did. Sophie felt "really strongly about monogamy" and did not want any intimacy beyond the marriage, but she knew that her wife "would be happy if she could have a one-night fling every once in a while." LGBQ individuals did not necessarily assume they had to marry partners who felt the same way about monogamy as they did. There appears to be a willingness to respect differing views and figure it out together. Nevertheless, after four years together, Sophie and her wife had not yet come up with a good solution for their different preferences. Knowing that it would hurt her, Sophie's wife had not pressed the issue. At the same time, Sophie thought that she might be willing to compromise in the future. She said: "I think it would depend on what it was. If it was that one-night thing that she would really love to do, I don't think it would be a deal-breaker. But I'll have to be in that situation to really see."

Several other people discussed the idea that it was "sad" to let nonmonogamy cause otherwise healthy marriages to end. If shifting sexual desires are understood as a natural and inevitable part of human nature, then it seemed unreasonable to expect everyone's needs to be met by one person across the marriage. In this sense, LGBQ individuals expressed a commitment to marriage over and above their commitment to monogamy. Kimberly, a twenty-six-year-old unmarried Assumer, put it this way:

> I think it's really sad when people are married but they find somebody else attractive and the lust they feel makes them leave their partner for that person.

But then they realize that they have made a mistake. I'm not interested in playing that game. If one of us found that we really just wanted to explore somebody else, I'd rather us do that while we're together and know that it's not going to ruin the relationship. Go have your lusty whatever-it-is and then come back to the relationship you wanted to begin with.

Hannah agreed. She said, "Breaking up because of nonmonogamy just seems tragic, especially where kids are involved. If it's something that can be fixed by opening up the relationship a little and allowing the couple to actually stay together, why wouldn't you do that?"

Maintaining Marital Monogamy Norms

Not all attitudes and behaviors exhibited by LGBQ individuals challenged marital monogamy norms. LGBQ individuals maintained heteronormative norms and expectations around marital monogamy in two primary ways: either because they themselves believed in them or because they felt socially constrained to adhere to them despite personal beliefs and preferences to the contrary.

NORMATIVE VIEWS IN DISGUISE?

Explicit normative statements in opposition to nonmonogamy were rare. In fact, only one participant—Cody, a thirty-six-year-old unmarried Marriage Assumer—expressed strong normative opposition to marital nonmonogamy. When I asked Cody if he and his partner of four years had discussed getting married, he said that one thing that put them off marrying was their disappointment with how other gay men are "using marriage."

> I have a lot of gay friends that are married and still have open relationships. And that disappoints me. They still do stuff that, to me, a single person should be doing. I love the *concept* of gay marriage, but personally when I look at marriage, I think of monogamy. It's kind of a sacred thing to me, not a religious sacred thing but where you're bonding two people. You're not single anymore, you need to act like you're bonded.

Cody stood out as a rare case of someone who expressed strong normative, moral opposition to marital nonmonogamy.

Importantly though, the survey suggests that Cody may be far from alone in holding such views. Just under a third of participants (27 percent) agreed with the normative statement that couples should "always be monogamous." Perhaps most LGBQ individuals did not feel comfortable expressing normative statements about nonmonogamy as openly and explicitly as Cody did.[30] Nonetheless, judgment about marital nonmonogamy was frequently articulated in more subtle forms.[31] One common viewpoint was that although individuals said that they did not "judge" those who were nonmonogamous, they did not believe that nonmonogamy could actually work in practice. For example, Esteban, a thirty-four-year-old married Assumer, said:

> I think in the long run, sooner or later [people in open marriages] get upset. Someone gets hurt. I can see how it's fun, right, if it's open. But god, it's so stressful. I think it potentially leads to people getting hurt emotionally or physically in terms of health issues. So, I don't see the benefit to that within a long-term plan with someone.

For Esteban, someone getting hurt was inevitable. He also could not understand why someone would want to introduce that likely "potential" into any relationship you wanted to last. Similarly, Kaitlyn, a twenty-nine-year-old married Assumer, said: "It's a nice idea in theory, nonmonogamy, but someone's always feeling hurt if you're being honest with yourself, so why do it?"

Josh, a forty-year-old married Assumer, thought that nonmonogamous relationships were "emotional," "tumultuous," and "drama-filled." Although he thought it possible that other people were better able to manage "drama" than he was, he was clearly skeptical that it could be healthy for anyone: "I think the people that say that it works for them have a completely different idea of what they want to get out of their life than I do." He sarcastically joked, "I'd have to quit my job if my personal life was that drama-filled. I already can't manage anything! And I can't imagine raising two kids! Like, daddy's going out on a date. What? How do you do that? But it happens. People do it." Josh simply could not imagine nonmonogamy as compatible with anything as ordinary as maintaining a job or raising children. In his mind, it required a completely different kind of life. (Contrary to such beliefs, nonmonogamous relationships in this study were not particularly "drama-filled," and arguing about sex outside the relationship was generally rare.[32])

These kinds of ideas show that it was possible to hold a reflexive view of nonmonogamy but not consider monogamy and nonmonogamy as equal relationship forms. And these statements were most frequently articulated by Marriage Assumers, highlighting a noteworthy difference across the groups.[33] Whereas Marriage Rejecters tended to believe that their own individual insecurity or social conditioning was to blame for not being able to be nonmonogamous, Marriage Assumers were more likely to believe it was not possible to practice nonmonogamy without "someone getting hurt." In other words, nonmonogamy itself was flawed, rather than individuals or society. Through statements like these, Marriage Assumers made clear their belief that monogamous relationships were superior, without couching such judgment in explicitly moral or normative terms.

Another form of judgment against nonmonogamous relationships was the belief that those who engaged in nonmonogamous relationships only did so because they had low self-esteem due to internalized homophobia. Internalized homophobia is the idea that LGBTQ+ individuals direct "negative social attitudes toward the self," consciously or unconsciously internalizing society's homophobic attitudes, resulting in poor self-esteem.[34] For instance, Jess, a thirty-one-year-old unmarried Marriage Rejecter, said:

> I think it's a broader issue of maintenance of couplehood within the community. I mean, we were talking about this before you got here, about open relationships. You know they are more widely embraced within the LGBT community but there's a lot of struggle with maintaining relationships, and a lot of it has to do with kind of the hurt that people bring from their previous experiences, from within society at large. Like, there's a lot of internalized homophobia and there's just a lot of pain, you know. So, we're not starting in the same place in a lot of cases.

Jess was not suggesting that the LGBTQ+ community was wrong to "embrace" open relationships, but she did think that the desire for open relationships was intrinsically connected to internalized homophobia. Although this was not an explicit normative judgment against "open relationships," they were understood as the product of something psychologically unhealthy.

Some suggested that because internalized homophobia would decline with marriage, so too would nonmonogamous relationships. They believed that as people felt more accepted by society in the wake of marriage equality, their self-esteem would improve, and the sexual practices of LGBQ individuals would therefore change. For example, Austin,[35] a married forty-eight-year-old, said:

> In Massachusetts, I think having the right to marry has really relaxed gay people, made them feel more comfortable with being in long-term relationships. I think a lot of gay people prior to marriage being legal were kind of forced by their own internalized homophobia to just have lots of one-night stands; now I think gay people are more apt to look for one long-term relationship.

For Austin, feeling "comfortable" in society was connected with an ability to focus on maintaining one long-term relationship and not needing "lots of one-night stands."[36]

Lastly, some LGBQ individuals assumed that other LGBQ individuals were not getting married because they did not want to be monogamous. Matt, a forty-two-year-old married Marriage Embracer, believed that the reason he and his husband were one of the few couples in his peer group to get married was because they were monogamous. He posited, "Certainly when we started to participate in mainstream gay culture of urban gay men, monogamy was not the default choice for a lot of gay couples. We were unusual because we had been monogamous from such a young age. So, we didn't know a lot of other people getting married at the time." Although these statements might not sound particularly judgmental, they reflected a (hetero)normative belief that only some kinds of relationships are suitable for marriage, and some kinds of people are committed enough for marriage.

Matt went so far as to describe marriage as incompatible with gay male culture, even for monogamous couples. In his mind, being married meant being ready and "mature enough" to stop participating in the "sexually charged" gay male culture that he had been used to. In fact, this perceived incompatibility between marriage and gay male culture had made it difficult for him to adjust to married life at first:

> Even though we were monogamous, at first it was still really hard for me to think that being married would make me not attractive to other men. That was a big part of my identity as a young gay man in my twenties and thirties. So, I was still always wanting to be in those high sexually charged environments, like gay clubs, so I would feel physically desired. We tried to kind of steer away from that into a different socializing pattern, and that was really hard for me to give up. [Being married] made me feel like "You're at a certain age"—at the time I was thirty-four—"You have a house, you have a husband, a career, this is what should be turning you on now." I matured a lot in that year in the sense that I willingly and joyfully gave that stuff up because I got all this other great stuff.

For Matt, marriage required a kind of "maturity" that necessitated giving up the more sexually charged life of gay partying—a sacrifice that he believed his nonmonogamous friends were not ready for or capable of.

This idea that nonmonogamous people avoid marriage because they are not ready to commit is not supported by the research evidence. No LGBQ individuals in this study were delaying or avoiding marriage because they did not want to be monogamous.[37] However, dominant cultural ideas about marital commitment do presume that it is incompatible with anything less than full focus on one's spouse, which includes both an emotional and sexual focus. It is for this reason that marriage scholars refer to contemporary marriage as "greedy"[38]: being ready for marriage means being ready to give one person your undivided attention, at the expense of other people in your family and community or, in this case, other forms of pleasure and fulfillment. The assumption that nonmonogamous people are avoiding marriage because they are not ready to fully commit to one person is therefore very much in line with normative cultural ideas about what contemporary marriage requires.

CONTENDING WITH THE HETERONORMATIVE EXPECTATIONS OF OTHERS

Same-sex couples were not doing marriage in a cultural vacuum. They had to contend with broader heteronormative expectations about the way marriage should be done. Nonmonogamous individuals all continued practicing nonmonogamy after getting married, but being married did shape their internal and interactional experiences of it because of their awareness and perceptions of what other people thought. Those who practiced nonmonogamy were still deeply aware of, and governed by, heteronormative beliefs that marriage equals monogamy, even if they did not personally subscribe to them. Regardless of the freedom they felt to make marriage their own, they still had to manage their marital choices based on the norms and beliefs others subscribed to. Enacting nonmonogamy in the context of legal marriage therefore entailed both individual and interactional adjustments—coming to terms with what it meant to be a married person who engages in outside sex, and navigating those decisions with others.

Even if individuals personally felt OK with being married and nonmonogamous, there was no escaping the reality that it remained at odds with the dominant cultural messaging on marriage. This made engaging in marital nonmonogamy feel awkward, at least at first. Patrick recalled this sense of uneasiness the first time he had engaged in sex outside his marriage: "I mean, it was a little more weird right after getting married when I did something, because I remember thinking 'now I'm a married man doing that.'" Despite being immersed in a gay culture and community, Patrick could not escape the deeply internalized heteronormative messaging that marriage equals monogamy. This did not, however, deter him from practicing marital nonmonogamy, and as Patrick adjusted to his new marital status, that "weird" feeling dissipated.

Yet others experienced a more permanent tension between heteronormative and gay cultural norms. For example, Liam described how being married ultimately deterred him from feeling comfortable exploring nonmonogamy:

> I guess maybe the monogamy discussion would be somehow more simplistic if it didn't have the marriage overlay. If we were still just boyfriends maybe it would be less awkward to navigate those waters. You just don't really start

seeing other people when you're married without really thinking hard about what you're doing.

For Liam, the mental work involved in trying nonmonogamy was "much harder" because he was married. Marriage and monogamy felt "like part and parcel" to him, and so "separating them out" in his mind was very difficult, even with his husband's blessing.

In addition to the mental work involved in navigating being married and nonmonogamous, others described interactional challenges to practicing nonmonogamy as a married person. Several perceived that other people interacted with them differently on the basis of their new status as a married individual. In particular, they believed that other people were less interested in engaging in sexual activity with them now that they were married. Ricardo, a fifty-two-year-old married Embracer, said:

> I think people kind of say, "OK, you're married" and then, you know, just sort of move on. I think now what a lot of us see is you go to a club to go dancing, and if you're not married, single guys think "Oh, OK, they're not serious. I still have a chance at them." But once they hear that you're married, it's kind of like, "Ohhhh, OK." [*laughs*] You know, your relationship is beyond serious. So, I think the mentality sort of changes.

This perceived disinterest that others had in engaging in sex with them now that there was "no chance" at a relationship did have some advantages. If someone only wanted to engage in sex with them because they hoped for a relationship, then nonmonogamous individuals were usually not interested anyway. As Tony, a sixty-nine-year-old married Rejecter, put it, "It's one of the advantages of being married because you're clear about what you're looking for. I'm not looking for another partner." Nonetheless, it was still frustrating to realize that other people were less interested in them simply because they had gotten married. They had not been available for a relationship prior to getting married either, but now their marital status limited their sexual options.

There was, however, some disagreement about what stating you were married meant in a gay sexual context. While some, like Tony and Ricardo, thought it signaled that you were no longer available, others were not so sure. Patrick argued, "In gay male culture, I actually don't think saying you're married really says much of anything in a sexual context. It's almost a red herring. It's more something to joke about, I think?" If LGBQ people are not on the same page about what being married means for nonmonogamy, this makes navigating sexual environments tricky. The ambiguity about how to enact nonmonogamy in the context of legal marriage might lessen over time, as new norms for same-sex marriage solidify, but at least in the first decade after same-sex marriage became legal, marital nonmonogamy still felt like unchartered territory.

Married nonmonogamous LGBQ individuals also spoke about feeling judged by others for being nonmonogamous and feeling pressure to keep their nonmonogamy hidden or discreet. Even though Cody—the one explicitly judgmental participant quoted earlier—had felt frustrated that nonmonogamous people were "making same-sex marriage look horrible" by "flaunting" their nonmonogamy, most married nonmonogamous people actually reported feeling social pressure to keep their nonmonogamy hidden so as *not* to make same-sex marriages "look bad." A common argument launched by opponents of same-sex marriage had been that gay men would "set a bad example to others" by being "openly adulterous."[39] But the opposite is actually true. Most LGBQ individuals were well aware of being stigmatized for their nonmonogamy and kept it well hidden outside of trusted LGBTQ+ circles. They were also acutely aware that nonmonogamy was politically precarious for the marriage equality movement. This kind of "respectability politics" contributed to the difficulty of being married and *openly* nonmonogamous.[40]

Nick,[41] a forty-year-old married man, told me that "over the last five years or so" he and his husband had become increasingly "uncomfortable" with "exploring nonmonogamy because of societal value judgments related to nontraditional sexual relationships within marriages." He was highly cognizant that "conservative converts to gay marriage have come to it with this lens around stability and commitment" and that "for them, commitment means that you're not going to be sleeping with one thousand partners." In the context of legal marriage, Nick and his husband were more careful not "to put the cards out on the table" with people who didn't already know what their thoughts were about nonmonogamy. Nick was acutely aware that, having only just gained access to legal marriage rights, to be openly nonmonogamous would put him squarely back in the position of an "abject sexual citizen."[42] Given that same-sex marriage was not yet legal nationwide at the time of data collection, participants may have been particularly vigilant not to make visible behaviors that could be damaging to the marriage equality cause. So long as marriage remains culturally and politically connected to monogamy, same-sex couples will likely continue to feel pressure to keep their nonmonogamous practices hidden. Having remained outside sexual citizenship for so long, and with legal rights remaining so vulnerable, they are unlikely to openly challenge heteronormative ways of doing marriage.

Conclusion

On the surface, nonmonogamous behaviors in marriage remain relatively rare, even among same-sex couples, and a more cynical observer might argue that until we see actual behavioral changes, same-sex couples are doing little to change the institution of marriage. But, when it comes to monogamy, the LGBQ individuals in this book were approaching and enacting marriage in fundamentally different ways than their heterosexual counterparts, challenging taken-for-granted aspects of the institution. Beliefs about sex and marriage matter as much as behavior. For the institution of marriage to become deinstitutionalized—to lose its institutional grip over individual behaviors—general attitudes about the importance of marital monogamy need to shift in addition to actual monogamous sexual behaviors in marriage.[43] And LGBQ individuals are posing a fundamental challenge to the cultural beliefs and assumptions undergirding the way couples do marriage: that marriage equals sexual ownership. Even if they never practice nonmonogamy, the fact that they openly discuss the possibility of nonmonogamy with their partners, believe that spouses should attend to changing sexual desires and needs, and prioritize relational commitment over fidelity, fundamentally contests taken-for-granted institutional meanings and beliefs relating to marriage.[44] If institutional norms and scripts for marriage are governing structures that lead to uniformity and stability, then the belief in sexual fluidity provides the potential for a greater focus on individual desires and changing needs within marriage. Attending to the way people think about sex in marriage also helps to highlight the role that women can play in challenging marital norms, as to date women have been relatively excluded from the literature that focuses solely on nonmonogamous behaviors.

Nonetheless, even as LGBQ individuals challenged norms and beliefs about marital monogamy, they adhered to other taken-for-granted cultural beliefs about marriage. When marriage allowed them to feel more secure and at ease with engaging with nonmonogamy it was because they subscribed to the cultural belief that it represented a unique form of relational commitment. They unconsciously bought into some cultural ideas about marriage even as they consciously rejected others. Additionally, sexual fluidity and an openness to nonmonogamy among LGBQ individuals was connected to the desire to maintain long-term relationships and marriage, not to undermine it. The desire for or pursuit of nonmonogamy was not an individualistic goal sought without concern for one's partner or relationship. Although individual sexual desires mattered, nonmonogamy was discussed openly in collaboration with one's partner as a means of supporting one another's shifting sexual desires and helped ensure honest communication, authenticity, and the ability to stay committed to relationships for the long-term. In this way, nonmonogamy was deployed in service of coupledom.

LGBQ people were not free from the institutional constraints of marriage. They felt free to make the institution of marriage their own, but only in private. They remained acutely aware of the demands of respectability politics and of undermining the broader movement for equality and rights if they were too open about their support for or participation in nonmonogamy. And because nonmonogamy remains deeply at odds with the dominant cultural messaging on marriage, practicing it in the context of legal marriage required LGBQ individuals to make internal and interactional adjustments: coming to terms with what it meant to be a married person who engages in outside sex and navigating those decisions with others.

In all these ways, then, we are left with a picture of LGBQ individuals both challenging and maintaining marital monogamy norms. This reflects the fact that they are navigating two equally powerful but competing cultural beliefs in their relationships: a strong commitment to sexual freedom from within LGBTQ+ culture and the still powerful expectation of sexual fidelity and respectability from broader heteronormative culture. These were not different individuals—one set internalizing beliefs about sexual freedom, and the other beliefs about sexual fidelity and respectability. Instead, these cultural beliefs coexist messily in their cultural repertoires, and LGBQ individuals struggle to navigate between them in their attitudes, practices, and interactions with others.

Looking to the future, there are some potential signs of change in the post-marriage equality era. Marriage Assumers (younger LGBQ individuals who started relationships after marriage was already legal) exhibited greater normative opposition to nonmonogamy than their older counterparts. Having access to legal marriage could be exerting greater heteronormative influence over the direction of new same-sex relationships, and the influence of LGBQ cultural norms around sexual freedom and equality may be beginning to wane in comparison. However, it is also possible that the direction of change could veer in the other direction. The data suggest that hesitation to be open about nonmonogamy with others stems in part from fear about the precariousness of marriage rights. If marriage rights become more secure,[45] greater openness about nonmonogamy could create more visible alternative models for younger LGBQ individuals and contribute to the continuation of sexual fluidity and nonmonogamy as a sexual practice in newer same-sex relationships.

Conclusion

The LGBQ people who took part in this study were often very grateful to have had the opportunity to share their stories. They sensed that they were historical trailblazers as the first group of people to enact legal same-sex marriage. And they knew that few people had yet taken the time to hear and document their experiences. Their detailed, in-depth stories help fill voids in both the family and sexualities scholarship about same-sex marriage. Yet this research was always motivated by sociological questions that extended beyond the case of same-sex marriage. From the start, I designed the project to advance our understanding of the changing and enduring meaning of contemporary marriage as an institution. Same-sex marriage was chosen as a case study to help achieve that. As new entrants into the institution, LGBQ people offer a unique vantage point into mechanisms of institutional governance and the potential for institutional change. I use this conclusion to revisit the broad sociological questions that motivated the research: How does the contemporary institution of marriage govern individual relationship choices and behaviors? How does marriage endure as an institution in the midst of historic changes to its meaning and practice? What role do individual marriage actors play in contributing to broader processes of institutional change in marriage?

Marriage Material

Sociological research on marriage today treats it as a greatly weakened institution. Consequently, the way it operates to shape individual's choices and behaviors remains poorly understood. What is the "marriage material" of today? The accounts in this book suggest we might be best served by imagining a patchwork quilt. The institution of marriage endures because it consists of multiple materials that each continue to shape individual behavior in varying ways. As discussed in the introduction, institutions are supported by three broad pillars of influence: regulative, normative, and cultural-cognitive.[1] Across the chapters, we saw all three institutional pillars operating to pull LGBQ people into the institution and shaping their behavior once married. Below, I revisit what we learned from the experiences of the newest entrants into marriage about how each of the three institutional pillars of marriage govern individual choices and behaviors.

THE NORMATIVE PILLAR

The normative pillar of an institution works to govern individual action through widely shared and internalized norms or ideas about which behaviors are expected and appropriate. It influences individuals to behave in particular ways because they feel a sense of duty or social pressure to do so, or because they have deeply internalized social expectations. Family scholars theorize that it is the weakening of this normative pillar that explains the deinstitutionalization of marriage over the past half century or so.[2] The findings in this book challenge this thinking in family sociology, both by illuminating how and why marital norms still hold sway and by showing that a weakening normative base does not signal a weakened institution.

Certainly the normative pillar of marriage was not the primary influence for any of the three marriage groups in this book. No one married solely because they felt they "should" or out of any social pressure to do so. But it still had some power over relationship choices and behaviors. Some Marriage Rejecters described being pulled into, or toward, marriage through social influences. As more people asked them when they were getting married, over time marriage became something that felt increasingly normative—an external, social influence that was harder to resist (chapter 2). Marriage Rejecters also described social expectations to prioritize their partner's marital needs above their own disinterest in marrying. If their partners wanted to marry and they did not, their own political rejection of marriage was made to feel "selfish" or "immature" in comparison to their partner's more socially approved of desire for marriage. In chapter 3, I showed that the normative pillar of marriage was shaping the marital choices of Marriage Assumers as well. Assumers spoke about marriage as "just what you do" if you want to have children, connecting to normative ideas about marriage creating a more secure and stable environment in which to raise children and establish a clear family unit.

The normative pillar of the institution had most influence over the relationship behaviors of Marriage Assumers. In chapter 4, I illustrated that

CONCLUSION 191

Marriage Assumers had deeply internalized the social expectation that there is a "right way" to get engaged, and they undertook self-policing work to achieve an "appropriate" proposal. In chapter 5, I described how some Marriage Assumers understood decisions to pool finances in marriage as resulting from adherence to social norms, both in the sense of a behavior they assumed all, or at least most, other married couples do, and as an expected behavior—something they felt they should do as a married couple. In chapter 6, I showed that Marriage Assumers were the most likely to express normative judgments against other LGBQ people who engaged in nonmonogamy in marriage. The fact that the normative pillar had most influence over these younger LGBQ people in newer relationships makes clear that it is not an outdated sphere of influence. If social norms are not as influential as they once were, and individuals have more freedom to decide their own behaviors within marriage, but it is the newest marriage participants who are most beholden to them, then their influence will likely endure.

The marriage accounts in this book also demonstrate how perceived social norms influence people to conform to social expectations within marriage. I illuminated this in chapter 6, as those who practiced nonmonogamy within their marriages felt judged by others and experienced social pressure to keep their nonmonogamy hidden or discreet. They managed their marital choices based on the norms they assumed others subscribed to. Moreover, they perceived diminishing sexual options in their social networks and communities based on the norms they assumed other people held about engaging in sex with married people.

THE REGULATIVE PILLAR

The regulative pillar of an institution refers to the way in which institutions govern action through formal rules that constrain and enable behavior. It is typically thought of as the most coercive, but at the same time as having weakened influence today. But the marriage accounts in this book show how the regulative pillar continues to exert influence over individual behaviors in a few important ways. Through the policies of state and federal governments, the institution of marriage continues to govern which rights, benefits, and protections individuals have access to. Entering the institution of marriage remains the only way to access a large number of these important sources of social support. Because only Marriage Rejecters spoke about these rights and benefits as the primary reason to marry, it is tempting to conclude that the institution of marriage has only a weak grip over individual behavior. Yet Marriage Rejecters show that even those who were very disinterested in or critical of marriage could ultimately be pulled into the institution by virtue of the fact it maintains a monopoly over these rights and protections (chapter 2). This reminds us of the continuing power, and coercive nature, of this pillar of the institution. By contrast, because Marriage Embracers and Assumers were also pulled into marriage through other pillars of influence, they were less cognizant of this source of power. It is worth remembering as well that at the time of participation in this study, LGBQ individuals did not have access to federal-level marriage benefits. As Marriage Rejecters noted, once the Defense of Marriage Act was overturned and the institution granted access to more rights and benefits, the strength of this pillar would likely have increased too.

Once married, the regulative pillar had a less direct influence over LGBQ people's choices and behaviors, but it still played an important supporting role. Contrary to dominant explanations in family sociology, married individuals were not significantly more likely to pool their financial assets because the regulative structure of marriage made it more financially advantageous for them to do so or because it coerced them into it in some way (chapter 5). Furthermore, they were not more committed to staying with their partners than unmarried people because the regulative structure of marriage made it too hard to leave them. The regulative structure of marriage does not force people to behave in particular ways; instead, it provides the structure for people to act in ways that demonstrate individual agency. Marriage offers a structural opportunity for partners to show their commitment by willingly choosing to enter a constraining institution. It was because their partners had freely chosen to legally marry them that married individuals felt more secure in their relationships. In this sense, the regulative structure of marriage plays a supporting role in providing the necessary structure for cultural beliefs about marriage to be enacted.

Lastly, it would be remiss not to emphasize that the regulative pillar of the institution also shaped LGBQ people's marriage choices and experiences through formal laws demarcating clear boundaries around who was allowed to marry. Just because same-sex marriage was now legal, historical experiences of institutional exclusion continued to shape the relationship choices and behaviors that individuals engaged in. Interestingly, although laws that include some and exclude others are clearly coercive in nature, the accounts in this research show that regulative exclusion could be institutionally liberating in some ways. Having already sustained relationships while being excluded from the institution of marriage, Marriage Embracers and Rejecters had developed alternative ways of doing relationships and were therefore much less susceptible than Marriage Assumers to its normative and cultural

CONCLUSION   193

institutional influences once they did gain access to it (chapters 4 and 5). By contrast, Marriage Assumers were much more susceptible to marriage's normative and cultural pillars of influence because their same-sex relationships had always been included in the regulative arm of the institution. In these ways, we see that the regulative pillar of the institution is more than just rules and incentives for behavior. It works in tandem with other parts of the institution in complex ways to shape behavior.

THE CULTURAL-COGNITIVE PILLAR

The cultural-cognitive pillar of the institution governs individual behaviors by establishing shared ideas about what has meaning. Individuals make certain choices and act in particular ways because of what they are able to conceive as possible and the meanings they attach to them. These cultural components of marriage are largely channeled through shared cultural scripts. While all three institutional pillars worked to pull LGBQ individuals into the institution of marriage, the cultural pillar dominated their marriage narratives (but in ways they were the least aware of). Given the recency of access to legal marriage, the extent to which LGBQ people had already internalized cultural scripts about marriage was somewhat surprising. Despite its recent legal status, the cultural-cognitive elements of marriage as an institution appeared to be already well institutionalized (taken-for-granted and unquestioned) among many LGBQ people.

In chapter 1, I made clear that the institution of marriage shaped the choices and behaviors of Marriage Embracers even before it became possible to legally marry because Embracers had internalized cultural beliefs about what marriage meant and could achieve for them. They followed available cultural scripts in order to attempt to gain those relational and social benefits from marriage. Believing that marriage offered unique access to relational commitment, social legitimacy, and family recognition, they participated in dominant cultural rituals to symbolize marriage, such as exchanging rings and having commitment ceremonies. When marriage became legal, Marriage Embracers jumped at the chance to legally marry because they understood it as offering the most culturally understood, recognized, and valued form of what they had already been trying to achieve for themselves. They had cultural ideas about marriage "on file" as part of their knowledge repertoire[3] and eagerly engaged in legal marriage as soon as they could.

In chapter 3, I showed, through the experiences of Marriage Assumers, just how much the strength of the cultural pillar of the institution has increased after legalization. Marriage Assumers took for granted cultural beliefs about marriage in ways that others did not. Having access to legal marriage from the outset of their relationships limited what options they were able to conceive and made marriage a requirement for relationship investment and success. Unlike Marriage Embracers, who were acutely aware of what marriage meant and why they were embracing it, Marriage Assumers were barely cognizant of the extent to which they subscribed to cultural beliefs about marriage and the scripts they were following in their relationships. As is typical of institutionalized experiences, they gave marriage little thought. It was taken for granted as "just what you do" when you love someone and are committed to them, the obvious "next step" in the "natural progression" of a relationship. Marriage Assumers also drew on a more limited range of cultural scripts than Embracers did. Whereas Marriage Embracers attached varied cultural meanings and capabilities to marriage, these younger LGBQ people in newer relationships drew on essentially one cultural idea to shape their choices and behaviors: specifically, the idea that marriage is a distinctive and special form of relational commitment. In fact, the marriage material they were drawing on was so uniform and limited that, after conducting so many interviews, I could essentially predict, sometimes word for word, what an interviewee was going to say in response to a question.

At the same time, Marriage Assumers understood the intricacies of popular cultural scripts surrounding marriage with impressive detail. In chapter 4, I described how they had no problem imagining themselves in existing scripts for how to get engaged and worked hard to enact them with precision and care. They did not acknowledge the gendered and heteronormative cultural beliefs underpinning proposal scripts, nor did they allow them to dissuade them of their relevance for their relationships. Following cultural scripts for proposals was so important that these scripts impacted multiple aspects of their relationships, including how they talked to their partners about the future and regulated their emotions with one another.

Marriage Rejecters stood out as being mostly free from the influence of the cultural pillar of marriage, but they were not completely beyond its influence (chapter 2). Some Marriage Rejecters described being pulled more toward marriage through their "emotions." Even as they maintained their rejection of the institution, they said that they "could not help" but feel happy for others who married and got emotional watching them participate in weddings. These emotions resulted from widely shared and very dominant cultural scripts about marriage that told them how they should feel during highly ritualized events such as weddings, prompting them to turn into "water fountains." Deeply ingrained cultural ideas about marriage symbolizing love, commitment, stability, and romance resonated with them on some level. Their emotional reactions to marriage were experienced as "beyond their control" because they had not been cognizant of the extent to which they were influenced by basic cultural beliefs about the meaning of marriage, in spite of their rejection of it as an institution.

Once LGBQ people were married, it was also the cultural pillar of the institution that had the most impact on how they behaved in their relationships. The influence was indirect but powerful: individuals internalized taken-forgranted cultural scripts about what marriage meant, which in turn changed the way they felt about their relationships, making them feel more committed and secure (chapter 5). These altered feelings shifted the kinds of choices and behaviors they engaged in within their relationships. These altered feelings often felt "intangible" to LGBQ people, more so than formal rules or informal social norms that outline how one "should" behave in marriage. But if marriage can shape behavior without reliance on external rules and social pressure, and individuals can act as if they are only responding to their own internal feelings, this points to a stronger, more firmly institutionalized governing structure.

The influence of cultural scripts on behavior within marriage was much stronger for Marriage Embracers and Assumers than for Rejecters, who did not subscribe to the same beliefs about marriage and commitment, limiting its power to shape the behaviors of all individuals within marriage. But comparing across the groups and attending to each of the institutional pillars illuminates the diverse, yet equally powerful, ways the institution continues to pull people in and shape their behaviors once within it. In doing so, it is clear that all LGBQ people are marriage material, with the potential to be governed, in one way or another, by the institution.

Remaking Same-Sex Relationships?

If the institution of marriage has the power to shape the choices and behaviors of LGBQ people, then does it transform the meaning and practice of their relationships, and if so, how? Drawing on mixed methods data and a varied sample of LGBQ people, I examined how the institution of marriage has changed same-sex relationships in multiple ways. Using both survey and interview data, I examined how LGBQ people understood their own relationships to have changed across the transition to marriage. I analyzed differences between married and unmarried relationships to identify ways in which they appeared to be significantly different in the context of legal marriage. And I looked at change *within* same-sex relationships (before and after marriage in individual relationships) and *across* same-sex relationships (from one cohort to another).

Within individual same-sex relationships, the data point to some notable changes after getting married but do not suggest that individual same-sex relationships are transformed by marriage. As one LGBQ person in the study so astutely put it: "It's not like the sky opens up." Marriage is not some all-powerful, magical institution that has the ability to transform the meaning and content of our individual relationships or who we are. We do not wake up the day after getting married in a fundamentally different relationship or as different people. So, on the one hand, I argue that the institution of marriage continues to have a powerful influence over individual choices and behaviors; but on the other, I claim that getting married does not substantially transform the content of individual same-sex relationships. This might sound contradictory or confusing to some. But the reason is that, as an institution, marriage exerts the most power over individual relationships *prior* to participation in it. The actual impact it has on one's relationship post-marriage is minimal by comparison.

Take Marriage Embracers, for instance. They had already embraced and integrated marriage into their relationships long before they were able to get legally married, and so being able to legally marry did not transform the meaning of their relationships, which were already centered on marriage-like commitments. Being legally married did deepen the commitment they already had with their partners, but this was not a fundamental change to the meaning or content of their relationships; rather, it resulted from the ability to enact a cultural script they had always internalized but never thought they would have access to. These deepened feelings of commitment led to some changes in relationship practices, including the way they fought with their partners and their willingness to merge finances. Their relationships altered in some important ways, but they were not transformed by marriage. We see a similar story for Marriage Assumers, whose relationships were premised and organized around being able to get legally married from the start. Because they could not fully trust partners without marital commitment, getting legally married did result in much stronger feelings of security, which, in turn, led to similar changes in relationship behaviors as with Marriage Embracers. These behavioral changes were evident in the data as robust and highly statistically significant differences between married and unmarried LGBQ people and certainly deserve attention. However, they were the logical outcome of being able to enact deeply internalized cultural beliefs LGBQ people already had, rather than resulting from qualitatively new meanings in their

CONCLUSION 197

relationships. Even if some of the relationship behaviors LGBQ people engaged in within marriage were new, the cultural beliefs underpinning them were not.

This was the case for relationship practices such as monogamy as well (chapter 6). Overall, there were no notable changes in practice. Those who were monogamous before getting married continued to be so afterward, while those who were nonmonogamous beforehand similarly continued to be so afterward. Those who conceptualized their relationships as sexually fluid continued to do so afterward. The primary difference being married made was to heighten LGBQ individuals' awareness of social expectations regarding appropriate behavior and increase their concerns over the public visibility of nonmonogamy in same-sex relationships, coupled with some increased difficulties in meeting outside partners for sex. Participating in the institution therefore had an impact, but the beliefs LGBQ individuals had about sex and their sexual practices were already securely established prior to entering marriage.

Turning to changes across same-sex relationships, the impact legal marriage has had on same-sex relationships is much more transformative. Here, I refer to changes in same-sex relationships that have occurred across cohorts of LGBQ individuals, as new groups of individuals with access to marriage understand and enact their relationships in ways that are fundamentally different from those who maintained them without it. To examine these changes, I took advantage of the fact that the LGBQ people in this study had formed relationships in two very different legal contexts—half prior to the availability of legal marriage, and half only afterward. The stark contrast between these groups made the impact of marital access on same-sex couple relationships abundantly clear. Those LGBQ people who started same-sex relationships with access to legal marriage had advantages in their relationships that those who had sustained relationships without it did not, including having a clearer way to evaluate their partners' commitment; having a surer model for relationship trajectories and long-term planning; having the enjoyment of participating in widely shared rituals and cultural scripts for relationships and romance; having a way to gain social recognition, validation and legitimacy for their relationships; and being able to create socially recognized family units together. Taken together, these represent the freedom to enact widely shared, dominant cultural meanings and practices in relationships, which serve to make them easily legible both between partners and to others.

We can also see that new same-sex relationships have lost something important—the freedom from marriage. Having access to legal marriage has limited what LGBQ people are able to conceive as possible for same-sex relationships. It shapes how they evaluate potential partners, becoming part of a necessary "checklist" as early as first dates, and then narrowly defines how they conceptualize commitment and security throughout their relationships. It has also created qualitatively new forms of work, anxiety, and conflict in their relationships. Younger LGBQ people who started relationships with access to marriage engage in new forms of relational work to meet the relationship and life goals considered prerequisites for marriage and to enact specific cultural scripts around how to get married. This involves the management of relationship dynamics that even impact the ways they talk to their partners and regulate their emotional responses to them. Partner interactions have become more intentional—a careful, more scripted game to be played in order to adhere to the norms and cultural scripts of marriage. Newer same-sex relationships contain more anxiety too. Partners rely on marriage to feel secure and trusting, and they doubt their partners more often. There is more conflict and less compromise when partners are not on the same page about relationship trajectories. Marriage has become a new source of conflict, one of the issues younger same-sex couples in newer relationships say they most regularly argue about.

I do not offer an evaluation here of whether legal marriage has changed same-sex relationships for better or for worse. As with all social changes, some things are gained, while others are lost. The point is that while individual LGBQ people might struggle to identify anything "tangible" about their own relationships that has changed since gaining access to legal marriage, sociological analysis of the data in this book makes clear that marriage has had a transformative impact on same-sex relationships. At the same time, it sheds some light on the potential of LGBQ individuals to resist the power of marriage as an institution and remake it to fit their needs.

Remaking Marriage?

As I was writing this book, one of the most common questions I would get about it from colleagues, friends, and acquaintances was some version of "do same-sex couples do marriage differently?" I knew that most people wanted a pithy answer, but which kinds of LGBQ people were they thinking of? What types of marriage behaviors were they imagining? When did LGBQ people do marriage differently? And why? Ultimately, I argue that LGBQ people draw on much of the same material as heterosexuals in their marriages. However, they sometimes ignored existing ways of doing marriage and attempted to remake marriage in potentially important ways. These moments offer insight into opportunities for change.

Counterintuitively, organizing the book around three marriage groups allowed me to see is that it is not just one kind of LGBQ person that is capable of remaking marriage, or that attempts to. It is tempting to imagine a particular kind of LGBQ individual, consciously trying to remake marriage. If that were the case, it would have been only among Marriage Rejecters that I offered evidence of institutional change work. But the reality is more complex. It is not the case that only certain kinds of people consciously resist marital norms and scripts and attempt to do marriage differently. To be clear, Marriage Rejecters were undoubtedly the ones most capable of remaking marriage. This is because they had not internalized cultural beliefs about what marriage means to the same degree as Marriage Embracers and Assumers, and this gave them greater freedom to ignore social expectations and cultural scripts about why and how to marry and be married. Yet throughout the book, I emphasized moments in which Marriage Embracers and Assumers also experienced freedom to do marriage differently. I examined these moments to explore how individuals can carve out space for change within the institution of marriage as well as the difficulties of doing so.

When cultural scripts for marital behavior did not seem relevant to LGBQ people, they felt free to ignore them. Existing sociological theory suggests that when norms and scripts for behavior are unclear, individuals should be confused about how to behave or stressed by the lack of clear guidance.[4] This was not the case for the LGBQ people in this book. Gaps in cultural guidance did not create anxiety or uncertainty; rather, they created some freedom from the need to adhere to expectations for behavior. Even though Marriage Embracers embraced the institution of marriage wholeheartedly, they felt free to ignore existing cultural scripts for marital behavior if and when they did not feel applicable. For example, when getting engaged by means of a proposal felt unnecessary and inappropriate given their long relationship history, they ignored that script (chapter 4). Even Marriage Assumers, who took so much about marriage for granted, sometimes ignored existing scripts for marital behavior when they did not apply easily to them. They wanted to adhere to the cultural script regarding getting engaged by means of a proposal, but ignored the presumption that who should propose be based on gender because the assumption of gender difference did not apply to their relationships. Unlike rules or social norms, scripts offered greater freedom to follow or ignore. However, in these ways LGBQ people were not remaking marriage, just making marriage fit them and their needs.

I further observed LGBQ people doing marriage differently when they had internalized alternative cultural beliefs that ran counter to (hetero)normative beliefs undergirding the institution of marriage. (Hetero)normative cultural beliefs about marriage are not the only ones in the repertoire of beliefs, or "tool box,"[5] that LGBQ people had to choose from. The existing institution of marriage had less power to shape behavior when it came up against beliefs and scripts that offered alternative models for behavior. Even though Marriage Assumers and Embracers had internalized many (hetero)normative beliefs about marriage, they often subscribed to other cultural beliefs that made them want to do marriage differently. For example, although they subscribed to the cultural belief that marriage was the most distinctive form of love and commitment, they had at the same time internalized cultural beliefs emanating from the LGBTQ+ community and feminism, including about the importance of egalitarianism and sexual freedom within relationships, and a belief in sexual fluidity. This resulted in a somewhat messy mix of marital behaviors. Marriage Assumers insisted on marriage proposals, but also often engaged in mutual proposals to achieve egalitarianism in their relationships (chapter 4). Marriage Assumers and Embracers idealized marriage but often refused to idealize or practice monogamy within it (chapter 6). This shows that it is only when there are other powerful cultural beliefs and scripts available that individuals even attempt to do marriage differently. They cannot forge new pathways alone; they need alternative models to follow.

The LGBQ people in this book had a limited cultural repertoire from which to draw (though arguably greater than many heterosexuals), and cultural beliefs and scripts relating to marriage dominated what they were able to conceive. Other possibilities for action only got selected when the cultural beliefs supporting them were as equally dominant, widely shared, and modeled. And this was not often the case. Put simply, for individuals to remake marriage, dominant (hetero)normative scripts need a wider variety of strong cultural contenders. Until then, individuals will struggle to enact change to marriage in meaningful, confident, and lasting ways.

As rules and norms have diminished in institutional influence, there is more room for individual choice in marriage and less obvious constraint, providing opportunities to make the institution fit individuals' desires and needs. But, given the strength of existing cultural scripts shaping behavior, this greater individual freedom still mostly occurs within the same overarching institutional structure. To be clear, this is not a critique of LGBQ people for failing to change the institution. As discussed in the introduction, institutional theory makes it abundantly clear how hard institutional change is. Only very skilled, strategic actors have the potential to change institutions.

Within the privacy of one's own relationship, few individuals could be as intentional or strategic as would be necessary for institutional change to happen. For more individuals to do marriage differently, there would need to be available more widely shared and visible alternative cultural scripts that pose challenges to some of the fundamental beliefs sustaining the institution and governing behavior within it. In the meantime, although the parameters of who is included in the institution have changed, not much else about the institution has. Instead, the institution of marriage has expanded its scope to govern the behaviors of a greater number of individuals.

Looking to the Future

To date, take-up rates of legal same-sex marriage have been high and fast, but some scholars have wondered whether they mostly represent a "backlog of couples who had lived together for many years" and who therefore took fast advantage of the opportunity to marry, while "younger couples may not marry in such large numbers in the future."[6] The data in this book predicts a different future. A record 7.1 percent of Americans now identify as LGBT, doubling in less than a decade.[7] The increase largely reflects the high prevalence of LGBT identification among the youngest US adults. One in five Gen Z adults—those born between 1997 and 2003—identify as LGBT. They all came of age and entered their first relationships with legal marriage as an option somewhere in the United States. They cannot remember, or sometimes even imagine, anything different. The data in this book makes clear that marriage has already become an institutionalized relationship experience among younger LGBQ individuals in new relationships—taken for granted, normalized, and internalized as the gold standard. If the young LGBQ people who participated in this book provide a glimpse into the future, it is a future in which everyone is free to legally marry the person they love but faces the pressure of finding the "right one" and doing it the "right way." It is a future in which lovers are measured, coveted, and abandoned based on their marriage material.

At the end of my interviews, I typically asked the LGBQ people who took part in this study to tell me where they imagined themselves in ten years' time. Most could only imagine happy futures. Some thought about the future in individual or family terms: they imagined getting old with their partners, having children, more children, or even grandchildren. Others imagined simply continuing to love one another and the joy of growing old together within the comfort and security of marriage. A few were less optimistic, wondering and worrying about whether they would be "sucked into" marriage or able to maintain commitment outside it instead. Others answered this question by looking outward and thinking about what the future held for same-sex couples more generally. They rightly predicted that same-sex couples would gain federal recognition for same-sex marriage, many more states would legalize same-sex marriage, and even that it would become legal nationwide. They correctly perceived that same-sex marriage in Massachusetts represented the beginning of ongoing changes to the legal parameters of marriage as an institution and what would be possible for same-sex couples in the United States.

Changes to the legal and social landscape around same-sex marriage are contradictory and far from linear. It would be a mistake to think of the status of legal same-sex marriage as progressing in a singular, forward fashion since the *Goodridge* decision in Massachusetts, or even the *Obergfell* decision that made same-sex marriage legal nationwide. It continues to face opposition and resistance. In a 2018 Supreme Court decision, heterosexual strangers were granted legal power to refuse to recognize same-sex marriages if doing so conflicted with their religious beliefs.[8] Then, in 2022, during the Supreme Court's *Dobbs v. Jackson Women's Health Organization* decision that overturned *Roe v. Wade*, Justice Clarence Thomas urged the court to overturn its ruling establishing the right of same-sex couples to marry. In response, Congress passed the Respect for Marriage Act,[9] designed to preemptively protect same-sex couples if the Supreme Court should move to remove same-sex marriage rights in the future. As of writing, that has not happened, but if the Supreme Court overturned *Obergefell v. Hodges*, the Respect for Marriage Act would not be able to stop any state from once again refusing to issue marriage licenses to same-sex couples.

The future of legal change is impossible to predict. But one thing is clear: marriage is not going anywhere any time soon, nor are same-sex marriages. Same-sex marriages existed before they were legal and will endure through any further legal challenges. It is also abundantly clear that LGBQ people have in no way undermined the institution of marriage by participating in it. They contribute to ongoing changes to marriage as they creatively adapt it to make it fit their individual relationship needs, but they sustain and strengthen its core institutional material while doing so. And, thanks to the 116 LGBQ people who generously shared their time and experiences for this book, we are now further along in understanding how contemporary marriage works, changes, and endures as an institution.

Acknowledgments

Researching and writing this book was very much a collaborative effort. It would not have been possible without the invisible labor and support of a host of colleagues, friends, and family, to whom I am immensely grateful.

First and foremost, I want to express my deepest thanks to all 116 people who took part in this study. Thanks for all the laughter, tears, food, wine, and pet snuggles while we spoke. It still astounds me that you took time out of your busy lives to sit and share with me raw parts of yourselves. You were thoughtful and introspective. You believed in the project and wanted your voices to matter. I feel privileged to be the person with whom you entrusted your marriage stories. In the years that have passed, your stories have intersected with my own family experiences, and I reflect on them often. Stepping back to do the kind of sociological analysis necessary for this book, it was not possible to do justice to all the intricacies and intimacies of everyone's lived experiences. But when people read my work, they often tell me how much it resonates with them, and so I hope that you will all find yourselves well reflected in it, too.

As a graduate student at the University of Chicago, I was fortunate to have Kristen Schilt as a mentor. She believed in this work and my ability to pull it off from the start. She pushed me to obtain rich and robust data. Many years on, I appreciate how she continues to champion my work and helps her mentees to build scholarly connections. Other members of my department were also each pivotal to my intellectual development. Lis Clemens took my curiosity about institutional scholarship seriously and gave me the confidence to approach this project more theoretically. Her feedback was immensely thorough and challenged me in ways that make me the scholar I am today. Thanks also go to Carla Pfeffer and Barbara Risman for their willingness to do the labor of reading and providing feedback on the work of a graduate student outside their own departments.

While writing this book, I had the steadfast support of many colleagues who I also consider friends. As graduate students at the University of Chicago, Alicia VandeVusse, Lizzy Gray, Maria Akchurin, Anjanette Chan Tack, and Piper Sledge provided countless hours of companionship in libraries and coffee shops as well as constructive feedback on my work. I also benefited from the feminist solidarity of the department's Sociology Women's Group, at a time when it was much needed. At the University of Notre Dame, I have been immensely fortunate to have many kind and generous colleagues. Special thanks go to Terry McDonnell, Erin McDonnell, Amy Langenkamp, Elizabeth McClintock, Calvin Zimmerman, Rory McVeigh, and Joel Mittleman, who all read or engaged with my work in some form or another. Thanks also to Bill Carbonaro for his years of mentorship and support as my Chair.

I owe many thanks to my wonderful writing group of other family and gender scholars—Ellen Lamont, Jessi Streib, Jacklyn Wong, and Monica Liu—for the years of feedback they have provided on this book in many stages of readiness. More than that, I am grateful to them for the truly supportive space they provided, and for helping to demystify the book-writing process. Each of them inspires me, not only through the content of their work but also by the kind, collaborative approach they take to it. I was also fortunate to find a true "buddy" in Meagan Ehlenz, whom the National Center for Faculty Development and Diversity "Faculty Success Program" paired me with after I completed their "boot camp." Despite not sharing my discipline or location, nor ever having met in person, Meagan has been a truly wonderful source of regular writing support and accountability.

Many others have provided thoughtful comments on my work, helping advance and sharpen my thinking and writing. Thanks especially to Rin Reczek, Mary Bernstein, Melanie Heath, Omar Lizardo, Sean Lauer, and Tim Hallett. I want to extend a special note of appreciation to Brian Powell for his advocacy. When my perfectionism risked unnecessarily delaying the book project, Brian gave me the confidence to submit the book proposal and recommended me to my editor. Though not directly included in this book, portions of work from this same project have also appeared in the *American Journal of Sociology* and *Journal of Marriage and Family*. The anonymous reviewers and editors of both journals helped shape my thinking for this book. I want to thank Michael Yarborough, Angela Jones, and Joseph DeFilippis for organizing the truly inspiring After Marriage conference and for their support of my chapter, "From Public Debate to Private Decision: The Normalization of Marriage among Critical LGBQ People," published in the subsequent edited volumes. I also received anonymous reviews on my book proposal and manuscript, which were especially useful and encouraging—a much-needed final push to finish writing.

Book writing also entails many tedious, arduous tasks that I was lucky enough at times to delegate to research assistants. Early on David Wood and Jonathan Schwartz contributed their quantitative analysis talents by helping me to get the most out of my survey data. Later, as I was finishing book writing, Eli Williams and Ashley Burk assisted with invaluable and tireless fact-finding for footnotes as well as much editing work.

My sincerest thanks also to Elizabeth Branch Dyson, my editor at the University of Chicago. I met Elizabeth during the COVID-19 pandemic over Zoom, and this afforded us the time away from busy conferences and crowded rooms to really connect. I am thankful for the time she spent with me chatting about my research and getting to know me. She was enthusiastic and thoughtful from the get-go. I am grateful to Mollie McFee, who facilitated the publication process, and to Tamara Ghattas and Olivia Aguilar and the rest of the book team. All of you provided expertise and guidance without ever undermining my vision.

This project would not have been possible without the financial support I received in conducting this research. An SBE Doctoral Dissertation Improvement Grant from the National Science Foundation (award ID: 1303621) and the Williams Institute's Small Grant allowed me to do the kind of rigorous data collection I wanted to. Support from the Institute for Scholarship in the Liberal Arts, University of Notre Dame, assisted with costs involved in the publishing process.

A few friends and family members deserve special acknowledgment. I'd like to extend my gratitude to Zac Nagel and John Montesdeoca for their company during my field work in Massachusetts. Eating good food and watching crappy TV with them sustained me while I was away from home. I am also deeply thankful to Meredith Whitnah, who was a source of enormous support for many years. I first met Meredith when I started working at the University of Notre Dame and she was finishing up her PhD. We have gone through the whole process of book writing together, regularly checking in, holding one another accountable, sharing the highs and lows, and generally supporting one another through it. It has made all the difference to have her with me on this journey. A special thanks also to Emma Planic, Dana Moss, and Susan Ford, who offered me much-needed coffee shop companionship as I worked on book writing. Having them around to complain to and gossip with (in short spurts in between serious writing of course) kept my spirits up. And to Raana Afzal—thank you for being my absolute rock in this world. I would be lost without you.

To my mum, Jonnie, and Maddi: I know that you will likely never get around to reading this book, but that does not matter. I am thankful for your unconditional love and support. I appreciate that you only care about whether I am happy, not what I write about. As a family scholar, I know I hit the jackpot with you as my family. To my dad: I know you will read this book, and you will try to talk to me about it when I really can't be bothered. I am thankful to you for sticking with me through our highs and lows. To my daughter, Ruby, who was born during the last year of my PhD program. It is crazy to think that I have been writing this book your whole life. You slowed down this book a lot, but also gave me perspective on what matters, and I wouldn't change it for the world. To my son, Leo: thank you for filling my life with joy, laughter, and cuddles whenever I need them the most. Finally, to my husband, Paul: thank you for being the kind of feminist, egalitarian partner about whom most people only dream. I can't imagine how I could have written this book without your unwavering support and co-parenting dedication. I have thought a lot about which marriage type in this book most reflects me. I think that perhaps I am a "Marriage Rejecter" at heart who just got extremely lucky finding you. If I had to be married to anyone, I am so glad it's you. And though I like to believe that we didn't need marriage, I also know that's not true.

Let me end by acknowledging that, in one way or another, our academic interests are all shaped by our personal histories, and mine is no different. It feels surreal to me that the year this book gets published I will be celebrating my twentieth wedding anniversary. If you had told the naive twenty-three-year-old me who married somewhat on a whim to move across an ocean to be with the person she loved that twenty years later she would still be married, she would not have believed you (my husband says: "She would have scoffed"). That twenty-three-year-old was not sure what marriage meant, nor how long hers would last, only that she wanted to be with her partner. Twenty years on, I am wowed by the impact that marriage has had on my life—taking me a world away from everything I knew growing up, and shaping my life trajectory in so many ways. That is why, in part, I have been so interested in studying and understanding this powerful institution.

But my interest in marriage likely began even earlier, subconsciously emerging out of all the times my mum told me what an unnecessary, patriarchal institution it is (and who has managed to sustain an unmarried committed relationship with my stepdad for twice as long as me and my husband). I am also the product of a complex, but loving blended family formed of multiple marriages. All these facts of my life contributed to my academic interest in marriage. I have always wanted to understand its social and cultural power. Most of all, I am thankful to have been surrounded by so many models of love and commitment in my life, and grateful to know that marriage is just one way to do it.

Methods Appendix

I designed this research study to achieve two things: to investigate, in detail, the ways that LGBQ individuals experience legal marriage and the impact that it has had on same-sex relationships; and to advance our understanding of the changing and enduring meaning of contemporary marriage as an institution. To do this, I collected in-depth interview and survey data from 116 individuals in married and unmarried same-sex relationships in Massachusetts in 2012 and 2013.

Recruitment

The people who took part in this research responded to a call for participants for a study about "how lesbian, gay, bisexual, and transgender people have experienced gaining the right to legally marry and how it impacts their lives." I made it clear on the recruitment materials that it did not matter what their views on marriage were. They found out about the study in a number of ways. Some saw fliers that I handed them directly at LGBTQ+ events or that I had posted at venues friendly to the LGBTQ+ community, such as coffee shops, bars, or community centers. Some received emails about the study from organizations and LISTERVs that agreed to help me advertise it. These included political, religious, and social organizations, such as MassEquality, the Metropolitan Community Church, and book clubs and sports leagues serving the LGBTQ+ community. I also drew on snowballing techniques[1] by asking participants to pass on information to others they knew. Although I advertised via one marriage organization, only a few participants had been involved in the marriage equality movement, and so the LGBQ people in this book were not marriage activists. No direct incentive was offered for participation.

Interested participants completed a brief online eligibility survey to make sure they met the criteria for inclusion in the study. They had to be over age eighteen, living in Massachusetts, and cohabiting with a same-sex partner for at least one year. I chose Massachusetts as the research site for several reasons. Because the few existing studies of same-sex marriage had taken place before or immediately after legalization, I wanted to try to gain a longer perspective on the impact of marriage on same-sex relationships. Massachusetts had provided access to legal marriage for much longer than other states. Massachusetts became the first state to make same-sex marriage legal in 2003 (put into effect in 2004), and it took another four years for another state to legalize same-sex marriage.[2] Massachusetts further made most sense as the research site for this study because it had overcome attempts to introduce constitutional amendments banning it,[3] whereas other states were still grappling with ongoing efforts to halt same-sex marriage. I wanted access to marriage to feel as secure as possible to the individuals in this study so that I could adequately examine its impact on their relationships. Massachusetts was well ahead of its time. However, Massachusetts is a politically and culturally liberal state with especially strong legal protections for LGBQ people, which make it distinctive. Now marriage is legal nationwide comparative research will be vital for investigating how differences in state and community contexts influence the impact of marriage on relationships.

I made specific efforts to include groups of individuals that had been excluded from prior research. The little existing research on same-sex marriage had only examined the experiences of individuals who married, but I knew from the outset that including both married and unmarried individuals was crucial. We know that institutions can shape individual behavior both before, and without, formal participation in them. To capture the full effects of marriage, I needed to explore how access to legal marriage impacted unmarried individuals too. In addition, I wanted to directly compare unmarried and married individuals to be able to evaluate the impact of being married. I made the decision to only include individuals cohabiting with a same-sex partner, and not single participants, because I wanted marriage to feel as if it could be a real possibility for them and their relationships, rather than only an abstract or imagined future. Single LGBQ people and those who are not in dyadic relationships are also likely impacted by gaining access to legal marriage, but this book cannot speak to their experiences. Only one partner from any couple was included in the study. I recognize that marriage is composed of two people who may have different experiences and that including both partners is important for research aimed at exploring variation within couples, but this was not my focus. My intent was to gain as wide a variety of perspectives on marriage as possible. Prior research that I conducted on same-sex marriage, in which I included both partners in each couple, additionally led me to conclude that including only one partner would be more advantageous.[4]

It was not my intention to recruit a sample that was representative of larger populations of same-sex couples or produce statistically generalizable findings. Rather, I designed the study to inform theory about sparsely investigated areas of scholarship. I approached recruitment and sample size using "case study logic."[5] Each person (or "case") I recruited was intended to provide an increasingly accurate understanding of my research questions. I continued recruiting until I had reached saturation and no further insights were gained from interviews. I actually reached saturation well before I stopped interviewing, but high interest in the study led me to continue interviewing for longer. Some groups were harder to recruit than others—unmarried men, for example—and I honed my recruitment efforts to reach those individuals. I made particular efforts to increase racial and class variation in my sample as well. I advertised the study via professional organizations and in community centers that catered to these underrepresented groups, reaching out to several Black churches and racially specific LGBTQ+ organizations. I also posted fliers in laundromats and tried recruiting via Craigslist. But these efforts did little to yield a more racially or class diverse sample. As others have described, it is especially difficult to recruit non-White sexual minority research participants.[6] I discuss the strengths and limitations of the sample characteristics below.

The timing of recruitment is important to keep in mind. The LGBQ people in this study had access to marriage in Massachusetts and the state-level benefits that this granted, but not to federal-level marriage recognition. This meant that they had no access to federal-level marriage rights and protections, as well as insecure marital status beyond their home state. I was finishing up data collection for this book when the Supreme Court struck down part of the federal Defense of Marriage Act,[7] requiring the federal government to recognize same-sex marriages from the states where they are legal. By then, same-sex couples in Massachusetts had had access to legal same-sex marriage for nine years, and a total of nine other states had made same-sex marriage legal. Participants sometimes expressed frustration about not having full legal equality. There was little evidence, however, that this had substantive impact on their participation in marriage. Same-sex marriage would not become legal nationwide until two years after I finished data collection—when, on June 26, 2015, the US Supreme Court ruled in *Obergefell v. Hodges* that all state bans on same-sex marriage were unconstitutional, granting same-sex couples in all fifty states the right to full, equal recognition under the law.[8] This book therefore captures a unique historic moment that social scientists will not have the opportunity to study again, analyzing the experiences of the first group of LGBQ individuals to gain access to legal marriage. They were marriage trailblazers, paving the way for others. It is possible that later experiences of same-sex marriage, after it became legal nationwide, differ from those in this book. But there is no reason to think they would be qualitatively different. If anything, the kinds of experiences documented here will have become more common as same-sex marriage has become more institutionalized over time (especially those of Marriage Assumers; see chapter 3). Moreover, the timing of data collection proved crucial for also being able to capture experiences that are likely becoming less common as marriage becomes more institutionalized (those of Marriage Embracers; see chapter 1).

Sample Characteristics

Using these recruitment methods resulted in a sample of 116 participants. Sixty-six were women and fifty were men. Seventy were legally married, and forty-six were in unmarried relationships. Relationship durations ranged from one to thirty-two years. They ranged in age from twenty-three to sixty-nine years. Ninety-two identified as gay or lesbian, ten as bisexual, and thirteen as queer. Participants were predominantly White (84 percent identified as White only) and highly educated (92 percent had a bachelor's degree or higher). I traveled all over the state conducting interviews and was not based in a single location, but most who took part described themselves as living in urban areas (53 percent described where they lived as an "urban area/city" and a further 33 percent described it as a "large town or city suburb"). Forty-two participants had children (48 percent of those in married relationships and 20 percent of those in unmarried relationships). For an overview of sample characteristics, see table A.1. Note that throughout the book, pseudonyms have been assigned to all participants, and identifying information has been removed.

In thinking about how the LGBQ people who took part in this study compare to the broader population of LGBQ people in the United States, a few things stand out.[9] Among all LGBTQ+ individuals in the United States, 58 percent are female and 42 percent are male, very similar proportions as those taking part in this study.[10] Twenty-nine percent of LGBTQ+ individuals in the United States are raising children (only slightly lower than the proportion in this study). The racial identification of LGBTQ+ individuals nationally is much more varied than those in this study (nationally, 58 percent identify as

TABLE A.1. Sample characteristics by marital status (%, [n])

	Married	Unmarried
*Relationship duration (mean = 10)***		
1–4 years	20% (14)	50% (23)
5–10 years	32% (22)	30% (14)
11–20 years	36% (25)	9% (4)
20+ years	12% (8)	11% (5)
Children		
Together*	35% (24)	7% (3)
From a prior relationship	9% (9)	13% (6)
*Age group (mean = 41)***		
18–29	7% (5)	33% (15)
30–49	61% (42)	43% (20)
50–69	32% (22)	24% (11)
Gender		
Female	58% (40)	54% (25)
Male	42% (29)	46% (21)
Race/ethnicity		
White only	84% (58)	85% (39)
American Indian/Alaska Native	1% (1)	7% (3)
Asian/Pacific Islander	1% (1)	0% (0)
African American/Black	6% (4)	7% (3)
Hispanic or Latino/a	7% (5)	2% (1)
*Education**		
Less than bachelor's degree	4% (3)	11% (5)
Bachelor's degree	22% (15)	50% (23)
Graduate degree	74% (51)	39% (18)
Religion		
Religious affiliation	59% (41)	50% (23)
No religious affiliation	41% (28)	50% (23)
Place of residence (self-reported)		
Urban area/city	57% (39)	46% (21)
Large town/city suburbs	28% (19)	43% (20)
Small town/rural area	16% (11)	11% (5)
Total	(69)	(46)

Notes: (1) One participant had a lot of missing survey data but completed the in-depth interview. As such, the table totals add up to 115 instead of 116. (2) As only one participant had a child from a prior same-sex relationship, I combined counts for all prior relationships together.
*Differences by marital status significant at the $p < 0.05$ level.
**Differences by marital status significant at the $p < 0.01$ level.

White only, but among those in couples, 74 percent identify as White only, more closely resembling the sample in this book). Nationally, White LBGQ individuals have higher rates of same-sex partnerships.[11] Nevertheless, the limited diversity of my sample does limit my ability to attend to potentially important differences in marriage by race and ethnicity.

The sample in this book was much less varied than the broader population of LGBTQ+ individuals when it comes to social class. Sociologists measure class in varying ways, but typically rely on education, occupation, and income. I did not collect occupation or income information, but my participants were more highly educated than the average LGBTQ+ American, placing them securely in the middle to upper-middle class. National data shows that only 17 percent of LGBTQ+ individuals hold a bachelor's degree, and only 13 percent hold a postgraduate degree. That said, partnered LGBTQ+ individuals are better educated than their single counterparts. Family sociologists have pointed to a "two-tier family system" emerging over the past half century in which family patterns have increasingly diverged by social class, especially education.[12] Educated Americans are significantly more likely to marry and stay married than their less-educated counterparts. These growing inequalities have resulted in widespread scholarly concern and debate about the "retreat from marriage" among lower social classes.[13] Yet sociological research also shows that Americans of different class backgrounds subscribe to the same beliefs about marriage and hold the same marital aspirations.[14] Inequalities have made it harder for all Americans to achieve their marriage goals, but the vast majority still want to marry and believe in its central tenets. The class-based limits of my sample mean that this book offers us the most insight into the LGBQ people most likely to marry. It uncovers the ways in which marriage shapes the behavior of those most able to accomplish social expectations around marriage. We should not necessarily expect less-educated LGBQ individuals to hold different cultural beliefs about marriage, but their experiences of marriage will likely differ in important ways.

The other way in which the sample in this book stands out as different from the national population of LGBTQ+ people is with regard to sexual identity.[15] Nationally, the largest sexual identity category is bisexual. Bisexuals are therefore underrepresented in this sample. This does, however, make sense given that high proportions of bisexuals are in different-sex relationships. Nonetheless, further research should attend to the experiences of bisexual individuals in same-sex marriages. Additionally, as noted in the introduction, no transgender individuals took part in the study. This study is therefore also unable to speak to their marital experiences.

It is important to keep in mind, however, that as a qualitative researcher, it was not my intention to produce a sample that was representative of larger populations of same-sex couples in any statistical sense. Rather, I expected my findings to be used to inform theory about how LGBQ people enact marriage and how marriage operates as an institution. In qualitative research the goal is not generalizability, but rather to be able to provide theoretical and empirical insights about the mechanisms one is studying—the why and how, not just the what. As Annette Lareau and Aliya Hamid Rao argue, focusing on whether qualitative samples are generalizable to broader populations misses the point.[16] I sought to be able to study marriage in enough depth that I could offer rich, detailed insights into the way it worked as an institution. To do this, I did need to recruit a varied sample, but not one that was statistically generalizable to the broader population. What was important was that I recruited a sample that contained variation in terms of the dimensions most relevant to my questions, and I am confident that I achieved this. Some of these dimensions I knew in advance, like the importance of recruiting both married and unmarried participants, and those both supportive and critical of marriage. Others emerged over the course of data collection, such as the timing of access to legal marriage. After realizing how important this was for answering my research questions, I made sure to recruit approximately half of participants who had started relationships before marriage became legal and half who started relationships afterward.

Mixed Methods

All participants completed an online survey and an in-depth face-to-face interview. The online survey took an average of thirty minutes to complete and was designed to collect a wide range of demographic information that would have been burdensome to collect during interviews. In addition, it covered some of the same questions I asked in the interview, including how participants thought marriage had impacted various aspects of their relationships and what kinds of relationship behaviors they engaged in. Collecting this quantitative data allowed me to provide detailed descriptive data about my sample and identify basic patterns within it. I conducted descriptive analysis of the survey data and chi-square analysis to test for associations between variables and identify significant differences between subgroups, for example by marital status, age, and relationship duration. Throughout the book, you will see that I draw on the survey data when doing so provides greater elaboration and clarification of results.[17]

Given the absence of prior research on the topic and the complexity of the research questions I had, qualitative research was crucial. I chose face-to-face in-depth interviews as my primary method because I wanted to be able to capture the meanings, beliefs, norms, and motivations that shaped the marital choices individuals made and the behaviors they engaged in. Furthermore, as one of the first in-depth studies of same-sex marriage, I wanted LGBQ people to have the opportunity to share what mattered to them. The interviews were semistructured but flexible. They covered a wide variety of topics, including relationship history, coming-out experiences, commitment decisions, relationship practices, relationships with families and friends, and community involvement. Participants were also asked how they thought marriage had impacted various aspects of their lives. I did not include all data from the survey and interviews in this book. In particular, I narrowed the focus of this book to couple-level processes and practices so that I could achieve depth rather than breadth. Other work I have published has focused more on the impact of marriage on social- and community-level processes and practices.[18]

My interview schedule followed a consistent set of overarching questions while still being flexible enough to offer participants the potential to shape the direction of the interview based on their own experiences and interests. I attempted to gain answers to the same overarching questions from everyone for comparability while also following detours and hunches when they came up in interviews. I took a short break halfway through data collection to reflect on the data I had and make sure I was asking the right questions.

Interviews lasted from forty-five minutes to three hours but averaged one and a half hours. They took place wherever participants felt most comfortable. Sometimes this meant being welcomed into people's homes, sharing dinner and drinks with them, and being introduced to their spouses, children, and pets. I held babies and ferrets, admired wedding albums and pornographic art. Other times, participants preferred to meet in public, and we did the interviews in offices, coffee shops, bars, community centers, and parks. Wherever and however the interviews took place, everyone was eager to talk and share their experiences, and they were grateful for the opportunity to reflect on and discuss a topic that felt important to them. I did not detect notable differences in the quality of interviews by location. There were benefits and downsides to both: some public spaces were noisy but offered fewer interruptions from family members, while homes felt more intimate and were easier to build rapport in but were more likely to be interrupted by familial and other intrusions. It was very common for participants to thank me for the "therapy session" or the chance to "reflect deeply" on their experiences and relationship after the interview.

METHODS APPENDIX

I transcribed all interviews verbatim and imported them into NVivo, a qualitative data analysis software program. I employed a blend of inductive and deductive approaches in analyzing the data, going back and forth between the existing theory and my data. I first coded the data utilizing an inductive method of open coding and allowed themes to emerge from participants' responses rather than prior conceptual categories.[19] Then I utilized a deductive method of coding and the extended case study method.[20] I knew in advance that I wanted to connect my data to institutional theory, so I looked at the data for evidence of institutional mechanisms and effects. After I identified initial themes, I aggregated and organized them into more precise or conceptual subcategories. This resulted in a codebook of approximately fifty major thematic codes, each with various subthemes associated with them. After all data had been coded, I created analytic memos to elaborate and theorize each major code and identify patterns across and within codes.

Insider/Outsider Status

I was both an insider and an outsider among the LGBQ people I was studying, sharing some background characteristics with my participants but not others. As I originally did the research as part of my PhD dissertation work, it was obvious to participants that I, like many of them, was highly educated and middle class. I wore a wedding ring as well, which made my coupled status visible. My married status only made me an insider among some participants, but it did situate me as having an obvious stake in the topic being discussed. Given that the study was about marriage, and I was wearing a wedding ring, participants were often eager to know more about my own marriage and personal interest in the topic: how long had I been married? About nine years at the time. What did I think of marriage? That was too complicated to answer succinctly. Was I married to a man or a woman? A man. Sharing characteristics with participants can be useful for helping to build comfort and rapport, but it can also mean that they do not explain themselves as clearly because they presume a shared understanding. Interviewees would sometimes respond to questions with phrases such as "well, you're married so you know," suggesting an assumption of shared knowledge and experience. In those cases, I would respond with something like "if you could explain it to me for the purposes of this interview that would be great."

Because I identify as heterosexual, I was an outsider among my participants, but not everyone could tell my sexual identity. In fact, some people incorrectly assumed that I was in a same-sex partnership. If people made incorrect assumptions about me, I corrected them immediately because I did not want them to feel misled. But if people asked me additional questions, I typically told them that I would be happy to answer any questions about myself but would prefer to wait until the interview was over. I often jokingly ended the interviews by saying something like "ok, my turn now, what would you like to ask me?" I think that participants appreciated my openness given how much they had shared with me. As someone who had not grown up in America and who has an accent (British), this also signaled an outsider status to participants. Overall, though, I think this helped because I could use the fact that I am not originally from the United States to suggest unfamiliarity with any issues I wanted participants to delve deeper into or clarify.

Notes

Introduction

1. Scholars have traced the emergence of the marriage equality movement and shifting public opinion on same-sex marriage; see Kaufman and Compton, "Post-Obergefell"; Rosenfeld, *Rainbow after the Storm*; Stone, *Ballot Box*; Taylor et al., "Culture and Mobilization." There remains, however, scant empirical research on how LGBTQ+ people experience marriage. Some early survey-based studies examined the possible impact of marriage on same-sex relationships; see Lannutti, "Influence of Same-Sex Marriage"; Shulman, Gotta, and Green, "Will Marriage Matter?" The Massachusetts Department of Public Health also conducted a survey in 2009 to celebrate the fifth anniversary of legal same-sex marriage. Respondents said that getting married had made them "more likely to be out," "more committed" to their partners, and "more accepted" by their families and communities; Ramos, Goldberg, and Badgett, "Effects of Marriage Equality." Kimberly Richman's survey and interview research with same-sex couples who were married during San Francisco's Winter of Love in 2004, and in Massachusetts during the first few years of it being legal, focused on the varying ways that LGBTQ+ people understood legal marriage and their reasons for getting married; Richman, *License to Wed*. She finds that love and romance are the most consistently rated important reasons for entering legal marriage. Richman also shows that people experience personal and social benefits after marrying, including greater security in their relationship, a heightened sense of love and commitment, and the validation of friends and family. Other work on same-sex marriage has emerged from queer theory and sexualities studies, centering around heteronormativity as a key area of inquiry. Kimport in *Queering Marriage* conducted interviews with individuals from twenty-seven couples who gained temporary access to legal marriage during the Winter of Love in San Francisco in February 2004, focusing on how marital intentions matter for their ability to challenge the heteronormative underpinnings of marriage.

2. Horowitz et. al., "Marriage and Cohabitation." The share of US adults who are currently married has declined modestly in recent decades, from 58 percent in 1995 to 53 percent today.

3. According to Fry, 25 percent of forty-year-olds have never been married today, compared with just 6 percent in 1980. During the same period the shares of adults currently cohabiting rose from 3 percent to 7 percent. Fry, "Record-High Share of 40-Year-Olds."

4. Hemez and Manning, "Thirty Years of Change."

5. Wu, "Trends in Births."

6. Cherlin, "Degrees of Change"; Lundberg, Pollak, and Stearns, "Family Inequality"; Wu, "Trends in Births."

7. Furstenberg, "Fifty Years of Family Change", 17–18; McLanahan, "Diverging Destinies;" see also Cherlin, *Labor's Love Lost*.

8. Manning, Smock, and Fettro. "Cohabitation and Marital Expectations"; Thornton and Young-DeMarco, "Attitudes Toward Family Issues"; Willoughby, Hall, and Goff, "Marriage Matters."

9. Taylor, "Decline of Marriage."

10. Bogle and Wu, "Thirty Years of Change"; Lichter, Batson, and Brown, "Welfare Reform"; Manning, Smock, and Fettro, "Cohabitation and Marital Expectations"; Taylor, "Decline of Marriage."

11. In 2001, Goldstein and Kenney found that at least 90 percent of American women would marry at some point in their lives; "Marriage Delayed or Marriage Forgone?," 511. However, more recent data by Bloome and Ang project significant declines in the odds of both men and women marrying by age forty across cohorts, with those born in the 1990s having significantly less likelihood of marrying by age forty than those born in earlier cohorts, as well as large and growing racial differences in the likelihood of marriage. Nonetheless, across a variety of statistical modeling techniques, somewhere between 63 percent and 80 percent of White Americans born in the 1990s are estimated to marry by age forty; "Marriage and Union Formation," 1766.

12. Manning, Westrick-Payne, and Gates, "Cohabitation and Marriage."

13. Liu and Umberson, "Times They Are a Changin"; Liu, Reczek, and Wilkinson, "Sexual Minority Couples"; Umberson and Montez, "Social Relationships"; Umberson, Thomeer, and Williams, "Family Status"; Waite and Gallagher, *Case for Marriage*.

14. Pew Research Center, "Marriage and Cohabitation in the U.S."

15. Brown and Kawamura, "Cohabitors and Marrieds"; Brown, Manning and Wu, "Relationship Quality in Midlife."

16. Amato, "Views of Marriage", 960–61; Axinn and Thornton, "Meaning of Marriage", 148–50; Cherlin, "Deinstitutionalization of American Marriage"; Coontz, "Transformation of Marriage", 977–79; Coontz, *Marriage, a History*, 263–304; Thornton, Axinn, and Xie, *Marriage and Cohabitation*, 4–6.

17. Burgess and Locke, *Family*, originally described the shift from the "institutional family" to the "companionship family," 22–23; See Amato, "Institutional, Companionate, and Individualistic" and Cherlin *Marriage-Go-Round*, 63–115, for fuller descriptions of these changes.

18. Bumpass and Lu, "Trends in Cohabitation"; Jones, "Is Marriage Becoming Irrelevant?"; Raley, "Increasing Fertility"; Smock, "Cohabitation."

19. Coontz, "Transformation of Marriage," 975.

20. Amato et al., *Alone Together*, 70–96; Cancian, *Love in America*, 11; Cherlin, "Deinstitutionalization of American Marriage", 851–53; Cherlin, *Marriage-Go-Round*, 88–90; Coontz, *Marriage, a History*, 305–13; Giddens, *Transformation of Intimacy*; Gross, "Detraditionalization of Intimacy Reconsidered"; Walker, "Marriage and Its Future"; Wilcox and Dew, "Flimsy Foundation."

21. Beck and Beck-Gernsheim, *Individualization*, 119–32; Giddens, *Transformation of Intimacy*, 190–209.

22. Giddens, *Transformation of Intimacy*, 56–58.

23. Of all articles published in the *Journal of Marriage and Family* over the last three decades, only two other articles have been cited more than Cherlin's 2004 article, "Deinstitutionalization of American Marriage" (based on an advanced search of all articles published in the journal ordered by highest number of citations).

24. Thornton, Axinn and Xie, *Marriage and Cohabitation*, 4.

25. Cherlin, "Degrees of Change"; Lauer and Yodanis, "Deinstitutionalization of Marriage Revisited."

26. Cherlin, "Deinstitutionalization of American Marriage."

27. Cherlin, "Degrees of Change," 74; Lauer and Yodanis, "Deinstitutionalization of Marriage Revisited," 63.

28. Kimport, *Queering Marriage*, 156. Kimport conducted interviews with individuals from twenty-seven couples who gained temporary access to legal marriage during what was termed the "Winter of Love" in San Francisco in February 2004. The Winter of Love refers to a brief period in which Gavin Newsom, then San Francisco mayor, decided to start marrying same-sex couples. During that time, over four thousand same-sex couples were married in City Hall. They came there from all over the country and even from outside the United States to get married. Eventually, the California Supreme Court halted the marriages, and six months later invalidated them.

29. Scott, *Institutions and Organizations*.

30. DiMaggio, "Interest and Agency."

31. Wilcox and Dew, "Flimsy Foundation."

32. DiMaggio and Powell, *New Institutionalism*.

33. DiMaggio and Powell, *New Institutionalism*, 9; Lauer and Yodanis, "Deinstitutionalization of Marriage Revisited," 59.

34. DiMaggio and Powell, *New Institutionalism*, 11.

35. DiMaggio and Powell, *New Institutionalism*, 15.

36. Swidler, "Culture in Action."

37. Cherlin, "Degrees of Change," 75.

38. See Ocobock, "Leveraging Legitimacy" for an in-depth discussion of findings from this study relating to marriage as a means of obtaining social legitimacy.

39. Ghaziani, Taylor, and Stone, "Cycles of Sameness and Difference."

40. *Obergefell v. Hodges*, 576 US 644 [2015], 13, 28.

41. The New York Times. "'Love Has Won': Reaction to the Supreme Court Ruling on Gay Marriage." June 26, 2015, sec. Opinion. https://www.nytimes.com/2015/06/27/opinion/love-has-won-reaction-to-the-supreme-court-ruling-on-gay-marriage.html.

42. Shesgreen, Deirdre. "Ohio Man 'fought for His Love,' Won Gay-Marriage Case." USA TODAY, June 26, 2015. https://www.usatoday.com/story/news/politics/2015/06/26/ohio-same-sex-marriage-plaintiff/29344307/.

43. President Obama [@POTUS44]. "Today Is a Big Step in Our March toward Equality. Gay and Lesbian Couples Now Have the Right to Marry, Just Like Anyone Else. #LoveWins." Tweet. Twitter, June 26, 2015. https://twitter.com/POTUS44/status/614435467120001024.

44. Swidler, *Talk of Love*, 113–14.

45. Swidler, *Talk of Love*, 127.

46. Berger and Luckmann, *Social Construction of Reality*, 44; DiMaggio and Powell, *New Institutionalism*, 21.

47. Meyer and Rowan, "Institutionalized Organizations," 343–44.
48. Clemens and Cook, "Politics and Institutionalism," 446.
49. DiMaggio and Powell, *New Institutionalism*, 9.
50. Tolbert and Zucker, "Institutional Sources"; Zucker, "Role of Institutionalization."
51. Heath, *One Marriage under God*.
52. Cherlin, "Degrees of Change," 66.
53. In rethinking his deinstitutionalization thesis, Cherlin theorized that deinstitutionalization would necessitate transformational changes, which he believed had *not* yet occurred to marriage; Cherlin, "Degrees of Change," 66.
54. Lauer and Yodanis, "Deinstitutionalization of Marriage Revisited."
55. Lauer and Yodanis, "Deinstitutionalization of Marriage Revisited."
56. Lauer and Yodanis, "Deinstitutionalization of Marriage Revisited," 62.
57. Geiger and Livingston, "8 Facts."
58. Yodanis and Lauer, "Is Marriage Individualized?"
59. Levine et al., "Open Relationships."
60. Norms surrounding the importance of marriage for having kids have shifted. Polling data shows that the numbers of Americans who believe that people who want to have children ought to get married decreased from 73 percent to 61 percent between 1988 and 2012; Nousak, "Attitudes Towards Births." Agreement that it is "very important" that couples with children get married decreased from 38 percent to 29 percent between 2013 and 2020; Jones, "Is Marriage Becoming Irrelevant?" Nonetheless, the numbers of married couples who have children has barely changed, meaning the actual experience of marriage and childbearing has not significantly altered, with most American still experiencing them as connected; United States Census Bureau, "American Community Survey." Moreover, not wanting children within marriage remains highly stigmatized; Carroll, "Intentionally Childless Marriage."
61. DiMaggio and Powell, "Iron Cage Revisited," 151; Lauer and Yodanis, "Deinstitutionalization of Marriage Revisited," 66.
62. DiMaggio and Powell, *New Institutionalism*, 14.
63. Barley and Tolbert, "Institutionalization and Structuration"; DiMaggio, "Interest and Agency"; Fligstein, "Social Skill and Institutional Theory"; Greenwood and Hinings, "Understanding Radical Organizational Change."
64. Battilana, Leca, and Boxenbaum, "How Actors Change Institutions"; DiMaggio, "Interest and Agency"; Garud, Jain, and Kumaraswamy, "Institutional Entrepreneurship"; Greenwood and Suddaby, "Institutional Entrepreneurship"; Maguire, Hardy, and Lawrence, "Institutional Entrepreneurship"; Rao, Morrill, and Zald, "Power Plays."
65. Powell and Colyvas, "Microfoundations," 277.
66. Barclay, Bernstein, and Marshall, *Queer Mobilizations*.
67. Ocobock, "Leveraging Legitimacy" describes the on-the-ground work LGBQ people engaged in. First, by making their relationships more visible and discussing them more openly, they worked to help others adapt their understanding of marriage from something that was taken for granted as inevitably heterosexual to something that is inclusive of same-sex relationships. Second, they worked to delegitimize continuing social exclusion and negative sanctioning of same-sex marriage by challenging it in interaction. By contrast, this study focuses on how what LGBQ individuals do in their couple relationships can change the institution of marriage.
68. In 1999, the Vermont Supreme Court ruled that the state must afford same-sex couples the same "benefits and protections" that different-sex couples can access through marriage.

NOTES TO PAGES 16–17

However, it gave the state legislature the right to determine whether to open marriage to same-sex couples or create a new status that provided the same protections and benefits. The Vermont Legislature responded in 2000 by creating civil unions, which granted all the state level benefits of marriage but denied symbolic equality with full marriage (*Baker v. State of Vermont*). Critics complained that this created a separate but equal standard, some even comparing civil unions to the "separate but equal" doctrine that defined racial segregation until *Brown v. Board of Education* in 1954. Nonetheless, several other states still followed suit, offering civil unions to same-sex couples, including New Jersey (in 2006), New Hampshire (in 2007), and Hawaii (in 2011). Most same-sex couples recognize a significant difference between full marriage and legal alternatives to marriage and prefer legal marriages to any other form of legal recognition. See Balsam et al., "Three-Year Follow-up"; Rothblum, Balsam and Solomon, "Comparison of Same-Sex Couples."

69. It was not until 2008 when another state, Connecticut, made same-sex marriage legal. Over the next few years, Iowa (2009), New Hampshire (2009), the District of Columbia (2009), and New York (2011) also made same-sex marriages legal. In 2012, voters in Maine, Maryland, and Washington state approved laws legalizing same-sex marriage, becoming the first states to do so through popular votes. For a more detailed history of the historical timeline of marriage equality see Freedom to Marry, "Winning the Freedom"; Pew Research Center, "Same-Sex Marriage."

70. Marriage equality activists faced off against a constitutional amendment banning same-sex marriage in 2007, which would have repealed the freedom to marry had voters supported it.

71. Between 2004 and 2006, twenty-four states approved constitutional amendments banning same-sex marriage. The antigay backlash against same-sex marriage was well-funded and managed. See Stone, *Ballot Box*.

72. Dedman and MacDonald, "About 2,500 Gay Couples."

73. Badgett and Herman, "Patterns of Relationship Recognition." Note that same-sex marriages in Massachusetts were only available to Massachusetts residents for the first four years.

74. US Census data calculates that, as of 2021, 64 percent of same-sex couples in Massachusetts were legally married. This suggests that the proportion has not altered much since 2010, which makes sense given rates of divorce and new marriages. However, it is difficult to gain reliable data on change over time between these two points of time as the US Census only started collecting direct data on numbers of same-sex married couples in 2019; United States Census Bureau, "American Community Survey."

75. United States v. Windsor, 570 U.S. 744 (2013).

76. Obergefell v. Hodges 576 U.S. 644 (2015).

77. Freedom to Marry, "Winning the Freedom."

78. Silver, "Change."

79. It was not just the legal landscape that changed rapidly, so too did social attitudes toward same-sex marriage. In 2004, when same-sex marriage first became legal in Massachusetts, Americans still opposed same-sex marriage by a margin of 60 percent to 31 percent. Just a decade later, as same-sex marriage became legal nationwide, Americans favored same-sex marriage by a margin of 55 percent to 39 percent; Pew Research Center, "Attitudes on Same-Sex Marriage." Public opinion had dramatically flipped. Support for same-sex marriage had steadily grown across political affiliations as well as religious and racial groups. The most recent polling finds that 71 percent of Americans support same-sex marriage; McCarthy, "Same-Sex Marriage Support."

80. Cherlin, *Marriage-Go-Round*; Cherlin, *Labor's Love Lost*; Ishizuka, "Economic Foundations"; Lamidi, "Trends in Cohabitation"; Lundberg, Pollak, and Stearns, "Family Inequality"; Manning, Smock, and Fettro, "Cohabitation and Marital Expectations"; McLanahan, "Diverging Destinies."

81. According to one projection, 84 percent of adults with college degrees will ever marry compared with 72 percent of those without college degrees; Martin, Astone, and Peters, "Fewer Marriages, More Divergence."

82. Martin, "Trends in Marital Dissolution"; Schwartz and Han, "Reversal of the Gender Gap."

83. In 2017, according to the American Community Survey, 63 percent of college graduates were currently married compared with 52 percent of those with some college education, 48 percent of those with a high school degree, and 49 percent of those without a high school degree; Ruggles et al., "Integrated Public Use Microdata Series."

84. Aragão et al., "Modern American Family."

85. Wu, "Trends in Births," finds that 55 percent of women aged younger than forty without college degrees had children outside of marriage in the 2010 to 2014 period.

86. Cherlin, "Degrees of Change"; McLanahan, "Diverging Destinies."

87. Married couples had higher levels of educational attainment than cohabiting couples among both same-sex and different-sex couples, but the marital status differential was greater among different-sex couples. Partnered gay men and lesbians are more likely to be college educated than unpartnered gay men and lesbians. See Carpenter and Gates, "Gay and Lesbian Partnership"; Rosenfeld, "Couple Longevity."

88. Cherlin, "Incomplete Institution." 646.

Chapter One

1. Dedman and MacDonald, "About 2,500 Gay Couples."

2. Collins, "Learning from the Outsider Within," 14–15; Schilt, *Just One of the Guys?*, 9. In her research on the experiences of transmen in the workplace, Schilt argues that, having worked on both sides of the gender binary, transmen have an "outsider-within" perspective on gendered workplace practices and are able to illuminate much about unequal gender relations between men and women more generally. Likewise, having sustained relationships without access to the institution of marriage and then transitioning to institutional inclusion, Marriage Embracers are able to articulate and illuminate much about the institutional mechanisms through which marriage shapes relationships.

3. Hull, *Same-Sex Marriage*; Lewin, *Recognizing Ourselves*. Existing literature suggests that commitment ceremonies started in earnest the 1970s but became more visible in the media starting in the 1990s.

4. There is no available public data on commitment ceremonies, so we do not know how many same-sex couples had one.

5. Holy Unions are religious marriage ceremonies that some churches perform for their same-sex congregants. Some churches, such as the Metropolitan Community Church, offered these as an alternative form of marriage well before same-sex marriage became legal. However, today, some churches continue to offer them because they refuse to provide "marriage" to their LGBTQ+ congregants in same-sex relationships.

6. Erin is an In-Betweener. She falls somewhere between the Marriage Embracer and Assumer groups. She was like those in the Embracer group in the sense that she insisted she didn't need marriage to be legal to get married. However, she had only gotten together with her partner shortly before marriage became legal and therefore had access to legal marriage for the vast majority of her relationship. When looking at her marital behaviors, she is therefore more akin

NOTES TO PAGES 32-38

to Marriage Assumers, demonstrating deeply internalized ideas about how to do marriage and what it means (see chapter 3). This is also the case for Maddy, quoted next.

7. It is noteworthy that having a religious background aided LGBQ people in being able to imagine marriage outside of the law. Some younger people in the Marriage Assumer group (chapter 3) also told me that they had "always thought" they would get married because when they imagined getting married, they thought first and foremost about a religious ceremony. However, there is an important cohort difference: whereas younger people in relationships that started after same-sex marriage became legal (Marriage Assumers) could only conceive of commitment ceremonies as an option in the context of religion, Marriage Embracers did not need a religious background to imagine having a commitment ceremony.

8. Hull, *Same-Sex Marriage*, 2, 24.

9. These included Cambridge, Northampton, Amherst, and Brookline. Cambridge, Massachusetts passed the first domestic partnership ordinance in 1992. Following this, however, a long, drawn-out fight ensued over the rights of local municipalities to offer domestic partnerships. See GLAD, "Connor v. City of Boston".

10. Eighteen participants had entered these alternative legal marriages statuses with their current partners and four with previous partners. Unfortunately, in the survey I asked about domestic partnerships and civil unions together so I cannot know how many had each type. However, interview data suggests it was more common for participants to get a domestic partnership than enter a civil union.

11. Relationship duration and cohabitation duration were both significant predictors of having a domestic partnership or civil union ($p = 0.010$ and $p = 0.002$, respectively).

12. Nine were in their thirties and forties, and nine were over age fifty.

13. Eleven of the eighteen who entered alternative legal marriage statuses did not invite anyone else to attend their civil unions or domestic partnerships, and of the remaining seven, most did not hold any sort of wedding to celebrate them. (No one mentioned having a wedding-like celebration for the domestic partnerships, but a few did for the civil unions.) By contrast, ten of the twelve people who had a commitment ceremony treated them as weddings.

14. States typically only consider requests for a divorce from their own residents. This made civil unions very difficult to dissolve for couples who traveled out of state to obtain one. A couple of people in this study had been in civil unions with previous partners and had to have them dissolved to legally marry their current partners. Sara, a thirty-eight-year-old, described it as "a legal drama." Ann, a fifty-four-year-old, described it as "having to get a divorce despite not having been legally married" and as a "pain in the butt."

15. Johannes, Forelle, and Tomsho, "Gay Couples Rush to Marry."

16. Johannes, Forelle, and Tomsho, "Gay Couples Rush to Marry"; CBS, "Same-Sex Couples Rush to the Altar"; Cooperman and Finer, "Gay Couples Marry."

17. Some participants were already living in Massachusetts and legally married in the month or two immediately after it became legal. Others did so within a couple of months of moving to Massachusetts.

18. The AIDS Coalition to Unleash Power (ACT UP), formed in 1987, was dedicated to political action and demonstrations. Ricardo described how the demonstration in Boston ended up at the Holy Cathedral in the South End, where people were there to perform commitment ceremonies. People were giving out bouquets of flowers to hold and taking photos, and the demonstrators took it in turns to get under a canopy and say vows.

19. When the Massachusetts Supreme Judicial Court ruled in November 2003 that same-sex couples had a constitutional right to marry, it also gave the legislature 180 days "to take such action as it may deem appropriate." This prompted opponents of same-sex marriage to attempt multiple actions to stop it. Then governor, Mitt Romney, tried to do so in multiple ways. His attempts to stop same-sex marriage are well documented in the media. See for example Kaczynski, "Mitt Romney's Long Fight."

20. In the years before legal marriage, many LGBQ people chose to symbolize their marriage-like relationships by wearing rings on their right-hand ring finger, instead of the left-hand ring finger that is typical to symbolize heterosexual marriage. There were several reasons for this: some felt that it would help them maintain privacy by not drawing attention to the nature of their relationship; some wanted to make a political statement that their marriages were different from heterosexual marriages; while others wanted to make a political statement of another kind—that their marriages were not equal, lacking legal recognition and rights. Whatever the reason, several participants mentioned the symbolic weight of switching ring fingers upon legally marrying.

21. Badgett and Herman, "Patterns of Relationship Recognition."

22. For a more in-depth analysis of the social legitimacy gains from legal marriage, see Ocobock, "Leveraging Legitimacy."

23. It is possible that only those LGBQ people who felt confident that a wedding would help them gain family acceptance and recognition chose to have commitment ceremonies. In other words, there may have been some selection into commitment ceremonies on the basis of expected effects. There is no way to know this, but it is clear that most of those who opted only to have domestic partnerships or civil unions had not experienced them as means of gaining family acceptance and inclusion, and so legal marriage was distinctive in this way.

24. To be clear, I am not suggesting that getting legally married was a sure means of gaining greater family recognition and acceptance, only that it was a motivation for getting married. These Marriage Embracers believed that marriage had the power to make a difference with their families and described marriage as deeply connected to family recognition and belonging. It's important to remember, though, that others had also believed commitment ceremonies could also serve that function. In this way, Marriage Embracers differed in their understanding of what outcomes of marriage were achievable without legal status and which were dependent on it. Nonetheless, the majority of Americans still do not view a couple as a family unless they are legally married; Powell et al., *Counted Out*; Powell, "Changing Counts." Other research I conducted with married gay men in Iowa found that even if same-sex couples had been together for decades, many families of origin only formally welcomed their partners into the family, started including them in family-only events, and began referring to them with family terminology (such as "son-in-law") after they were legally married; Ocobock, "Power and Limits of Marriage." Yet marital outcomes are also more complex than marital motivations, and even legal marriage sometimes failed to achieve the kind family recognition LGBQ people hoped to gain from it.

25. This move was distinct to Connecticut. Civil unions in other states, such as Vermont, were not automatically converted into legal marriages.

26. It may also be the case that LGBQ people with children had achieved family recognition through their parental status and so felt less need for a wedding, though this is not something my participants discussed. For more information about how LGBQ parenting is connected to family recognition and support, see, for example, Hequembourg, "Unscripted Motherhood"; Leal et al., "Social Support."

27. Others have also found that same-sex couples prefer marriage over commitment ceremonies, civil unions, or domestic partnerships. Gates, Badgett, and Ho, "Marriage, Registration and Dissolution"; Hull, "Same-Sex Marriage"; Reczek, Elliott, and Umberson, "Commitment without Marriage"; Richman, *License to Wed*.

28. Badgett and Herman, "Patterns of Relationship Recognition," draw on data from state administrative agencies and the US Bureau of the Census to analyze the take-up rates of various marital statuses. They propose that the "rush" to marry in the first year each status is available suggests that full legal marriage is much more popular among same-sex couples than any other marital status. As soon as they could, large numbers of same-sex couple residents rushed to get married—33 percent of all resident same-sex couples in the first year it was legal in their state. By comparison, only 18 percent entered into civil unions or broad (state-level) domestic partnerships in the first year states offered these other statuses. When domestic partnerships were more limited (for example, at the county or city level), only 8 percent of same-sex couples entered them the first year they were made available.

29. Swidler, *Talk of Love*, 37.

30. Swidler, *Talk of Love*, 157.

31. Pew Research shows that the proportion of LGBT adults citing love, companionship, and making a lifelong commitment as "very important reasons" for getting legally married are similar to those for the general public (between 70 and 90 percent); Taylor, "Marriage and Parenting." Double as many LGBT people cite "legal rights and benefits" as important reasons to marry compared to the general public, yet still fewer than half do. Others have also found that love and commitment rank highly as reasons LGBTQ+ people give for getting legally married. See Ramos, Goldberg, and Badgett, "Effects of Marriage Equality"; Richman, *License to Wed*. In the survey for this study, "love and commitment" was most frequently cited as an "extremely important" reason to marry.

32. As I show in chapter 2, Marriage Rejecters thought of love and commitment very differently from Marriage Embracers, conceptualizing their ability to sustain their relationships without marriage as the truest, strongest form of love and commitment. And, as I show in chapter 3, Marriage Assumers, who always assumed they would have access to legal marriage from the start of their relationships, depended on legal marriage as the *only* setting within which to express long-term love and commitment.

33. Hull, "Same-Sex Marriage," 3.

Chapter Two

1. This kind of commitment outside and beyond a marital model that Personal Marriage Rejecters spoke about could be considered in line with what sociologist Anthony Giddens sees as typical of a trend toward "pure relationships" in the late twentieth century. Pure relationships are a form of relationship with no overarching structure to sustain them, sustained instead by mutual self-disclosure and an appreciation of each other's unique qualities. With external criteria and structures absent, the relationship exists solely for whatever rewards the relationship can deliver, and is maintained only so long as it can do so; Giddens, *Transformation of Intimacy*, 6. For Giddens, this trend toward "pure relationships" is paralleled by a more responsive and creative form of sexuality—what he terms "plastic sexuality," 2. This refers to a heightened self-awareness of the plasticity of sexuality, a freedom from pre-given ways of being sexual. Because

equality and sexual freedom are key to pure relationships, they might be more common in same-sex relationships; Jamieson, *Intimacy Transformed?*

2. Relationship duration was significantly correlated with the likelihood of marriage among unmarried participants, with the likelihood of marriage decreasing the longer one had been with their partners (p = 0.02). I can be confident that this finding is driven by those in the Rejecter group because all other unmarried participants were Marriage Assumers, wanted to marry, and were actively working toward it (chapter 3). Being older also mattered for the importance unmarried participants placed on getting married. Just 36 percent of unmarried participants aged fifty and above said that it was "important" to them if they legally married their partners in the future, compared to 76 percent of those under age fifty. But although the data reveal both relationship duration and age-based patterns, relationship duration was highly significant (p = 0.007), whereas age was not (p = 0.09).

3. Bosley-Smith and Reczek, "Before and After 'I Do,'" conducted one of the only other qualitative studies of same-sex marriage in Massachusetts in 2013 that I know of. Their research with thirty "mid-life couples" finds that "marital ambivalence" is a common experience among this generation who had sustained relationships for a long time prior to gaining access to legal marriage (1988–1989). The experiences are most akin to the Personal Rejecters in this chapter. However, the Marital Embracers in chapter 1 are of a similar "mid-life" stage and show no such ambivalence. Moreover, the Intellectual Marriage Rejecters in this chapter come from different life and relationship stages and reject marriage on different grounds. As such, my findings build upon and offer a more complex account of marriage experiences.

4. Epstein, "Queer Encounter," 195.

5. Gamson, "Must Identity Movements Self-Destruct?," 395.

6. See Bernstein and Taylor, *Marrying Kind?*, for an overview of queer critiques of marriage.

7. Duggan, "New Homonormativity," 179; Bernstein and Taylor, *Marrying Kind?*, 13–14; Robinson, "Heteronormativity and Homonormativity."

8. Bechdel, "Dykes to Watch Out For."

9. Becky is referring to The New Yorker cartoon by Michael Shaw first published in March 2004, with the headline "Gays and Lesbians Getting Married—Haven't they Suffered Enough?"

10. Hardy and Easton, *Ethical Slut*.

11. Ruby is likely referring to controversies over "conflict" or "blood" diamonds: diamonds sold to fund armed conflict and civil war in Angola, the Democratic Republic of Congo, and Sierra Leone. She may also be referring more generally to the use of child labor in the diamond industry in India and Africa.

12. Bernstein and Burke, "Normalization," showed cultural representations of and discourse about marriage in LGBT newspapers opened up space for critical discussions of marriage as an institution. In their overview of debates about same-sex marriage within the lesbian and gay movement, Bernstein and Taylor also argued that the marriage equality movement "opened up discursive space" for conflicting feelings toward marriage; Bernstein and Taylor, *Marrying Kind?*, 20.

13. Art is one of the LGBQ participants in the In-Betweener group. He is one of the few participants who was involved in activism for marriage equality. He and his partner had also been planning a commitment ceremony prior to same-sex marriage becoming legal (when it became legal, they got legally married instead). This seems to position him as a Marriage Embracer. However, Art also expresses a lot of critiques of marriage, positioning him more as a Marriage Rejecter.

14. Ghaziani, Taylor, and Stone, "Cycles of Sameness and Difference," 176–77.

NOTES TO PAGES 64–76

15. Meyer, "Prejudice, Social Stress, and Mental Health."
16. Baumle and Compton, *Legalizing LGBT Families*.
17. Although many employers offered access to healthcare benefits once legally married, this was at the discretion of employers and not an automatic right. No private employer is mandated to offer health benefits to spouses of employees. As of 2020, while the number of employers offering same-sex spousal coverage has increased since the legalization of same-sex marriage, it remains less common than opposite-sex spousal coverage; Dawson, Rae, and Kates, "Access to Employer-Sponsored Health Coverage."
18. See Baumle and Compton, *Legalizing LGBT Families*, for more information about the legal landscape around same-sex parenting and the continuing challenges that same-sex couples face even after gaining access to legal marriage.
19. Murray, "Nonmarriage Inequality Essays," 1243.
20. This situation was so common in the LGBTQ+ community that, when I asked him about it, the AIDS activist and documentarian Jim Hubbard said: "This situation [of the rejecting family coming in and taking over a dying person's possessions or medical decisions] was so normal that I don't think we even gave it as much thought as maybe we ought to have" (personal communication with the author, Nov 30, 2021). For more information about the work of Jim Hubbard, see Hubbard, "AIDS Activist Video."
21. Socio-legal scholars identify different kinds of legal consciousness, with individuals exhibiting different degrees of awareness of and understanding of the law, applying different meanings to the law, and using it in different ways. See Baumle and Compton, *Legalizing LGBT Families*, for a detailed examination of the varying ways LGBT individuals approach and use the law in relation to parenting, and specifically pages 5–6 for a succinct overview of the main forms of legal consciousness.
22. For reference, Marriage Embracers (chapter 1) are all older LGBQ people in long-term relationships that predated access to legal marriage. Marriage Rejecters (chapter 2) are the most varied of the three groups with regard to age. They include some younger LGBQ people in newer relationships, but are still mostly older LGBQ people in long-term relationships that predated legal marriage. As I will show in chapter 3, Marriage Assumers are all younger people in newer relationships that started only after marriage was legal.
23. Coontz, *Marriage, a History*, 229–30.
24. Dianne worked for a company that already offered same-sex partner benefits (which were not dependent on marriage), their families were already supportive, and they were already very committed. As such, Dianne could not imagine what they would gain from marriage. By contrast, her partner felt that "if there is no barrier to marrying, why not do it?" Interestingly, after marrying, Dianne said she had "come to see the light" about marriage. She said, "I see now that marriage has social meaning. It offers so much legitimacy. And I guess I would've gotten married right away if I'd known that!" See Ocobock, "Leveraging Legitimacy," for more research on same-sex marriage and legitimacy.
25. As part of my semi-structured interview schedule, I typically asked participants both what they thought the best thing and worst thing about having access to legal marriage was.
26. Lamont, "Negotiating Courtship"; Robnett and Leaper, "Girls Don't Propose!"; Schweingruber, Cast, and Anahita, "'Story and a Ring.'" See chapter 4 for more information on same-sex proposals.
27. The term "collective effervescence" was coined by the French sociologist Emily Durkheim who used it to describe the heightened emotion and communal energy that arises when

people come together to participate in shared cultural rituals. Weddings are often described as moments of collective effervescence because heightened emotions, shared rituals, and communal energy create an atmosphere of unity and shared experience regardless of an individual's personal views of marriage as an institution.

Chapter Three

1. Massachusetts passed the Safe Schools Program for Gay and Lesbian Students in 1993. More information about the program can be found at https://www.doe.mass.edu/sfs/lgbtq/.

2. Gallup data shows that 64 percent of heterosexuals say that it is important that when a couple plans to spend the rest of their lives together they should legally marry, and 60 percent say it is important for an unmarried couple to legally marry when they have a child together. Eighty-one percent of never-married adults in the United States would like to get married someday; Jones, "Is Marriage Becoming Irrelevant?" Pew Research Center data from 2014 found similar results, with 68 percent of Americans believing that it was important for couples to marry if they planned to spend the rest of their lives together; Wang and Parker, "Never Married."

3. Bawer, *Place at the Table*, 88; Sullivan, *Virtually Normal*.

4. Warner, *Trouble with Normal*, 53.

5. Bernstein and Taylor, *Marrying Kind?*, 13.

6. Processes of institutionalization are discussed in more detail in the book's introduction.

7. Although it is possible that Marriage Embracers had also imagined hypothetical (but nonlegal) marriage futures early in their relationships, they did not tell me about such daydreams or conversations. Instead, they described marriage as something that was embraced only gradually or later on in the course of their already committed relationships.

8. Nationally, married same-sex couples have higher rates of childrearing than unmarried same-sex couples, suggesting a link between marital status and childrearing patterns; Goldberg and Conron, "Raising Children."

9. The legal landscape is still changing regarding the relationship between same-sex marriage and parenting rights. For example, in *Pavan v. Smith* in 2017, the Supreme Court found that the wife of a woman who gives birth is entitled to the same presumption of parentage that a similarly situated husband would be, even when the spouse explicitly does not contribute genetic material. The court considered the presumption in that case to be part of the "constellation of benefits" and rights linked to marriage to which same-sex couples are entitled under *Obergefell v Hodges*. This ruling and others have effectively left biology behind and expanded the presumption of parentage to all spouses of gestational parents, making it accessible for many more members of the LGBTQ+ community and giving greater recognition to parenthood based on intent rather than biology. However, the current legal landscape remains very unclear and uncertain.

10. "Some states permit state-licensed child welfare agencies to refuse to place and provide services to children and families, including LGBTQ people and same-sex couples, if doing so conflicts with their religious beliefs." At the time of writing, this was true for twelve states: https://www.lgbtmap.org/equality-maps/foster_and_adoption_laws.

11. The 2019 LGBTQ Family Building Survey provided data on how many lesbian, gay, bisexual, transgender, and queer (LGBTQ) people are interested in becoming parents. Most significantly, the data revealed dramatic differences in expectations around family between LGBTQ Millennials (aged eighteen to thirty-five) and older generations of LGBTQ people. Seventy-seven percent of LGBTQ Millennials are either already parents or are considering becoming

parents in the coming years, a 44 percent increase over older LGBTQ generations; Family Equality, "LGBTQ Family Building Survey."

12. The stereotype that women in same-sex relationships move in together very quickly is one of the most pervasive and has been referred to as the "U-Haul syndrome"; Miller, "Beyond the U-Haul." However, Orth and Rosenfeld's analysis of survey data finds no significant differences in how quickly lesbian and heterosexual couples move in together, with couples across the United States moving in together on average a year and a half after they start dating. The only major difference is that same-sex couples tended to be older when they met: age thirty-four for members of female-female couples compared with age twenty-six for male-female couples. This age difference might make it seem like lesbians tend to get together more quickly, but the analysis demonstrates that it is the age of meeting that really matters, not whether both partners are women. These age-based differences in timing of meeting for same and different-sex couples are also likely to dissipate in the context of legal same-sex marriage and growing cultural acceptance of same-sex relationships. See Orth and Rosenfeld, "Commitment Timing."

13. Cherlin, *Marriage-Go-Round*, 139–40.

14. It is worth noting that, based on the current research on heterosexual unmarried cohabitation, not all these Marriage Assumers will necessarily end up marrying the partners they were currently cohabiting with. In the United States, much of the literature on the function of cohabitation frames it as a precursor to marriage; Sassler and Miller, *Cohabitation Nation*. However, although US cohabiting unions have increased in duration, over time fewer cohabiting unions are transitioning into marriages; Guzzo, "Trends in Cohabitation Outcomes"; Kuperberg, "Premaritial Cohabitation"; Lamidi, Manning, and Brown, "First Premarital Cohabitation"; Lichter et al., "Pathways to a Stable Union?" In fact, US data have suggested that cohabitation seems to serve, at least initially, as an intensive form of dating among recent cohorts. Serial cohabitation (experiencing the dissolution of one cohabitation and then entering another) has increased significantly during the past decade; Lichter, Turner, and Sassler, "Serial Cohabitation." Unfortunately, the paucity of data on sexual-minority adults, particularly longitudinal data, means that few studies explore whether the factors shaping the union formation processes of same-sex individuals are similar to or different from those influencing different-sex adults; Sassler and Lichter, "Cohabitation and Marriage."

15. Findings from the 2019 Generations study, based on a representative sample of lesbians, gay men, and bisexuals (LGB) in the United States, show differences in the proportion of LGB people who are legally married across three cohorts: younger (eighteen to twenty-five years old), middle (thirty-four to forty-one years old) and older (forty-two to fifty-nine years old). Only 6 percent of the younger cohort of LGB individuals were legally married, while 37 percent of the middle cohort were; Meyer and Krueger, "Legally Married."

16. Swidler identified two dominant cultural forms of love present in people's narratives: "mythic" and "prosaic." Dominant portrayals of love involve ideas such as a clear, all or nothing choice, of a unique other, made in defiance of social forces. But the middle-class adults Swidler interviewed debunked this mythic vision, drawing on "prosaic realism" instead. This is the idea that love grows slowly and takes hard work, for example. However, Swidler argues that this version of love is just as "cultural" as the mythic view it claims to debunk; Swidler, *Talk of Love*, 114.

17. Kefalas et al. in "More Than Being Together" (866–67) describe marriage planners as only able to feel ready for marriage when a particular "marriage mentality" had been achieved—a cognitive framework that allows them to give up the self-interested ways of an unattached single so they can commit to the obligations and responsibilities of being a spouse.

18. Marriage scholars argue that contemporary marriage is "individualized marriage," meaning that, in contrast to prior historical eras, marriage is conceptualized in individual terms and should not get in the way of individual goals; Cherlin, *Marriage-Go-Round*, 88–89; Finkel, *All-or-Nothing Marriage*.

19. Pew Research ("Attitudes on Same-Sex Marriage") found that two-thirds of heterosexual cohabiters who wanted to get married someday cited either their own or their partner's finances as a reason why they're not engaged or married; Pew Research Center, "Attitudes on Same-Sex Marriage" and "Many Cohabiters Cite Finances." Pew Research also found in 2017 that being a good financial provider is still seen as particularly important for men to be a good husband or partner. About seven-in-ten adults (71 percent) said it was very important for a man to be able to support a family financially to be a good husband or partner, while just 32 percent said the same for a woman to be a good wife or partner; Parker and Stepler, "Men as Financial Providers."

20. Cherlin, *Labor's Love Lost*; Edin, Kefalas, and Reed, "Peek inside the Black Box"; Gibson-Davis, Gassman-Pines, and Lehrman "'His' and 'Hers'"; Parker and Stepler, "Education Gap"; Schneider and Hastings, "Socioeconomic Variation"; Smock, Manning, and Porter, "'Everything's There Except Money'"; Wilcox, Wolfinger, and Stokes, "One Nation, Divided."

21. Swidler, *Talk of Love*, 119.

22. Swidler, *Talk of Love*, 114.

23. According to an estimate by Gallup from 2017, 61 percent of all same-sex couples who were living together had married. Cherlin also predicts that younger people may not marry in such large numbers; Cherlin, "Degrees of Change," 75.

Chapter Four

1. For more information about scripting theory and how people use scripts in personal relationships see Ginsburg, "Rules, Scripts and Prototypes"; Goddard and Wierzbicka, "Cultural Scripts"; Klinkenberg and Rose, "Dating Scripts"; Simon and Gagnon, "Permanence and Change"; Simon and Gagnon, "Origins, Influences and Changes."

2. Schweingruber, Anahita, and Berns, "'Popping the Question.'"

3. Hamilton and Armstrong, "Gendered Sexuality"; Lamont, "Negotiating Courtship"; Ridgeway, *Framed by Gender*.

4. Robnett and Leaper, "Girl's Don't Propose!"; Schweingruber, Cast, and Anahita, "'Story and a Ring.'"

5. Cherlin, "Incomplete Institution"; Cherlin, "Deinstitutionalization of American Marriage"; see also Hequembourg, "Unscripted Motherhood"; Lauer and Yodanis, "Individualized Marriage."

6. Pfeffer, "Normative Resistance," 578; see also Green, "Queer Unions."

7. In an interview study with forty LGBTQ-identified people in the San Francisco Bay Area, Lamont found that they consciously rejected heterosexual dating and marriage norms in an effort to achieve more egalitarian relationships; Lamont, "'Write the Scripts Ourselves.'" In their study of women in heterosexual and same-sex marriages in Ontario, Canada, sociologists Fetner and Heath also concluded that whereas most heterosexuals are "nonreflexive adopters" of conventional wedding practices, same-sex couples take an "actively critical approach," thinking deeply about how their choices relate and contribute to heteronormativity; Fetner and Heath, "Women's Conformity and Resistance," 727, 732.

8. Seventy-three out of the 116 people in this study were legally married or engaged to be married. Of these, half (thirty-six) had become engaged via a proposal, in which one partner proposed marriage to the other, while the other half (thirty-seven) became engaged without one.

9. See for example Weiss, "Wedding Marketing."

10. Lamont, *Mating Game*; Sassler and Miller, "Waiting to Be Asked"; Sassler and Miller, *Cohabitation Nation*.

11. Half of the men who were or had been engaged (fifteen) had a proposal, and half (fifteen) did not; as did half of the women (twenty-one and twenty-two respectively).

12. Linear regression analyses showed that those who had been with their partners for eleven to fifteen years were 26 percent less likely, those together more than fifteen years were 46 percent less likely, and those together more than twenty-five years were 63 percent less likely to have had a proposal than their counterparts who were in relationships of less than ten years (all significant at $p < 0.05$ or higher). Compared to those in their thirties, those aged forty to forty-nine were 30 percent less likely, those aged fifty to fifty-nine were 42 percent less likely, and those aged over sixty were 58 percent less likely to have had a proposal (all significant at $p < 0.05$ or higher). Additionally, regardless of relationship duration or age, those who began their relationships before same-sex marriage was legal were 38 percent less likely to have had a proposal than those who started their relationships after it was already an option to legally marry ($p < 0.01$).

13. Patrick indicated that there was an "age gap" between him and his partner, and that his partner was younger, but I did not collect data on age differences between partners and so I do not know by how much. However, we know that same-sex couples are more likely to have significant age differences between partners than heterosexuals, and so divergent engagement expectations might be more widespread for same-sex couples; see Schwartz and Graft, "Assortative Matching."

14. As I showed in chapter 2, some Rejecters had partners who surprised them with proposals, putting them on the spot, and ignoring their reservations about marriage because they assumed (correctly) that they would say yes in the moment.

15. Sassler and Miller, "Waiting to Be Asked"; Sassler and Miller, *Cohabitation Nation*.

16. Goffman, *Presentation of Self*, 112, 128.

17. Schweingruber, Anahita, and Berns, "'Popping the Question,'" 158.

18. See Davis, "Contesting Intersex," for further information about differences of sex development.

19. In the survey, I asked participants to locate themselves and their partners on a scale from one to ten, with one being a person whose physical attributes are "very feminine" and ten being a person whose physical attributes are "very masculine." The survey wording and scale was developed by Moore in *Invisible Families*. I analyzed gender presentation differences between partners in two ways. First, I used a simple binary measure of whether one partner was on the masculine end (six or above) and the other on the feminine end (four or below) of the spectrum. Second, I used a linear measure calculating the point difference between partners—i.e., the distance between where partners were on the spectrum. For example, both partners could be on the feminine end of the spectrum, but one could identify as a one and the other a four, representing a three-point difference. By contrast, one partner could situate themselves on the feminine end (four) and the other the masculine end (six) of the spectrum, representing just a two-point difference between them. Neither measure of gender presentation was significantly correlated with which partner proposed ($p > 0.05$).

20. Swidler, "Culture in Action," 277, 284.
21. Green, "Queer Unions," 428–29.
22. Sassler and Miller, "Waiting to Be Asked."
23. Blumstein and Schwartz, *American Couples*; Carrington, *No Place Like Home*; Kurdek, "Developmental Changes"; Lamont, "'Write the Scripts Ourselves'"; Lamont, *Mating Game*; Shechory and Ziv, "Perception of Equity."
24. Cherlin, "Degrees of Change," 72.

Chapter Five

1. Scott, *Institutions and Organizations*, 4th ed. See also the introduction for more information on the three institutional pillars that shape individual behavior.
2. Lamidi, Manning, and Brown, "First Premarital Cohabitation"; see also Sassler and Lichter, "Cohabitation and Marriage."
3. To be clear, married and unmarried LGBQ relationships in this study were not *completely* different from one another. There was no evidence that being married had any significant impact on how much time couples spent together, how often they socialized with friends, how much sex they had, or how they expressed affection, for example.
4. Marital status was a statistically significant predictor of the odds of seriously considering ending relationships ($p = 0.002$).
5. Marital status remained the only statistically significant factor when all these other variables were included.
6. Heimdal and Houseknecht, "Income Organization"; Kenney, "Cohabiting Couple, Filing Jointly?"; Pahl, "Family Finances"; Vogler, "Cohabiting Couples."
7. Lauer and Yodanis, "Individualized Marriage," 675.
8. They tended to say that they either had both joint savings and checking accounts or no joint accounts, with fewer adopting partial pooling and having only a joint checking *or* joint savings account.
9. Sixty-two percent of participants in this study owned their own place of residence. Income and age were the main determinants of whether or not an individual owned their own place of residence, but these figures also varied significantly by marital status, with 77 percent of married individuals owning their own place of residence, compared to just 39 percent of unmarried individuals.
10. Marital status was a statistically significant predictor of the likelihood of sharing joint accounts ($p = 0.004$) and owning property together ($p = 0.005$). It is possible that the greater proportion of financial pooling in married relationships results from self-selection, whereby those people most likely to merge finances are also those especially likely to get married. Others have found that although heterosexual cohabiting couples are less likely to pool their finances than married couples, those with the intention to get married are more likely to do so than couples without any intention to get married; Blumstein and Schwartz, *American Couples*; Lyngstad, Noack, and Tufte, "Pooling of Economic Resources." However, my data offers little support for this kind of selection effect for same-sex couples. Unmarried participants who said that they were "very likely" to get married were no more likely to have joint accounts or property in both names than unmarried couples who said that they were not very likely to get married. Marital intentions did not shape financial practices in the same way as actually being married. Instead, there is something transformative about the experience of marriage itself.

NOTES TO PAGES 142–147

11. Cherlin, "Deinstitutionalization of American Marriage"; Coontz, *Marriage, a History*.

12. Cohen, "Liberalization of Divorce Attitudes."

13. Cherlin, "Deinstitutionalization of American Marriage," 854.

14. Cherlin, "Deinstitutionalization of American Marriage," 855.

15. Swidler, *Talk of Love*, 156.

16. The limited data we have available suggests that same-sex and heterosexual couples divorce at similar rates; Rosenfeld, "Couple Longevity."

17. Coontz, *Marriage, a History*; Zelizer, "Social Meaning of Money."

18. Blumstein and Schwartz, *American Couples*, 96–98.

19. Amato et al., *Alone Together*; Beck and Beck-Gernsheim, *Individualization*; Giddens, *Transformation of Intimacy*.

20. Pepin, "Beliefs about Money."

21. Scott, *Institutions and Organizations*, 4th ed.

22. When no-fault divorce was first introduced in California in 1970, there was a surge in the divorce rate, leading some to argue that if you make divorce easier, more people will do it. However, family scholars have since shown that although making divorce easier led to a temporary surge it had little long-term impact. The initial surge had more to do with the fact that marriage was still fairly mandatory as a social norm, and divorce was freshly tolerated. The surge was the result of a previous generation of couples who had felt obligated to marry, and been in unhappy marriages, now divorcing. But now that marriage is more voluntary, the availability of no-fault divorce has little impact on the likelihood of divorce. See Phillip Cohen's analysis of data in Baer, "Divorce Rate."

23. Evan is one of the few participants who did not fit into the Embracer, Rejecter, or Assumer groups and is therefore categorized instead as an In-Betweener.

24. Blumstein and Schwartz, *American Couples*; Brines and Joyner, "Ties That Bind"; Vogler, "Cohabiting Couples"; Winkler, "Economic Decision-Making."

25. Although in some ways there is a "marriage penalty" in the US tax code many couples, especially those in which one spouse earns significantly more than the other, end up saving money by filing taxes jointly; Bradley, "Tax and Inequality." Badgett found that in Massachusetts, 66 percent of gay and lesbian couples would have saved an average of $2,325 if they had been allowed to file their taxes jointly. About 11 percent would have seen no change, and about 23 percent would have had to pay an average of $502 more; Badgett, "Economic Value of Marriage."

26. The Supreme Court decision that ultimately overturned the Defense of Marriage Act (DOMA) was based on the inequality of estate taxes. Under federal tax law, a spouse who dies can leave their assets, including the family home, to the other spouse without incurring estate taxes. Edie Windsor and Thea Spyer lived together as a couple in New York City for forty-four years and married in Canada in 2007. Thea passed away two years later from multiple sclerosis. Windsor was forced to pay $363,053 in estate tax, which she would not have had to pay if she had been Spyer's husband or if their same-sex marriage had been recognized by the federal government. On June 26, 2013, the Supreme Court argued that the Defense of Marriage Act violated the Equal Protection principles of the US Constitution and ruled that section three of DOMA was unconstitutional. I was just finishing up data collection for this study when this occurred, but the people who took part had no access to federal level rights and protections.

27. Because most couples do not earn the same salaries over their careers, when a married American retires the Social Security Administration allows them to either receive their own benefits based on their years of earnings or receive one half of their spouse's monthly

benefit—whichever is higher. If the breadwinner of a couple dies, the surviving spouse is entitled to receive their spouse's more generous benefits instead of their own. However, until the Defense of Marriage Act was overturned in 2013 this did not apply to same-sex marriage. Bennett and Gates calculate that the lack of survivor benefits cost elderly same-sex widows and widowers an average of $5,528 a year; Bennett and Gates, "Cost of Marriage Inequality."

28. When employees enroll their families in their employer's health insurance plan, the federal government does not tax employee health benefits. However, as the federal government did not recognize same-sex marriage, it did not recognize same-sex spouses as "family." Badgett estimates that the average LGBTQ+ individual receiving benefits for their spouse was taxed $1,069 in additional federal income and payroll taxes because their state-level marriages were not recognized by the federal government; Badgett, "Unequal Taxes."

29. Swidler, *Talk of Love*, 123–24.

30. Art is one of the few participants who did not fit into the Embracer, Rejecter, or Assumer groups and is therefore categorized instead as an In-Betweener.

31. To be clear, Marriage Assumers often had one joint account out of which to pay for house expenses, but they kept the rest of their earnings and assets separate. They also more casually helped one another financially when their partners needed assistance, but did not conceptualize their assets as shared.

32. Relationship duration was a statistically significant predictor of having joint account ($p = 0.045$) and owning joint property ($p = 0.004$).

33. This occurred prior to moving to Massachusetts, and was a large impetus for their decision to move there, where they would be able to be on one another's health insurance benefits as unmarried partners.

34. Relationship duration is no longer a statistically significant predictor of financial pooling once marital status is included in the model.

35. Blumstein and Schwartz, *American Couples*, 105.

36. Blumstein and Schwartz, *American Couples*, 109.

Chapter Six

1. Haas and Lannutti, "Influence of Marriage"; Green, Valleriani, and Adam, "Marital Monogamy."

2. Coverture legally enshrined monogamy mostly for the wife. Men were always much freer to engage in outside sexual relationships because they had rights that women did not have; Coontz, *Marriage, a History*, 186–87.

3. Barker and Landridge, "Whatever Happened to Non-monogamies?," 750; Pieper and Bauer, "Call for Papers." We are beginning to see some signs of change. Mainstream news outlets are increasingly covering nonmonogamous relationships in a positive light, and celebrities have begun to openly discuss their nonmonogamous marriages (Dominus, "Open Marriage"; Essence, "Will Smith Gets Real"; Khazan, "Multiple Lovers"; Solomon, "Challenging Family Norms"; Fitzpatrick, "'Ethical Slut'"). Nonetheless, monogamy remains the normative and assumed relationship form in the vast majority of cultural depictions of coupledom.

4. Cherlin, "Deinstitutionalization of American Marriage"; Cherlin, "Degrees of Change."

5. Lauer and Yodanis, "Deinstitutionalization of Marriage Revisited."

6. Levine et al., "Open Relationships."

7. Vangelisti and Gernstenberger, "Communication and Marital Infidelity"; see also Duncombe et al., *State of Affairs*.

8. Researchers have consistently found higher rates of nonmonogamy among same-sex couples; Adam, "Relationship Innovation"; Blumstein and Schwartz, *American Couples*; Haupert et al., "Prevalence of Experiences"; Levine et al., "Open Relationships." But some data suggest that the HIV/AIDS epidemic had an impact on increasing monogamy in male same-sex relationships as a protective health measure; Perry et al., "Decision-Making Power." However, as Adam found in his interviews with gay men in the early 2000s, although a decline in nonmonogamy among gay men might be a result of increasing HIV concerns, generational shifts in the focus of gay activism from liberation to marriage rights may also play a role: with the rise of marital equality, so too came the rise of heteronormative and mononormative marital scripts; Adam, "Relationship Innovation."

9. Normative masculinity ideals likely play a large role here. Despite hegemonic cultural assumptions that gay men are "less than real men," masculinity ideals, such as competition and sexual prowess, have long been idealized as a basis for sexual attraction in the gay male and bisexual communities; Haas and Lannutti, "Influence of Marriage," 166.

10. See Klesse, "Polyamory and Its 'Others' "; Munson and Stelboum, "Lesbian Polyamory Reader."

11. See Mint, "Power Mechanisms of Jealousy"; Munson and Stelboum, "Lesbian Polyamory Reader"; Ringer, "Constituting Nonmonogamies." However, other authors have questioned the feminist, queer, and liberatory claims that have been made about nonmonogamies, often pointing out the largely apolitical motivations given by people involved in such relationships themselves; Wilkinson, "What's Queer."

12. Foucault, *History of Sexuality*; Giddens, *Transformation of Intimacy*.

13. Hoffarth and Jost, "When Ideology Contradicts Self-Interest"; Pinsof and Haselton, "Political Divide over Same-Sex Marriage." Importantly, Hoffarth and Jost show that stereotypes associating promiscuity with homosexuality are relevant for understanding opposition to same-sex marriage among sexual minorities as well as heterosexuals. Political conservatism is associated (a) with implicit and explicit endorsement of the stereotype that gay people are more promiscuous than heterosexuals and (b) with opposition to same-sex marriage.

14. Bernstein and Taylor, *Marrying Kind?*; Duggan, "New Homonormativity."

15. Adam, "Relationship Innovation."

16. Sheff, *Polyamorists Next Door*.

17. Carlson et al., "Gendered Division."

18. Dan Savage, a popular gay columnist, coined the term "monogamish" in 2011; Savage, "Monogamish." Since then it has become part of popular vernacular in the LGBTQ+ community and has been used in a variety of ways. Savage used it broadly to describe those married or partnered couples who were not actively seeking outside partners, who were "perceived to be [a] monogamous couple," but who had an understanding about when outside sexual contact was permissible. However, given that much research now suggests this is also how many nonmonogamous individuals would define their relationships, such a broad conceptualization of monogamish has lost conceptual clarity. Other LGBTQ+ individuals use the term to describe something more specific, more in line with the phenomenon I outline, as do other sexualities scholars; Haas and Lannutti, "Influence of Marriage," 165.

19. Haas and Lannutti examined nonrepresentative survey data across the fifty states and also found that married and unmarried same-sex couples were nonmonogamous at similar rates

(72 percent were monogamous; 27 percent nonmonogamous); Haas and Lannutti, "Influence of Marriage."

20. The vast majority (87 percent) said no, while 10 percent said yes, and an additional 3 percent said maybe.

21. Polling data does not ask about a question about nonmonogamy, and so it is difficult to know how the average American feels about it, or if they even know what it is. Gallup polling data on "polygamy" shows a rapid increase in the "moral acceptability" of polygamy from 7 percent in 2003 to 20 percent in 2020, but with 80 percent of Americans still opposed to it; Gallup, "Marriage." Polling data also includes a question on "infidelity," and here Americans are staunchly morally opposed, with only 6 percent of Americans saying that it is "morally acceptable" for married men and women to "have an affair."

22. Green, Valleriani, and Adam, "Marital Monogamy" define the difference between normative and reflexive views of marital monogamy. In this study of Canadian couples, Green et al. found that almost all same-sex couples hold a reflexive view of marital arrangements, and only about half of heterosexuals tend to continue to hold a normative view, 426–27.

23. The "disagree" category includes "strongly disagree and disagree," as does the agree category.

24. Although not about sex in marriage, Lamont finds that young LGBTQ individuals are less judgmental than their heterosexual counterparts when it comes to sex and express less "stigma" around casual sex; Lamont, *Mating Game*, 125–30.

25. Deploying rhetoric about what is "natural" or "innate" has become increasingly common for the LGBTQ+ community. "Born this way" rhetoric became a rallying cry for many LGBTQ+ people and a succinct slogan for the political logic behind mainstream US-based gay and lesbian equality activism in the late 2000s. Here we see Marriage Rejecters utilizing the same kind of essentialist rhetoric that is typically deployed to describe sexual identity to discuss same-sex sexual behaviors. Rejecting dominant ideas about what is "natural" and "normal" does not necessarily entail rejecting dominant forms of essentialist thinking about sexuality. Rejecters still fundamentally convey an understanding of sexual behavior as having some kind of "natural" basis to it (nonmonogamy), just not the one typically promoted by heteronormative society (monogamy). As Schilt points out, however, such understandings stand in contrast to much sociological theorizing that situates sexual identity categories—and here I would add sexual behaviors—as social constructs that emerge and shift across particular political, historical, and geographical contexts. See Schilt, "Born This Way," 1–2.

26. This was similar to the way that many women described not being willing to let their fathers "give them away" when they got married. They did not experience it as a big decision or issue; rather they simply adapted the wedding to suit their own interpretation of what marriage was.

27. The Common Book of Prayer asks spouses to "forsake all others," "live in fidelity," and be "faithful so long as you both shall live" (http://justus.anglican.org/resources/bcp/marriage.pdf).

28. Existing research on sexual fluidity has almost exclusively examined changes to sexual attractions, orientations, and identity; Budnick, "'Straight Girls Kissing'?"; Diamond, *Sexual Fluidity*; Everett, "Sexual Orientation Identity Change"; Katz-Wise, "Sexual Fluidity"; Mittleman, "Sexual Fluidity"; Ott et al., "Repeated Changes." Here, however, I am utilizing the concept of sexual fluidity to think about shifting sexual desires and behaviors in the context of committed relationships rather than within individuals. We know that sexual desires and behaviors change significantly over the life course, but this does not adequately capture the kind of flexibility and openness we see in same-sex relationships with regard to nonmonogamy practices;

see Carpenter and DeLamater, *Sex for Life*. It is not only that desires and behaviors change, it is that same-sex couples expected them to.

29. Green et al., "Marital Monogamy," 424.

30. Social desirability bias likely plays a role here. This is the phenomenon in which respondents seek to give socially appropriate answers to questions, even if this involves distorting the truth. The LGBQ individuals in this study may have wanted to withhold stronger normative expressions of disapproval regarding nonmonogamy, knowing that it is at odds with queer norms that demand respect for sexual freedom in the LGBTQ+ community. For more about the effects of social desirability bias in research, see Pager and Quillian, "Walking the Talk?," and Phillips and Clancy, "'Social Desirability.'"

31. LGBQ individuals appear between a rock and a hard place on the topic of nonmonogamy. If they express strong normative opposition to nonmonogamy they risk countering norms from within the LGBTQ+ community regarding support for sexual freedom and diversity. At the same time, if they express too open support for nonmonogamy to heterosexuals they risk countering heteronormative norms for marital monogamy and the broader movement for marital equality and the politics of respectability.

32. Only 6 percent said that they argued with their partners about "sex outside the relationship" regularly (once every few months or more). Another 79 percent said they never argued about it and 14 percent argued about it rarely (once a year or less). Unfortunately, I have no way of telling whether those who were nonmonogamous argued about it more than those who were not. However, gender was highly significant ($p = 0.000$). Because men in this study were much more likely to be nonmonogamous, this might suggest that those who are nonmonogamous argue more than those who are monogamous, for whom it's just not an issue at all most of the time. Forty-one percent of men said that they ever argued about sex outside the relationship, compared to just 5 percent of women. Though only 12 percent of men said that they argued about it regularly (2 percent of women did).

33. The social science evidence on the quality of nonmonogamous relationships is somewhat mixed. For years, research studies found no significant difference in relationship quality and satisfaction between same-sex couples who were monogamous and those were nonmonogamous; see Blumstein and Schwartz, *American Couples*; Kurdek and Schmitt, "Relationship Quality"; Whitton, Weitbrecht, and Kuryluk, "Monogamy Agreements." But Haas and Lannutti found significant differences in relationship quality by monogamy status; Haas and Lannutti, "Influence of Marriage." It is possible that the quality of nonmonogamous relationships has declined. If Marriage Assumers do not have as many successful nonmonogamous role models available to them, this might help explain why they expressed greater judgment against their nonmonogamous LGBQ peers than older Marriage Embracer and Rejecters did. It is also possible that the availability of legal marriage has shifted normative beliefs about how same-sex relationships should be done, increasing prejudice against nonmonogamy.

34. Meyer and Dean, "Internalized Homophobia," 161.

35. Austin is one of the few participants who did not fit into the Embracer, Rejecter, or Assumer groups and is therefore categorized instead as an In-Betweener.

36. As a minority stressor, internalized homophobia has been linked to several negative outcomes in romantic relationships, but none specifically associated with nonmonogamy. Some research connects internalized homophobia to an avoidance of sexual intimacy, as those who feel uncomfortable with their same-sex attractions avoid sexual intimacy; see Herek and Glunt, "AIDS, Identity, and Community"; Meyer, "Minority Stress and Mental Health"; Meyer and

Dean, "Internalized Homophobia." Yet those who avoid sexual intimacy would be unlikely to maintain nonmonogamous relationships. A growing body of research also implicates internalized homophobia as a factor contributing to HIV-related sexual risk behavior in gay and bisexual men; see review in Huebner et al., "Impact of Internalized Homophobia." However, there is no reason to assume nonmonogamous relationships are sexually risky, especially as we know a lot of boundary work is undertaken by nonmonogamous couples. See Barker and Landridge, *Understanding Non-monongamies*, for a review. Nevertheless, mainstream popular conceptions of internalized homophobia do connect it to broader relationship issues, including "struggling with having healthy, long-term committed relationships" or "allowing oneself to consistently be in inequitable, dysfunctional, neglectful, unstable, unfaithful, and/or abusive relationships"; Ni 2020. It therefore makes sense that some LGBTQ+ individuals would regard nonmonogamous relationships as a sign that someone might be struggling with self-esteem or relationship problems. However, when individuals cannot imagine that others would choose to maintain nonmonogamous relationships if they were *not* suffering from internalized homophobia, this upholds heteronormative ideas about the inherent superiority of monogamous relationships.

37. Older research offered limited evidence of a kind of selection effect into (nonlegal) marriage, with only monogamous individuals being willing to take that step. Solomon, Rothblum, and Balsam found that gay men who entered into civil unions in Vermont were more likely to have agreed with their partners not to have sexual partners outside the relationship than were gay men who were not in civil unions; Solomon, Rothblum, and Balsam, "Money, Housework, Sex." This might point to some change over time, or something specific to civil unions versus legal marriage.

38. Gerstel and Sarkisian, "Marriage"; Ocobock, "Status or Access?"

39. Rauch, *Gay Marriage*, 151.

40. Jonathan Rauch, a gay conservative proponent of same-sex marriage, predicted that it was "far-fetched" to assume that married LGBQ people would flaunt their nonmonogamy: "Gay male spouses will value respectability. They will have parents and in-laws and other family members whom they will not want to disappoint. Candid discussions of sexual exclusivity will be for intimate friends, most of them gay"; Rauch, *Gay Marriage*, 152. But respectability is more than just a private concern. In mass democracies, marginalized communities must typically find ways to appeal to majority opinion to secure their rights; Jones, "Respectability Politics." One common strategy is respectability politics, whereby groups portray themselves as adhering to mainstream norms of "proper" behavior. This has been the strategy adopted by the LGBTQ+ movement over the past several decades; see Beam, "What's Love Got to Do with It?"; Moscowitz, *Battle over Marriage*. Respectability politics for the LGBTQ+ movement has been particularly focused on relationship norms of monogamy, casting "other forms of gay identity (*not* being part of a monogamous, married, child-rearing couple) to the margins"; Moscowitz, *Battle over Marriage*, 133, emphasis in original. However, as other scholars have pointed out, respectability politics is the hallmark of members of marginalized groups who are socially privileged, and this kind of marital experience may therefore only reflect this book's sampling of middle- and upper-middle class and predominantly White individuals; Dazey, "Rethinking Respectability Politics."

41. Nick is one of the few participants who did not fit into the Embracer, Rejecter, or Assumer groups and is therefore categorized instead as an In-Betweener.

42. Phelan, *Sexual Strangers*, 11–12, 31.

43. Cherlin, "Deinstitutionalization of American Marriage"; Lauer and Yodanis, "Deinstitutionalization of Marriage Revisited."

44. In their Canadian study, Green, Valleriani, and Adam, concluded that where we see the most change to marriage is in "abstract ideals about marital monogamy" rather than any "concrete shift in orientations toward monogamy as these apply to one's own marital relationship." They found that LGBQ individuals increasingly respected diverse sexual practices among *other people* but had not increased the practice of nonmonogamy for their own marriages; Green, Valleriani, and Adam "Marital Monogamy," (426–27). By contrast, the data from this study suggests that shifts in orientation toward monogamy *do* apply to one's own marital relationship, if one looks beyond current monogamous status.

45. Although marriage rights are now legal nationwide, these rights are currently far from secure. In *Dobbs v. Jackson Women's Health Organization*, the Supreme Court's Mississippi abortion decision that overturned *Roe v. Wade*, Justice Thomas urged the court to overturn its rulings establishing the right of same-sex couples to marry. If the Supreme Court overturns *Obergefell v. Hodges*, states would be free to refuse to issue marriage licenses to same-sex couples once again. Without Obergefell, the data suggests that most states would have same-sex marriage bans; Povich, "Without Obergefell."

Conclusion

1. Scott, *Institutions and Organizations*, 4th ed. See the introduction to this book for a fuller description.
2. Cherlin, "Deinstitutionalization of American Marriage."
3. Swidler, *Talk of Love*, 37.
4. Cherlin, "Incomplete Institution"; Hequembourg, "Unscripted Motherhood."
5. Swidler, "Culture in Action."
6. Cherlin predicts that younger people may not marry in such large numbers; Cherlin, "Degrees of Change," 75.
7. Jones, "LGBT Identification."
8. Masterpiece Cakeshop v. Colorado Civil Rights Commission, 584 U.S. (2018).
9. The Respect for Marriage Act (RFMA; H.R. 8404)

Methods Appendix

1. Weiss, *Learning from Strangers*.
2. It was not until 2008 when another state, Connecticut, made same-sex marriage legal. Over the next few years, Iowa (2009), New Hampshire (2009), the District of Columbia (2009), and New York (2011) also made same-sex marriages legal. In 2012, voters in Maine, Maryland, and Washington state approved laws legalizing same-sex marriage, becoming the first states to do so through popular votes. For a more detailed history of the historical timeline of marriage equality see Freedom to Marry, "Winning the Freedom"; Pew Research Center, "Same-Sex Marriage."
3. Marriage equality activists faced off against a constitutional amendment banning same-sex marriage in 2007, which would have repealed the freedom to marry had voters supported it.
4. Ocobock, "Power and Limits of Marriage."
5. Small, "'How Many Cases,'" 25.
6. Moore, *Invisible Families*.
7. United States v. Windsor, 570 U.S. 744 (2013).

8. Obergefell v. Hodges, 576 U.S. 644 (2015).

9. Until recently, it was difficult to gain accurate data on how many same-sex couples in the United States had legally married. The US Census Bureau's 2013 American Community Survey (ACS) marked the first time that a large national demographic survey explicitly identified both married and unmarried same-sex couples, allowing for separate analyses of these two groups. Prior to its release, the US Census Bureau reported married same-sex couples as "unmarried partners"; O'Connell and Feliz, "Household Statistics"; Williams Institute, "Census Snapshot." We know that, as of 2021, there were about 1.2 million same-sex couple households and about 710,000 of them—nearly 60 percent—were married; United States Census Bureau, "American Community Survey." Survey data has also provided information about how married same-sex couples compare to their unmarried same-sex and different-sex counterparts; Badgett and Herman, "Patterns of Relationship Recognition"; Gates "Demographics." We know that female same-sex couples are more likely than male couples to get legally married. Compared to their unmarried counterparts, married same-sex couples have a higher household median income, are more likely to own homes, and are more likely to have children.

10. These national comparisons all come from The Williams Institute, "LGBT Demographic Data Interactive."

11. Gates, "Demographics"; Moore, *Invisible Families*.

12. Cherlin, *Labor's Love Lost*; Furstenberg, "Fifty Years of Family Change," 17–18.

13. Gibson-Davis, Edin, and McLanahan, "High Hopes," 1310; Schoen and Cheng, "Partner Choice."

14. Edin, Kefalas, and Reed, "Peek inside the Black Box"; Edin and Kefalas, *Promises I Can Keep*.

15. Jones, "LGBT Identification."

16. Also see Small, "'How Many Cases.'"

17. Small, "Mixed Methods Study."

18. Ocobock, "Power and Limits of Marriage"; "From Public Debate to Private Decision"; "Status or Access?"; "Leveraging Legitimacy."

19. Strauss and Corbin, *Basics of Qualitative Research*.

20. Burawoy, "Extended Case Method."

References

Adam, Barry D. "Relationship Innovation in Male Couples." *Sexualities* 9, no. 1 (2006): 5–26. https://doi.org/10.1177/1363460706060685.

Amato, Paul R. "Institutional, Companionate, and Individualistic Marriage: A Social Psychological Perspective on Marital Change." In *Marriage at the Crossroads: Law, Policy, and the Brave New World of Twenty-First-Century Families*, edited by Marsha Garrison and Elizabeth S. Scott, 75–90. Cambridge University Press, 2012. https://doi.org/10.7312/pete14408-007.

———. "Tension between Institutional and Individual Views of Marriage." *Journal of Marriage and Family* 66, no. 4 (2004): 959–65.

Amato, Paul R., Alan Booth, David R. Johnson, and Stacy J. Rogers. *Alone Together: How Marriage in America Is Changing*. Cambridge, MA: Harvard University Press, 2007.

Aragão, Carolina, Kim Parker, Shannon Greenwood, Chris Baronavski, and John Carlo Mandapat. "The Modern American Family: Key Trends in Marriage and Family Life." Pew Research Center, September 14, 2023. https://www.pewresearch.org/social-trends/2023/09/14/the-modern-american-family/.

Axinn, William G., and Arland Thornton. "The Transformation in the Meaning of Marriage." In *The Ties That Bind: Perspectives on Marriage and Cohabitation*, edited by Linda J. Waite, 147–65. New York: Aldine de Gruyter, 2000.

Badgett, M. V. Lee. "The Economic Value of Marriage for Same-Sex Couples." *Drake Law Review* 58: 1081–1116.

———. "Unequal Taxes on Equal Benefits: The Taxation of Domestic Partner Benefits." Center for American Progress and the Williams Institute, December 2007. https://escholarship.org/uc/item/25c0n9rx.

Badgett, M. V. Lee, and Jody L. Herman. "Patterns of Relationship Recognition by Same-Sex Couples in the United States." UCLA School of Law: The Williams Institute, 2011. https://escholarship.org/uc/item/72h2n794.

Baer, Drake. "Let's Stop Treating the Divorce Rate Like the Crime Rate." *The Cut*. February 17, 2017. https://www.thecut.com/2017/02/is-it-good-for-the-divorce-rate-to-go-down.html.

———. "Maybe Monogamy Isn't the Only Way to Love." *The Cut*, March 6, 2017. https://www.thecut.com/2017/03/science-of-polyamory-open-relationships-and-nonmonogamy.html.

Balsam, Kimberly F., Theodore P. Beauchaine, Esther D. Rothblum, and Sondra E. Solomon. "Three-Year Follow-up of Same-Sex Couples Who Had Civil Unions in Vermont, Same-Sex Couples Not in Civil Unions, and Heterosexual Married Couples." *Developmental Psychology* 44, no. 1 (2008): 102–16. https://doi.org/10.1037/0012-1649.44.1.102.

Barclay, Scott, Mary Bernstein, and Anna-Maria Marshall. *Queer Mobilizations: LGBT Activists Confront the Law*. New York: New York University Press, 2009.

Barker, Meg, and Darren Langdridge. *Understanding Non-monogamies*. New York: Routledge, 2010.

———. "Whatever Happened to Non-monogamies? Critical Reflections on Recent Research and Theory." *Sexualities* 13, no. 6 (2010): 748–72. https://doi.org/10.1177/1363460710384645.

Barley, Stephen R., and Pamela S. Tolbert. "Institutionalization and Structuration: Studying the Links between Action and Institution." *Organization Studies* 18, no. 1 (1997): 93–117. https://doi.org/10.1177/017084069701800106.

Battilana, Julie, Bernard Leca, and Eva Boxenbaum. "How Actors Change Institutions: Towards a Theory of Institutional Entrepreneurship." *Academy of Management Annals* 3, no. 1 (2009): 65–107. https://doi.org/10.1080/19416520903053598.

Baumle, Amanda K., and D'Lane R. Compton. *Legalizing LGBT Families: How the Law Shapes Parenthood*. New York: New York University Press, 2017.

Bawer, Bruce. *A Place at the Table: The Gay Individual in American Society*. New York: Poseidon Press, 1993.

Beam, Myrl. "What's Love Got to Do with It? Queer Politics and the 'Love Pivot.'" In *Queer Activism after Marriage Equality*, edited by Joseph Nicholas DeFilippis, Michael W. Yarbrough, and Angela Jones. New York: Routledge, 2018.

Bechdel, Allison. "Dykes to Watch Out For: Get Me to the Clerk on Time." *Off Our Backs*, 2004.

Beck, Ulrich, and Elisabeth Beck-Gernsheim. *Individualization: Institutionalized Individualism and its Social and Political Consequences*. London: SAGE, 2001.

Bennett, Lisa, and Gary Gates. "The Cost of Marriage Inequality to Gay, Lesbian and Bisexual Seniors: A Human Rights Campaign Foundation Report." *Urban Institute*, January 21, 2004. https://www.urban.org/sites/default/files/publication/57881/410939-The-Cost-of-Marriage-Inequality-to-Gay-Lesbian-and-Bisexual-Seniors.PDF.

Berger, Peter L., and Thomas Luckmann. *The Social Construction of Reality: A Treatise in the Sociology of Knowledge*. New York: Open Road Media, 2011.

Bernstein, Mary. "Same-Sex Marriage and the Future of the LGBT Movement: SWS Presidential Address." *Gender and Society* 29, no. 3 (2015): 321–37. https://doi.org/10.1177/0891243215575287.

Bernstein, Mary, and Mary C. Burke. "Normalization, Queer Discourse, and the Marriage-Equality Movement in Vermont." In *The Marrying Kind? Debating Same-Sex Marriage within the Lesbian and Gay Movement*, edited by Mary Bernstein and Verta Taylor, 319–44. Minneapolis: University of Minnesota Press, 2013.

Bernstein, Mary, and Verta Taylor. *The Marrying Kind? Debating Same-Sex Marriage within the Lesbian and Gay Movement*. Minneapolis: University of Minnesota Press, 2013.

Bloome, Deirdre, and Shannon Ang. "Marriage and Union Formation in the United States: Recent Trends across Racial Groups and Economic Backgrounds." *Demography* 57, no. 5 (2020): 1753–86. https://doi.org/10.1007/s13524-020-00910-7.

Blumstein, Philip, and Pepper Schwartz. *American Couples: Money, Work, Sex*. New York: William Morrow & Co., 1983.

Bogle, R., and Hsueh-Sheng Wu. "Thirty Years of Change in Marriage and Union Formation Attitudes, 1976–2008." Family Profile FP-10-139. Bowling Green, OH: National Center for Family and Marriage Research, 2010. https://scholarworks.bgsu.edu/ncfmr_family_profiles/139/.

Bosley-Smith, Emma R., and Corinne Reczek. "Before and After 'I Do': Marriage Processes for Mid-Life Gay and Lesbian Married Couples." *Journal of Homosexuality* 65, no. 14 (2018): 1985–2004. https://doi.org/10.1080/00918369.2017.1423213.

Bradley, Stephanie L. "Tax and Inequality in the United States." *Sociology Compass* 12, no. 2 (2018): e12559. https://doi.org/10.1111/soc4.12559.

Brines, Julie, and Kara Joyner. "The Ties That Bind: Principles of Cohesion in Cohabitation and Marriage." *American Sociological Review* 64, no. 3 (1999): 333–55. https://doi.org/10.2307/2657490.

Brown, Susan L., and Sayaka Kawamura. "Relationship Quality among Cohabitors and Marrieds in Older Adulthood." *Social Science Research* special issue 39, no. 5 (2010): 777–86. https://doi.org/10.1016/j.ssresearch.2010.04.010.

Brown, Susan L., Wendy D. Manning, and Huijing Wu. "Relationship Quality in Midlife: A Comparison of Dating, Living Apart Together, Cohabitation, and Marriage." *Journal of Marriage and Family* 84, no. 3 (2022): 860–78. https://doi.org/10.1111/jomf.12813.

Budnick, Jamie. "'Straight Girls Kissing'? Understanding Same-Gender Sexuality beyond the Elite College Campus." *Gender & Society* 30, no. 5 (2016): 745–68. https://doi.org/10.1177/0891243216657511.

Bumpass, Larry, and Hsien-Hen Lu. "Trends in Cohabitation and Implications for Children's Family Contexts in the United States." *Population Studies* 54, no. 1 (2000): 29–41. https://doi.org/10.1080/713779060.

Burawoy, Michael. "The Extended Case Method." *Sociological Theory* 16, no. 1 (1998): 4–33.

Burgess, E. W., and H. J. Locke. *The Family: From Institution to Companionship*. Oxford: American Book Co., 1945.

Cancian, Francesca M. *Love in America: Gender and Self-Development*. Cambridge: Cambridge University Press, 1987.

Carlson, Daniel L., Amanda J. Miller, Sharon Sassler, and Sarah Hanson. "The Gendered Division of Housework and Couples' Sexual Relationships: A Reexamination." *Journal of Marriage and Family* 78, no. 4 (2016): 975–95. https://doi.org/10.1111/jomf.12313.

Carpenter, Christopher, and Gary J. Gates. "Gay and Lesbian Partnership: Evidence from California." *Demography* 45, no. 3 (2008): 573–90. https://doi.org/10.1353/dem.0.0014.

Carpenter, Laura, and John DeLamater. *Sex for Life: From Virginity to Viagra, How Sexuality Changes throughout Our Lives*. New York: New York University Press, 2012.

Carrington, Christopher. *No Place Like Home: Relationships and Family Life among Lesbians and Gay Men*. Worlds of Desire: The Chicago Series on Sexuality, Gender, and Culture. Chicago: University of Chicago Press, 1999.

Carroll, Laura. "The Intentionally Childless Marriage." In *Voluntary and Involuntary Childlessness: The Joys of Otherhood?*, edited by Natalie Sappleton, 217–35. Bingley, UK: Emerald, 2018. https://doi.org/10.1108/978-1-78754-361-420181010.

CBS News. "Same-Sex Couples Rush to the Altar." May 25, 2004. https://www.cbsnews.com/news/same-sex-couples-rush-to-the-altar/.

Cherlin, Andrew J. "Degrees of Change: An Assessment of the Deinstitutionalization of Marriage Thesis." *Journal of Marriage and Family* 82, no. 1 (2020): 62–80. https://doi.org/10.1111/jomf.12605.

———. "The Deinstitutionalization of American Marriage." *Journal of Marriage and Family* 66, no. 4 (2004): 848–61. https://doi.org/10.1111/j.0022-2445.2004.00058.x.

———. *Labor's Love Lost: The Rise and Fall of the Working-Class Family in America*. New York: Russell Sage Foundation, 2014.

———. *The Marriage-Go-Round: The State of Marriage and the Family in America Today*. New York: Knopf Doubleday, 2009.

———. "Remarriage as an Incomplete Institution." *American Journal of Sociology* 84, no. 3 (1978): 634–50. https://doi.org/10.1086/226830.

Clemens, Elisabeth S., and James M. Cook. "Politics and Institutionalism: Explaining Durability and Change." *Annual Review of Sociology* 25, no. 1 (1999): 441–66. https://doi.org/10.1146/annurev.soc.25.1.441.

Cohen, Philip N. "The Liberalization of Divorce Attitudes Proceeds Apace." *Family Inequality* (blog). October 12, 2016. https://familyinequality.wordpress.com/2016/10/12/the-liberalization-of-divorce-attitudes-proceeds-apace/.

Collins, Patricia Hill. "Learning from the Outsider Within: The Sociological Significance of Black Feminist Thought." *Social Problems* 33, no. 6 (1986): 14–32. https://doi.org/10.2307/800672.

Coontz, Stephanie. *Marriage, a History: From Obedience to Intimacy or How Love Conquered Marriage*. New York: Viking, 2005.

———. "The World Historical Transformation of Marriage." *Journal of Marriage and Family* 66, no. 4 (2004): 974–79. https://doi.org/10.1111/j.0022-2445.2004.00067.x.

Cooperman, Alan, and Jonathan Finer. "Gay Couples Marry in Massachusetts." *Washington Post*, May 18, 2004. https://www.washingtonpost.com/wp-dyn/articles/A34642-2004May17.html.

Davis, Georgiann. *Contesting Intersex: The Dubious Diagnosis*. New York: NYU Press, 2015.

Dawson, Lindsey, Matthew Rae, and Jennifer Kates. "Access to Employer-Sponsored Health Coverage for Same-Sex Spouses: 2020 Update." *KFF*, November 30, 2020. https://www.kff.org/private-insurance/issue-brief/access-to-employer-sponsored-health-coverage-for-same-sex-spouses-2020-update/.

Dazey, Margot. "Rethinking Respectability Politics." *British Journal of Sociology* 72, no. 3 (2021): 580–93. https://doi.org/10.1111/1468-4446.12810.

Dedman, Bill, and Christine MacDonald. "About 2,500 Gay Couples Sought Licenses in 1st Week." *Boston Globe*, June 17, 2004. http://www.boston.com/news/local/massachusetts/articles/2004/06/17/about_2500_gay_couples_sought_licenses_in_1st_week/.

Diamond, Lisa M. *Sexual Fluidity: Understanding Women's Love and Desire*. Cambridge, MA: Harvard University Press, 2008.

DiMaggio, Paul J. "Interest and Agency in Institutional Theory." In *Institutional Patterns and Organizations: Culture and Environment*, edited by Lynne G. Zucker, 3–22. Cambridge, MA: Ballinger, 1988.

DiMaggio, Paul J., and Walter W. Powell. "Introduction." In *The New Institutionalism in Organizational Analysis*, 1–38. Chicago: University of Chicago Press, 1991.

———. "The Iron Cage Revisited: Institutional Isomorphism and Collective Rationality in Organizational Fields." *American Sociological Review* 48, no. 2 (1983):147–60. https://doi.org/10.2307/2095101.

Dominus, Susan. "Is an Open Marriage a Happier Marriage?" *New York Times Magazine*, May 11, 2017. https://www.nytimes.com/2017/05/11/magazine/is-an-open-marriage-a-happier-marriage.html.

Duggan, Lisa. "The New Homonormativity: The Sexual Politics of Neoliberalism." In *Materializing Democracy: Toward a Revitalized Cultural Politics*, edited by Russ Castronovo, Dana D. Nelson, and Donald E. Pease, 175–94. New York: Duke University Press, 2002.

REFERENCES 245

Duncombe, Jean, Kaeren Harrison, Graham Allan, and Dennis Marsden. *The State of Affairs: Explorations in Infidelity and Commitment.* Milton: Taylor & Francis, 2004.

Edin, Kathryn, and Maria J. Kefalas. *Promises I Can Keep: Why Poor Women Put Motherhood before Marriage.* Berkeley: University of California Press, 2011.

Edin, Kathryn, Maria J. Kefalas, and Joanna M. Reed. "A Peek inside the Black Box: What Marriage Means for Poor Unmarried Parents." *Journal of Marriage and Family* 66, no. 4 (2004): 1007–14. https://doi.org/10.1111/j.0022-2445.2004.00072.x.

Epstein, Steven. "A Queer Encounter: Sociology and the Study of Sexuality." *Sociological Theory* 12, no. 2 (1994): 188–202. https://doi.org/10.2307/201864.

Essence. "Will Smith Gets Real about His Nonmonogamous Marriage to Jada Pinkett-Smith." September 27, 2021. https://www.essence.com/entertainment/will-smith-opens-up-nonmonogamous-jada-pinkett-smith/.

Everett, Bethany. "Sexual Orientation Identity Change and Depressive Symptoms: A Longitudinal Analysis." *Journal of Health and Social Behavior* 56, no. 1 (2015): 37–58. https://doi.org/10.1177/0022146514568349.

Family Equality. "LGBTQ Family Building Survey." 2019. https://www.familyequality.org/resources/lgbtq-family-building-survey/.

Fetner, Tina, and Melanie Heath. "Do Same-Sex and Straight Weddings Aspire to the Fairytale? Women's Conformity and Resistance to Traditional Weddings." *Sociological Perspectives* 59, no. 4 (2016): 721–42. https://doi.org/10.1177/0731121415601269.

Finkel, Eli J. *The All-or-Nothing Marriage: How the Best Marriages Work.* New York: Penguin, 2017.

Fitzpatrick, Anna. "'The Ethical Slut': Inside America's Growing Acceptance of Polyamory." *Rolling Stone*, September 16, 2017. https://www.rollingstone.com/culture/culture-features/the-ethical-slut-inside-americas-growing-acceptance-of-polyamory-112319/.

Fligstein, Neil. "Social Skill and Institutional Theory." *American Behavioral Scientist* 40 (1997): 397–405. https://doi.org/10.1177/000276429704000403.

Foucault, Michel. *The History of Sexuality: An Introduction.* 1981. Reprint, Harmondsworth: Penguin, 1990.

Freedom to Marry. "Winning the Freedom to Marry Nationwide: The Inside Story of a Transformative Campaign." Accessed April 29, 2023. http://www.freedomtomarry.org/pages/how-it-happened.

Fry, Richard. "A Record-High Share of 40-Year-Olds in the U.S. Have Never Been Married." Pew Research Center, June 28, 2003. https://www.pewresearch.org/short-reads/2023/06/28/a-record-high-share-of-40-year-olds-in-the-us-have-never-been-married/.

Furstenberg, Frank F. "Fifty Years of Family Change: From Consensus to Complexity." *The Annals of the American Academy of Political and Social Science* 654, no. 1 (2014): 12–30.

Gallup. "Marriage." *In Depth: Topics A to Z.* Gallup, Inc., 2003. https://news.gallup.com/poll/117328/Marriage.aspx.

Gamson, Joshua. "Must Identity Movements Self-Destruct? A Queer Dilemma." *Social Problems* 42, no. 3 (1995): 390–407. https://doi.org/10.2307/3096854.

Garud, Raghu, Sanjay Jain, and Arun Kumaraswamy. "Institutional Entrepreneurship in the Sponsorship of Common Technological Standards: The Case of Sun Microsystems and Java." *Academy of Management Journal* 45, no. 1 (2002): 196–214. https://doi.org/10.2307/3069292.

Gates, Gary J. "Demographics of Married and Unmarried Same-Sex Couples: Analyses of the 2013 American Community Survey." UCLA School of Law: The Williams Institute, 2015. https://escholarship.org/uc/item/3td6n3q0.

Gates, Gary J., M. V. Lee Badgett, and Deborah Ho. "Marriage, Registration and Dissolution by Same-Sex Couples in the US." UCLA School of Law: The Williams Institute, 2008. https://escholarship.org/uc/item/5tg8147x.

Geiger, A. W., and Gretchen Livingston. "8 Facts about Love and Marriage in America." Pew Research Center, February 13, 2019. https://www.pewresearch.org/fact-tank/2019/02/13/8-facts-about-love-and-marriage/.

Gerstel, Naomi, and Natalia Sarkisian. "Marriage: The Good, the Bad, and the Greedy." *Contexts* 5, no. 4 (2006): 16–21. https://doi.org/10.1525/ctx.2006.5.4.16.

Ghaziani, Amin, Verta Taylor, and Amy Stone. "Cycles of Sameness and Difference in LGBT Social Movements." *Annual Review of Sociology* 42, no. 1 (2016): 165–83. https://doi.org/10.1146/annurev-soc-073014-112352.

Gibson-Davis, Christina, Anna Gassman-Pines, and Rebecca Lehrman. "'His' and 'Hers': Meeting the Economic Bar to Marriage." *Demography* 55, no. 6 (2018): 2321–43. https://doi.org/10.1007/s13524-018-0726-z.

Gibson-Davis, Christina M., Kathryn Edin, and Sara McLanahan. "High Hopes but Even Higher Expectations: The Retreat from Marriage among Low-Income Couples." *Journal of Marriage and Family* 67, no. 5 (2005): 1301–12. https://doi.org/10.1111/j.1741-3737.2005.00218.x.

Giddens, Anthony. *The Transformation of Intimacy: Sexuality, Love, and Eroticism in Modern Societies*. Cambridge: Polity Press, 1992.

Ginsburg, G. P. "Rules, Scripts and Prototypes in Personal Relationships." In *Handbook of Personal Relationships: Theory, Research and Interventions*, edited by Steve Duck, 23–39. Oxford: Wiley, 1988.

GLAD. "Connors v. City of Boston." GLAD. Accessed October 25, 2023. https://www.glad.org/cases/connors-v-city-of-boston/.

Goddard, Cliff, and Anna Wierzbicka. "Cultural Scripts: What Are They and What Are They Good For?" *Intercultural Pragmatics* 1, no. 2 (2004): 153–66. https://doi.org/10.1515/iprg.2004.1.2.153.

Goffman, Erving. *The Presentation of Self in Everyday Life*. New York: Knopf Doubleday, 1959.

Goldberg, Shoshana K., and Kerith J. Conron. "How Many Same-Sex Couples in the US Are Raising Children?" UCLA School of Law: The Williams Institute, 2018. https://williamsinstitute.law.ucla.edu/publications/same-sex-parents-us/.

Goldstein, Joshua R., and Catherine T. Kenney. "Marriage Delayed or Marriage Forgone? New Cohort Forecasts of First Marriage for U.S. Women." *American Sociological Review* 66, no. 4 (2001): 506–19. https://doi.org/10.2307/3088920.

Green, Adam Isaiah. "Queer Unions: Same-Sex Spouses Marrying Tradition and Innovation." *Canadian Journal of Sociology* 35, no. 3 (2010): 399–436. https://doi.org/10.29173/cjs7435.

———. "Until Death Do Us Part? The Impact of Differential Access to Marriage on a Sample of Urban Men." *Sociological Perspectives* 49, no. 2 (2006): 163–89. https://doi.org/10.1525/sop.2006.49.2.163.

Green, Adam Isaiah, Jenna Valleriani, and Barry Adam. "Marital Monogamy as Ideal and Practice: The Detraditionalization Thesis in Contemporary Marriages." *Journal of Marriage and Family* 78, no. 2 (2016): 416–30. https://doi.org/10.1111/jomf.12275.

Greenwood, Royston, and C. R. Hinings. "Understanding Radical Organizational Change: Bringing Together the Old and the New Institutionalism." *Academy of Management Review* 21, no. 4 (1996): 1022–54. https://doi.org/10.5465/amr.1996.9704071862.

Greenwood, Royston, and Roy Suddaby. "Institutional Entrepreneurship in Mature Fields: The Big Five Accounting Firms." *Academy of Management Journal* 49, no. 1 (2006): 27–48. https://doi.org/10.5465/amj.2006.20785498.

Gross, Neil. "The Detraditionalization of Intimacy Reconsidered." *Sociological Theory* 23, no. 3 (2005): 286–311. https://doi.org/10.1111/j.0735-2751.2005.00255.x.

Guzzo, Karen Benjamin. "Trends in Cohabitation Outcomes: Compositional Changes and Engagement among Never-Married Young Adults." *Journal of Marriage and Family* 76, no. 4 (2014): 826–42. https://doi.org/10.1111/jomf.12123.

Haas, Stephen M., and Pamela J. Lannutti. "The Influence of Marriage and (Non)Monogamy Agreements on Relationship Quality in LGBT Relationships." In *The Social Science of Same-Sex Marriage: LGBT People and Their Relationships in the Era of Marriage Equality*, 163–78. Abingdon: Routledge, 2002.

Hamilton, Laura, and Elizabeth A. Armstrong. "Gendered Sexuality in Young Adulthood: Double Binds and Flawed Options." *Gender & Society* 23, no. 5 (2009): 589–616. https://doi.org/10.1177/0891243209345829.

Hardy, Janet W., and Dossie Easton. *The Ethical Slut: A Practical Guide to Polyamory, Open Relationships, and Other Freedoms in Sex and Love*. 3rd ed. New York: Ten Speed Press, 2017.

Haupert, M. L., Amanda N. Gesselman, Amy C. Moors, Helen E. Fisher, and Justin R. Garcia. "Prevalence of Experiences with Consensual Nonmonogamous Relationships: Findings from Two National Samples of Single Americans." *Journal of Sex & Marital Therapy* 43, no. 5 (2017): 424–40. https://doi.org/10.1080/0092623X.2016.1178675.

Heath, Melanie. *One Marriage under God: The Campaign to Promote Marriage in America*. New York: New York University Press, 2012.

Heimdal, Kristen R., and Sharon K. Houseknecht. "Cohabiting and Married Couples' Income Organization: Approaches in Sweden and the United States." *Journal of Marriage and Family* 65, no. 3 (212): 525–38. https://doi.org/10.1111/j.1741-3737.2003.00525.x.

Hequembourg, Amy. "Unscripted Motherhood: Lesbian Mothers Negotiating Incompletely Institutionalized Family Relationships." *Journal of Social and Personal Relationships* 21, no. 6 (2004): 739–62. https://doi.org/10.1177/0265407504047834.

Hemez, Paul, and Wendy D. Manning. "Thirty Years of Change in Women's Premarital Cohabitation Experience." Family Profile FP-17-05. Bowling Green, OH: National Center for Family and Marriage Research, 2017. https://www.bgsu.edu/ncfmr/resources/data/family-profiles/hemez-manning-30-yrs-change-women-premarital-cohab-fp-17-05.html.

Herek, Gregory, and Eric Glunt. "AIDS, Identity, and Community: The HIV Epidemic and Lesbians and Gay Men." In *AIDS, Identity, and Community: The HIV Epidemic and Lesbians and Gay Men*, edited by Beverly Greene and Gregory M. Herek, 55–84. Thousand Oaks, CA: SAGE, 1995.

Hoffarth, Mark R., and John T. Jost. "When Ideology Contradicts Self-Interest: Conservative Opposition to Same-Sex Marriage Among Sexual Minorities—A Commentary on Pinsof and Haselton (2016)." *Psychological Science* 28, no. 10 (2017): 1521–24. https://doi.org/10.1177/0956797617694866.

Horowitz, Juliana Menasce, Nikki Graf, and Gretchen Livingston. "Marriage and Cohabitation in the U.S." Pew Research Center, November 6, 2019. https://www.pewresearch.org/social-trends/2019/11/06/marriage-and-cohabitation-in-the-u-s/.

Hubbard, Jim. "AIDS Activist Video and the Evolution of the Archive." *Jim Hubbard* (blog), February 14, 2018. https://www.jimhubbardfilms.com/writing/aids-activist-video-and-the-evolution-of-the-archive.

Huebner, David M., Mary C. Davis, Carol J. Nemeroff, and Leona S. Aiken. "The Impact of Internalized Homophobia on HIV Preventive Interventions." *American Journal of Community Psychology* 30, no. 3 (2002): 327–48. https://doi.org/10.1023/A:1015325303002.

Hull, Kathleen. *Same-Sex Marriage: The Cultural Politics of Love and Law*. Cambridge: Cambridge University Press, 2006.

Ishizuka, Patrick. "The Economic Foundations of Cohabiting Couples' Union Transitions." *Demography* 55, no. 2 (2018): 535–57. https://doi.org/10.1007/s13524-018-0651-1.

Jamieson, Lynn. "Intimacy Transformed? A Critical Look at the 'Pure Relationship.'" *Sociology* 33, no. 3 (1999): 477–94.

Johannes, Laura, Charles Forelle, and Robert Tomsho. "Gay Couples Rush to Marry in Massachusetts." *Wall Street Journal*, May 18, 2004. https://www.wsj.com/articles/SB108484054026214117.

Jones, Jeffrey M. "Is Marriage Becoming Irrelevant?" Gallup, December 28, 2020. https://news.gallup.com/poll/316223/fewer-say-important-parents-married.aspx.

———. "LGBT Identification in U.S. Ticks Up to 7.1%." Gallup, February 17, 2022. https://news.gallup.com/poll/389792/lgbt-identification-ticks-up.aspx.

Jones, P. E. "Respectability Politics and Straight Support for LGB Rights." *Political Research Quarterly* 75, no. 4 (2022): 935–49. https://doi.org/10.1177/10659129211035834.

Kaczynski, Andrew. "Mitt Romney's Long Fight against Gay Marriage." *BuzzFeed News*, May 4, 2012. https://www.buzzfeednews.com/article/andrewkaczynski/mitt-romneys-crusade-against-gay-marriage.

Katz-Wise, Sabra L. "Sexual Fluidity in Young Adult Women and Men: Associations with Sexual Orientation and Sexual Identity Development." *Psychology & Sexuality* 6, no. 2 (2015): 189–208. https://doi.org/10.1080/19419899.2013.876445.

Kaufman, Gayle, and D'Lane Compton. "Attitudes toward LGBT Marriage and Legal Protections Post-Obergefell." *Sexuality Research and Social Policy* 18, no. 2 (2021): 321–30. https://doi.org/10.1007/s13178-020-00460-y.

Kefalas, Maria J., Frank F. Furstenberg, Patrick J. Carr, and Laura Napolitano. "'Marriage Is More Than Being Together': The Meaning of Marriage for Young Adults." *Journal of Family Issues* 32, no. 7 (2011): 845–75. https://doi.org/10.1177/0192513X10397277.

Kenney, Catherine. "Cohabiting Couple, Filing Jointly? Resource Pooling and U.S. Poverty Policies." *Family Relations* 53, no. 2 (2004): 237–47. https://doi.org/10.1111/j.0022-2445.2004.00014.x.

Khazan, Olga. "Multiple Lovers, without Jealousy." *Atlantic*, July 21, 2014. https://www.theatlantic.com/health/archive/2014/07/multiple-lovers-no-jealousy/374697/.

Kimport, Katrina. *Queering Marriage: Challenging Family Formation in the United States*. New Brunswick: Rutgers University Press, 2014.

Klesse, Christian. "Polyamory and Its 'Others': Contesting the Terms of Non-monogamy." *Sexualities* 9, no. 5 (2006): 565–83. https://doi.org/10.1177/1363460706069986.

Klinkenberg, Dean, and Suzanna Rose. "Dating Scripts of Gay Men and Lesbians." *Journal of Homosexuality* 26, no. 4 (1994): 23–35. https://doi.org/10.1300/J082v26n04_02.

Kuperberg, Arielle. "Premarital Cohabitation and Direct Marriage in the United States: 1956–2015." *Marriage & Family Review* 55, no. 5 (2019): 447–75. https://doi.org/10.1080/01494929.2018.1518820.

Kurdek, Lawrence A. "Developmental Changes in Relationship Quality in Gay and Lesbian Cohabiting Couples." *Developmental Psychology* 31, no. 1 (1995): 86–94. https://doi.org/10.1037/0012-1649.31.1.86.

Kurdek, Lawrence A., and J. Patrick Schmitt. "Relationship Quality of Gay Men in Closed or Open Relationships." *Journal of Homosexuality* 12, no. 2 (1986): 85–99. https://doi.org/10.1300/J082v12n02_06.

Lamidi, Esther O., Wendy D. Manning, and Susan L. Brown. "Change in the Stability of First Premarital Cohabitation among Women in the United States, 1983-2013." *Demography* 56, no. 2 (2019): 427–50. https://doi.org/10.1007/s13524-019-00765-7.

Lamidi, Esther. "Trends in Cohabitation: The Never Married and Previously Married, 1995–2014." Family Profile FP-15-86. Bowling Green, OH: National Center for Family and Marriage Research, 2015. https://scholarworks.bgsu.edu/ncfmr_family_profiles/86.

Lamont, Ellen. *The Mating Game: How Gender Still Shapes How We Date.* Oakland: University of California Press, 2020.

———. "Negotiating Courtship: Reconciling Egalitarian Ideals with Traditional Gender Norms." *Gender & Society* 28, no. 2 (2014): 189–211. https://doi.org/10.1177/0891243213503899.

———. " 'We Can Write the Scripts Ourselves': Queer Challenges to Heteronormative Courtship Practices." *Gender & Society* 31, no. 5 (2017): 624–46. https://doi.org/10.1177/0891243217723883.

Lannutti, Pamela J. "The Influence of Same-Sex Marriage on the Understanding of Same-Sex Relationships." *Journal of Homosexuality* 53, no. 3 (2007): 135–51. https://doi.org/10.1300/J082v53n03_08.

Lareau, Annette, and Aliya Hamid Rao. "It's about the Depth of Your Data." *Contexts* (blog), March 19, 2016. https://contexts.org/blog/its-about-the-depth-of-your-data/.

Lauer, Sean R., and Carrie Yodanis. "Individualized Marriage and the Integration of Resources." *Journal of Marriage and Family* 73, no. 3 (2011): 669–83.

Lauer, Sean, and Carrie Yodanis. "The Deinstitutionalization of Marriage Revisited: A New Institutional Approach to Marriage." *Journal of Family Theory & Review* 1, no. 2 (2010): 58–72. https://doi.org/10.1111/j.1756-2589.2010.00039.x.

Leal, Daniela, Jorge Gato, Susana Coimbra, Daniela Freitas, and Fiona Tasker. "Social Support in the Transition to Parenthood among Lesbian, Gay, and Bisexual Persons: A Systematic Review." *Sexuality Research and Social Policy* 18, no 4 (2021): 1165–79. https://doi.org/10.1007/s13178-020-00517-y.

Levine, Ethan Czuy, Debby Herbenick, Omar Martinez, Tsung-Chieh Fu, and Brian Dodge. "Open Relationships, Nonconsensual Nonmonogamy, and Monogamy among U.S. Adults: Findings from the 2012 National Survey of Sexual Health and Behavior." *Archives of Sexual Behavior* 47, no. 5 (2018): 1439–50. https://doi.org/10.1007/s10508-018-1178-7.

Lewin, Ellen. *Recognizing Ourselves: Ceremonies of Lesbian and Gay Commitment.* New York: Columbia University Press, 1998.

Lichter, Daniel T., Christie D. Batson, and J. Brian Brown. "Welfare Reform and Marriage Promotion: The Marital Expectations and Desires of Single and Cohabiting Mothers." *Social Service Review* 78, no. 1 (2004): 2–25. https://doi.org/10.1086/380652.

Lichter, Daniel T., Katherine Michelmore, Richard N. Turner, and Sharon Sassler. "Pathways to a Stable Union? Pregnancy and Childbearing among Cohabiting and Married Couples." *Population Research and Policy Review* 35, no. 3 (2016): 377–99. https://doi.org/10.1007/s11113-016-9392-2.

Lichter, Daniel T., Richard N. Turner, and Sharon Sassler. "National Estimates of the Rise in Serial Cohabitation." *Social Science Research* special issue 39, no. 5 (2010): 754–65. https://doi.org/10.1016/j.ssresearch.2009.11.002.

Liu, Hui, Corinne Reczek, and Lindsey Wilkinson. "Introduction. The Health and Well-Being of Sexual Minority Couples." In *Marriage and Health: The Well-Being of Same-Sex Couples*, 1–10. New Brunswick, NJ: Rutgers University Press, 2020.

Liu, Hui, and Debra J. Umberson. "'The Times They Are a Changin': Marital Status and Health Differentials from 1972 to 2003." *Journal of Health and Social Behavior* 49, no. 3 (2008): 239–53. https://doi.org/10.1177/002214650804900301.

Lundberg, Shelly, Robert A. Pollak, and Jenna Stearns. "Family Inequality: Diverging Patterns in Marriage, Cohabitation, and Childbearing." *Journal of Economic Perspectives* 30, no. 2 (2016): 79–102. https://doi.org/10.1257/jep.30.2.79.

Lyngstad, Torkild Hovde, Turid Noack, and Per Arne Tufte. "Pooling of Economic Resources: A Comparison of Norwegian Married and Cohabiting Couples." *European Sociological Review* 27, no. 5 (2011): 624–35. https://doi.org/10.1093/esr/jcq028.

Maguire, Steve, Cynthia Hardy, and Thomas B. Lawrence. "Institutional Entrepreneurship in Emerging Fields: HIV/AIDS Treatment Advocacy in Canada." *Academy of Management Journal* 47, no. 5 (2004): 657–79. https://doi.org/10.5465/20159610.

Manning, Wendy D., Pamela J. Smock, and Marshal Neal Fettro. "Cohabitation and Marital Expectations among Single Millennials in the U.S." *Population Research and Policy Review* 38, no. 3 (2019): 327–46. https://doi.org/10.1007/s11113-018-09509-8.

Manning, Wendy D., Krista K. Westrick-Payne, and Gary J. Gates. "Cohabitation and Marriage among Same-Sex Couples in the 2019 ACS and CPS: A Research Note." *Demography* 59, no. 5 (2022): 1595–1605. https://doi.org/10.1215/00703370-10181474.

Martin, Steven P. "Trends in Marital Dissolution by Women's Education in the United States." *Demographic Research* 15 (2006): 537–60. https://doi.org/10.4054/DemRes.2006.15.20.

Martin, Steven P., Nan Marie Astone, and H. Elizabeth Peters. "Fewer Marriages, More Divergence: Marriage Projections for Millennials to Age 40." *Urban Institute*, 2014. https://eric.ed.gov/?id=ED575460.

McCarthy, Justin. "Same-Sex Marriage Support Inches Up to New High of 71%." Gallup, June 1, 2022. https://news.gallup.com/poll/393197/same-sex-marriage-support-inches-new-high.aspx.

McLanahan, Sara. "Diverging Destinies: How Children Are Faring under the Second Demographic Transition." *Demography* 41, no. 4 (2004): 607–27. https://doi.org/10.1353/dem.2004.0033.

Meyer, Ilan H. "Minority Stress and Mental Health in Gay Men." *Journal of Health and Social Behavior* 36, no. 1 (1995): 38–56. https://doi.org/10.2307/2137286.

———. "Prejudice, Social Stress, and Mental Health in Lesbian, Gay, and Bisexual Populations: Conceptual Issues and Research Evidence." *Psychological Bulletin* 129, no. 5 (2003): 674–97. https://doi.org/10.1037/0033-2909.129.5.674.

Meyer, Ilan H., and Laura Dean. "Internalized Homophobia, Intimacy, and Sexual Behavior among Gay and Bisexual Men." In *Stigma and Sexual Orientation: Understanding Prejudice against Lesbians, Gay Men, and Bisexuals*, edited by Gregory M. Herek, 160–86. Thousand Oaks, CA: SAGE, 1998.

Meyer, Ilan H., and Evan A. Krueger. "Legally Married LGB People in the United States." UCLA School of Law: The Williams Institute, 2019. https://williamsinstitute.law.ucla.edu/publications/legally-married-lgb-people-us/.

REFERENCES

Meyer, John W., and Brian Rowan. "Institutionalized Organizations: Formal Structure as Myth and Ceremony." *American Journal of Sociology* 83, no. 2 (1977): 340–63. https://doi.org/10.1086/226550.

Miller, Shauna. "Beyond the U-Haul: How Lesbian Relationships Are Changing." *Atlantic*, July 3, 2013. https://www.theatlantic.com/sexes/archive/2013/07/beyond-the-u-haul-how-lesbian-relationships-are-changing/277495/.

Mint, Pepper. "The Power Mechanisms of Jealousy." In *Understanding Non-monogamies*, edited by Meg Barker and Darren Langdridge, 201–6. London: Routledge, 2009.

Mittleman, Joel. "Sexual Fluidity: Implications for Population Research." Unpublished manuscript, shared via personal communication.

Moore, Mignon. *Invisible Families: Gay Identities, Relationships, and Motherhood among Black Women*. Berkeley: University of California Press, 2011.

Moscowitz, Leigh. *The Battle over Marriage: Gay Rights Activism through the Media*. Urbana: University of Illinois Press, 2013.

Munson, Marsha and Judith P. Stelboum. "The Lesbian Polyamory Reader: Open Relationships, Non-monogamy, and Casual Sex." *Journal of Lesbian Studies* 3, no. 1 (1999): 1–7. https://doi.org/10.1300/J155v03n01_01.

Murray, Melissa. "Obergefell v. Hodges and Nonmarriage Inequality Essays." *California Law Review* 104, no. 5 (2016): 1207–58.

Ni, Preston. "10 Signs of Internalized Homophobia and Gaslighting." *Psychology Today*, May 31, 2020. https://www.psychologytoday.com/us/blog/communication-success/202005/10-signs-internalized-homophobia-and-gaslighting.

Nousak, Samantha. "Attitudes towards Births Outside of Marriage, 1988 & 2012." Family Profile FP-18-13. Bowling Green, OH: National Center for Family and Marriage Research, 2018. https://www.bgsu.edu/ncfmr/resources/data/family-profiles/nousak-attitudes-births-outside-mar-fp-18-13.html.

Ocobock, Abigail. "From Public Debate to Private Decision: The Normalization of Marriage among Critical LGBQ People." In *Queer Families and Relationships after Marriage Equality*, edited by Michael W. Yarbrough, Angela Jones, and Joseph Nicholas DeFilippis. Abingdon: Routledge, 2018.

——— . "Leveraging Legitimacy: Institutional Work and Change in the Case of Same-Sex Marriage." *American Journal of Sociology* 126, no. 3 (2020): 513–44. https://doi.org/10.1086/712501.

——— . "The Power and Limits of Marriage: Married Gay Men's Family Relationships." *Journal of Marriage and Family* 75, no. 1 (2013): 191–205. https://doi.org/10.1111/j.1741-3737.2012.01032.x.

——— . "Status or Access? The Impact of Marriage on Lesbian, Gay, Bisexual, and Queer Community Change." *Journal of Marriage and Family* 80, no. 2 (2018): 367–82. https://doi.org/10.1111/jomf.12468.

O'Connell, Martin, and Sarah Feliz. "Same-Sex Couple Household Statistics from the 2010 Census." Fertility and Family Statistics Branch, Social, Economic and Housing Statistics Division, United States Census Bureau, 2011. https://www.census.gov/library/working-papers/2011/demo/SEHSD-WP2011-26.html.

Orth, Taylor, and Michael Rosenfeld. "Commitment Timing in Same-Sex and Different-Sex Relationships." *Population Review* 57, no. 1 (2018): 1–19. https://doi.org/10.1353/prv.2018.0000.

Ott, Miles Q., David Wypij, Heather L. Corliss, Margaret Rosario, Sari L. Reisner, Allegra R. Gordon, and S. Bryn Austin. "Repeated Changes in Reported Sexual Orientation Identity

Linked to Substance Use Behaviors in Youth." *Journal of Adolescent Health* 52, no. 4 (2013): 465–72. https://doi.org/10.1016/j.jadohealth.2012.08.004.

Pager, Devah, and Lincoln Quillian. "Walking the Talk? What Employers Say versus What They Do." *American Sociological Review* 70, no. 3 (2005): 355–80. https://doi.org/10.1177/000312 240507000301.

Pahl, Jan. "Family Finances, Individualisation, Spending Patterns and Access to Credit." *Journal of Socio-Economics* special issue 37, no. 2 (2008): 577–91. https://doi.org/10.1016/j .socec.2006.12.041.

Parker, Kim, and Renee Stepler. "Americans See Men as the Financial Providers, Even as Women's Contributions Grow." Pew Research Center, September 20, 2017. https://www.pewresearch.org /short-reads/2017/09/20/americans-see-men-as-the-financial-providers-even-as-womens -contributions-grow/.

———. "As U.S. Marriage Rate Hovers at 50%, Education Gap in Marital Status Widens." Pew Research Center, September 4, 2017. https://www.pewresearch.org/fact-tank/2017/09/14 /as-u-s-marriage-rate-hovers-at-50-education-gap-in-marital-status-widens/.

Pepin, Joanna R. "Beliefs about Money in Families: Balancing Unity, Autonomy, and Gender Equality." *Journal of Marriage and Family* 81, no. 2 (2019): 361–79. https://doi.org/10.1111 /jomf.12554.

Perry, Nicholas S., David M. Huebner, Brian R. W. Baucom, and Colleen C. Hoff. "The Complex Contribution of Sociodemographics to Decision-Making Power in Gay Male Couples." *Journal of Family Psychology* 30, no. 8 (2016): 977–86. https://doi.org/10.1037/fam0000234.

Pew Research Center. "Attitudes on Same-Sex Marriage." Pew Research Center's Religion & Public Life Project. May 14, 2019. https://www.pewresearch.org/religion/fact-sheet /changing-attitudes-on-gay-marriage/.

———. "Many Cohabiters Cite Finances as a Reason Why They Are Not Engaged or Married to Their Partner." November 1, 2019. https://www.pewresearch.org/social-trends/2019/11/06 /marriage-and-cohabitation-in-the-u-s/psdt_11-06-19_cohabitation-00-05/.

———. "Marriage and Cohabitation in the U.S." Pew Research Center report. November 6, 2019. https://www.pewresearch.org/social-trends/2019/11/06/marriage-and-cohabitation-in -the-u-s/.

———. "Same-Sex Marriage, State by State." Pew Research Center's Religion & Public Life Project. June 26, 2015. https://www.pewresearch.org/religion/2015/06/26/same-sex-marriage -state-by-state-1/.

Pfeffer, Carla A. "Normative Resistance and Inventive Pragmatism: Negotiating Structure and Agency in Transgender Families." *Gender & Society* 26, no. 4 (2012): 574–602. https://doi .org/10.1177/0891243212445467.

———. *Queering Families: The Postmodern Partnerships of Cisgender Women and Transgender Men*. Oxford: Oxford University Press, 2017.

Phelan, Shane. *Sexual Strangers: Gays, Lesbians, and Dilemmas of Citizenship*. Philadelphia: Temple University Press, 2001.

Phillips, Derek L., and Kevin J. Clancy. "Some Effects of 'Social Desirability' in Survey Studies." *American Journal of Sociology* 77, no. 5 (1972): 921–40. https://doi.org/10.1086/225231.

Pieper, M, and R Bauer. "Call for Papers: International Conference on Polyamory and Mono-Normativity." University of Hamburg. November 5, 2005. http://www.wiso.uni-hamburg.de /index.php?id.3495.

Pinsof, David, and Martie Haselton. "The Political Divide over Same-Sex Marriage: Mating

Strategies in Conflict?" *Psychological Science* 27, no. 4 (2016): 435–42. https://doi.org/10.1177/0956797615621719.

Povich, Elaine S. "Without Obergefell, Most States Would Have Same-Sex Marriage Bans." *Stateline*, July 7, 2022. https://stateline.org/2022/07/07/without-obergefell-most-states-would-have-same-sex-marriage-bans/.

Powell, Brian. "Changing Counts, Counting Change: Toward a More Inclusive Definition of Family." *Journal of the Indiana Academy of the Social Sciences* 17, no. 1 (2014).

Powell, Brian, Catherine Blozendahl, Claudia Geist, and Lala Carr Steelman. *Counted Out: Same-Sex Relations and Americans' Definitions of Family*. New York: Russell Sage Foundation, 2010.

Powell, Walter W., and Jeannette A. Colyvas. "Microfoundations of Institutional Theory." In *The SAGE Handbook of Organizational Institutionalism*, by Royston Greenwood, Christine Oliver, Roy Suddaby, and Kerstin Sahlin, 276–98. London: SAGE, 2008.

Raley, R. Kelly. "Increasing Fertility in Cohabiting Unions: Evidence for the Second Demographic Transition in the United States?" *Demography* 38, no. 1 (2001): 59–66. https://doi.org/10.1353/dem.2001.0008.

Ramos, Christopher, Naomi G. Goldberg, and M. V. Lee Badgett. "The Effects of Marriage Equality in Massachusetts: A Survey of the Experiences and Impact of Marriage on Same-Sex Couples." UCLA School of Law: The Williams Institute, 2009. https://escholarship.org/uc/item/9dx6v3kj.

Rao, Hayagreeva, Calvin Morrill, and Mayer N. Zald. "Power Plays: How Social Movements and Collective Action Create New Organizational Forms." *Research in Organizational Behavior* 22 (2000): 237–81. https://doi.org/10.1016/S0191-3085(00)22007-8.

Rauch, Jonathan. *Gay Marriage: Why It Is Good for Gays, Good for Straights, and Good for America*. New York: Holt Paperbacks, 2005.

Reczek, Corinne, Sinikka Elliott, and Debra Umberson. "Commitment without Marriage: Union Formation among Long-Term Same-Sex Couples." *Journal of Family Issues* 30, no. 6 (2009): 738–56. https://doi.org/10.1177/0192513X09331574.

Richman, Kimberly D. *License to Wed: What Legal Marriage Means to Same-Sex Couples*. New York: New York University Press, 2013.

Ridgeway, Cecilia L. *Framed by Gender: How Gender Inequality Persists in the Modern World*. New York: Oxford University Press, 2011.

Ringer, J. R. "Constituting Nonmonogamies." In *Queer Families, Queer Politics: Challenging Culture and the State*, edited by Mary Bernstein and Renate Reimann, 137–51. New York: Columbia University Press, 2001.

Robinson, Brandon Andrew. "Heteronormativity and Homonormativity." In *The Wiley Blackwell Encyclopedia of Gender and Sexuality Studies*, edited by Angela Wong, Maithree Wickramasinghe, Renee Hoogland, and Nancy A. Naples, 1–3. Chichester: John Wiley & Sons, Ltd., 2016.

Robnett, Rachael D., and Campbell Leaper. "'Girls Don't Propose! Ew.': A Mixed-Methods Examination of Marriage Tradition Preferences and Benevolent Sexism in Emerging Adults." *Journal of Adolescent Research* 28, no. 1 (2013): 96–121. https://doi.org/10.1177/0743558412447871.

Rosenfeld, Michael J. "Couple Longevity in the Era of Same-Sex Marriage in the United States." *Journal of Marriage and Family* 76, no. 5 (2014): 905–18. https://doi.org/10.1111/jomf.12141.

———. *The Rainbow after the Storm: Marriage Equality and Social Change in the U.S.* Oxford: Oxford University Press, 2021.

Rothblum, Esther D., Kimberly F. Balsam, and Sondra E. Solomon. "Comparison of Same-Sex Couples Who Were Married in Massachusetts, Had Domestic Partnerships in California, or

Had Civil Unions in Vermont." *Journal of Family Issues* 29, no. 1 (2008): 48–78. https://doi.org/10.1177/0192513X07306087.

Ruggles, Steven, Sarah Flood, Ronald Goeken, Josiah Grover, Erin Meyer, Jose Pacas, and Matthew Sobek. "Integrated Public Use Microdata Series: Version 9.0." Minneapolis: University of Minnesota, 2019. http://doi.org/10.18128/D010.V9.0.

Sassler, Sharon, and Daniel T. Lichter. "Cohabitation and Marriage: Complexity and Diversity in Union-Formation Patterns." *Journal of Marriage and Family* 82, no. 1 (2020): 35–61. https://doi.org/10.1111/jomf.12617.

Sassler, Sharon, and Amanda Miller. *Cohabitation Nation: Gender, Class, and the Remaking of Relationships*. Oakland: University of California Press, 2017.

Sassler, Sharon, and Amanda J. Miller. "Waiting to Be Asked: Gender, Power, and Relationship Progression among Cohabiting Couples." *Journal of Family Issues* 32, no. 4 (2011): 482–506. https://doi.org/10.1177/0192513X10391045.

Savage, Dan. "Monogamish." *Dan Savage* (blog), July 20, 2011. https://savage.love/savagelove/2011/07/20/monogamish/.

Schilt, Kristen. "Born This Way: Thinking Sociologically about Essentialism." In *Emerging Trends in the Social and Behavioral Sciences*, edited by Robert A. Scott, Robert H. Scott, Stephen Michael Kosslyn, and Marlis C. Buchmann, 1–14. Hoboken, NJ: John Wiley & Sons, 2015.

———. *Just One of the Guys? Transgender Men and the Persistence of Gender Inequality*. Chicago: University of Chicago Press, 2010.

Schneider, Daniel, and Orestes P. Hastings. "Socioeconomic Variation in the Effect of Economic Conditions on Marriage and Nonmarital Fertility in the United States: Evidence from the Great Recession." *Demography* 52, no. 6 (2015): 1893–1915. https://doi.org/10.1007/s13524-015-0437-7.

Schoen, Robert, and Yen-hsin Alice Cheng. "Partner Choice and the Differential Retreat from Marriage." *Journal of Marriage and Family* 68, no. 1 (2006): 1–10. https://doi.org/10.1111/j.1741-3737.2006.00229.x.

Schwartz, Christine R., and Nikki L. Graf. "Assortative Matching among Same-Sex and Different-Sex Couples in the United States, 1990–2000." *Demographic Research* 21, no. 28 (2009): 843–78. https://doi.org/10.4054/demres.2009.21.28.

Schwartz, Christine R., and Hongyun Han. "The Reversal of the Gender Gap in Education and Trends in Marital Dissolution." *American Sociological Review* 79, no. 4 (2014): 605–29. https://doi.org/10.1177/0003122414539682.

Schweingruber, David, Sine Anahita, and Nancy Berns. "'Popping the Question' When the Answer Is Known: The Engagement Proposal as Performance." *Sociological Focus* 37, no. 2 (2004): 143–61. https://doi.org/10.1080/00380237.2004.10571239.

Schweingruber, David, Alicia D. Cast, and Sine Anahita. "'A Story and a Ring': Audience Judgments about Engagement Proposals." *Sex Roles: A Journal of Research* 58, no. 3 (2009): 165–78. https://doi.org/10.1007/s11199-007-9330-1.

Scott, W. Richard. *Institutions and Organizations*. Thousand Oaks, CA: SAGE, 1995.

———. *Institutions and Organizations: Ideas, Interests, and Identities*. 4th ed. Thousand Oaks, CA: SAGE, 2013.

Shechory, Mally, and Riva Ziv. "Relationships between Gender Role Attitudes, Role Division, and Perception of Equity among Heterosexual, Gay and Lesbian Couples." *Sex Roles* 56, no. 9 (2007): 629–38. https://doi.org/10.1007/s11199-007-9207-3.

Sheff, Elisabeth. *The Polyamorists Next Door: Inside Multiple-Partner Relationships and Families*. Lanham, MD: Rowman & Littlefield, 2013.

Shesgreen, Deirdre. "Ohio Man 'Fought for His Love,' Won Gay-Marriage Case." *USA Today*, 26 June 2015. https://www.usatoday.com/story/news/politics/2015/06/26/ohio-same-sex-marriage-plaintiff/29344307/.

Shulman, Julie L., Gabrielle Gotta, and Robert-Jay Green. "Will Marriage Matter? Effects of Marriage Anticipated by Same-Sex Couples." *Journal of Family Issues* 33, no. 2 (2012): 158–81. https://doi.org/10.1177/0192513X11406228.

Silver, Nate. "Change Doesn't Usually Come This Fast." *FiveThirtyEight*, June 26, 2015. https://fivethirtyeight.com/features/change-doesnt-usually-come-this-fast/.

Simon, William, and John H. Gagnon. "Sexual Scripts: Origins, Influences and Changes." *Qualitative Sociology* 26, no. 4 (2003): 491–97. https://doi.org/10.1023/B:QUAS.0000005053.99846.e5.

———. "Sexual Scripts: Permanence and Change." *Archives of Sexual Behavior* 15, no. 2 (1986): 97–120. https://doi.org/10.1007/BF01542219.

Small, Mario Luis. "'How Many Cases Do I Need?': On Science and the Logic of Case Selection in Field-Based Research." *Ethnography* 10, no. 1 (2009): 5–38. https://doi.org/10.1177/1466138108099586.

———. "How to Conduct a Mixed Methods Study: Recent Trends in a Rapidly Growing Literature." *Annual Review of Sociology* 37, no. 1 (2011): 57–86. https://doi.org/10.1146/annurev.soc.012809.102657.

Smock, Pamela J. "Cohabitation in the United States: An Appraisal of Research Themes, Findings, and Implications." *Annual Review of Sociology* 26, no. 1 (2000): 1–20. https://doi.org/10.1146/annurev.soc.26.1.1.

Smock, Pamela J., Wendy D. Manning, and Meredith Porter. "'Everything's There Except Money': How Money Shapes Decisions to Marry Among Cohabitors." *Journal of Marriage and Family* 67, no. 3 (2005): 680–96. https://doi.org/10.1111/j.1741-3737.2005.00162.x.

Solomon, Andrew. "How Polyamorists and Polygamists Are Challenging Family Norms." *New Yorker*, March 15, 2021. https://www.newyorker.com/magazine/2021/03/22/how-polyamorists-and-polygamists-are-challenging-family-norms.

Solomon, Sondra E., Esther D. Rothblum, and Kimberly F. Balsam. "Money, Housework, Sex, and Conflict: Same-Sex Couples in Civil Unions, Those Not in Civil Unions, and Heterosexual Married Siblings." *Sex Roles* 52, no. 9–10 (2005): 561–75. https://doi.org/10.1007/s11199-005-3725-7.

Stone, Amy L. *Gay Rights at the Ballot Box*. Minneapolis: University of Minnesota Press, 2012.

Strauss, Anselm, and Juliet Corbin. *Basics of Qualitative Research: Techniques and Procedures for Developing Grounded Theory*. 2nd ed. Thousand Oaks, CA: SAGE, 1998.

Sullivan, Andrew. *Virtually Normal: An Argument about Homosexuality*. New York: Knopf Doubleday, 1995.

Swidler, Ann. "Culture in Action: Symbols and Strategies." *American Sociological Review* 51, no. 2 (1986): 273–86. https://doi.org/10.2307/2095521.

———. *Talk of Love: How Culture Matters*. Chicago: University of Chicago Press, 2001.

Taylor, Paul. "The Decline of Marriage and Rise of New Families." Social & Demographic Trends. *Pew Research Center*, November 18, 2010. https://www.pewresearch.org/social-trends/2010/11/18/the-decline-of-marriage-and-rise-of-new-families/.

———. "Marriage and Parenting." In *A Survey of LGBT Americans: Attitudes, Experiences and Values in Changing Times*, 64–74. Washington, D.C.: Pew Research Center, 2013. https://www.pewresearch.org/social-trends/2013/06/13/chapter-4-marriage-and-parenting/.

Taylor, Verta, Katrina Kimport, Nella Van Dyke, and Ellen Ann Andersen. "Culture and Mobilization: Tactical Repertoires, Same-Sex Weddings, and the Impact on Gay Activism." *American Sociological Review* 74, no. 6 (2009): 865–90. https://doi.org/10.1177/000312240907400602.

Thornton, Arland, William G. Axinn, and Yu Xie. *Marriage and Cohabitation*. Chicago: University of Chicago Press, 2007.

Thornton, Arland, and Linda Young-DeMarco. "Four Decades of Trends in Attitudes toward Family Issues in the United States: The 1960s through the 1990s." *Journal of Marriage and Family* 63, no. 4 (2001): 1009–37. https://doi.org/10.1111/j.1741-3737.2001.01009.x.

Tolbert, Pamela S., and Lynne G. Zucker. "Institutional Sources of Change in the Formal Structure of Organizations: The Diffusion of Civil Service Reform, 1880–1935." *Administrative Science Quarterly* 28, no. 1 (1983): 22–39. https://doi.org/10.2307/2392383.

Umberson, Debra, and Jennifer Karas Montez. "Social Relationships and Health: A Flashpoint for Health Policy." *Journal of Health and Social Behavior* 51, no. 1 supplement (2010): S54–66. https://doi.org/10.1177/0022146510383501.

Umberson, Debra, Mieke Beth Thomeer, and Kristi Williams. "Family Status and Mental Health: Recent Advances and Future Directions." In *Handbook of the Sociology of Mental Health*, edited by Carol S. Aneshensel, Jo C. Phelan, and Alex Bierman, 405–31. Dordrecht: Springer Netherlands, 2013. https://doi.org/10.1007/978-94-007-4276-5_20.

United States Census Bureau. "2021: American Community Survey 1-Year Estimates Detailed Tables, B11009: Coupled Households by Type." Accessed March 22, 2023. https://data.census.gov/table?g=040XX00US25&d=ACS+1-Year+Estimates+Detailed+Tables.

Vangelisti, Anita L., and Mandi Gerstenberger. "Communication and Marital Infidelity." In *The State of Affairs: Explorations in Infidelity and Commitment*, edited by Jean Duncombe, Kaeren Harrison, Graham Allan, and Denis Marsden. 59–78. London: Routledge, 2004.

Vogler, Carolyn. "Cohabiting Couples: Rethinking Money in the Household at the Beginning of the Twenty-First Century." *Sociological Review* 53, no. 1 (2005): 1–29. https://doi.org/10.1111/j.1467-954X.2005.00501.x.

Waite, Linda J., and Maggie Gallagher. *The Case for Marriage: Why Married People Are Happier, Healthier, and Better Off Financially*. New York: Doubleday, 2000.

Walker, Alexis. "A Symposium on Marriage and Its Future." *Journal of Marriage and Family* 66, no. 4 (2004): 843–47. https://doi.org/10.1111/j.0022-2445.2004.00057.x.

Wang, Wendy, and Kim Parker. "Record Share of Americans Have Never Married." Pew Research Center, September 24, 2014. https://www.pewresearch.org/social-trends/2014/09/24/record-share-of-americans-have-never-married/.

Warner, Michael. *The Trouble with Normal: Sex, Politics, and the Ethics of Queer Life*. New York: Free Press, 1999.

Weiss, Robert S. *Learning from Strangers: The Art and Method of Qualitative Interview Studies*. New York: Simon and Schuster, 1995.

Weiss, Suzannah. "The Sexist Undertones of Wedding Marketing." *New York Times*, October 5, 2019. https://www.nytimes.com/2019/10/05/fashion/weddings/the-sexist-undertones-of-wedding-marketing.html.

Whitton, Sarah W., Eliza M. Weitbrecht, and Amanda D. Kuryluk. "Monogamy Agreements in Male Same-Sex Couples: Associations with Relationship Quality and Individual Well-

REFERENCES

Being." *Journal of Couple & Relationship Therapy* 14, no. 1 (2015): 39–63. https://doi.org/10.1080/15332691.2014.953649.

Wilcox, W. Bradford, and Jeffrey Dew. "Is Love a Flimsy Foundation? Soulmate versus Institutional Models of Marriage." *Social Science Research* special issue 39, no. 5 (2010): 687–99. https://doi.org/10.1016/j.ssresearch.2010.05.006.

Wilcox, W. Bradford, Nicholas H. Wolfinger, and Charles E. Stokes. "One Nation, Divided: Culture, Civic Institutions, and the Marriage Divide." *Future of Children* 25, no. 2 (2015): 111–27. https://doi.org/10.1353/foc.2015.0015.

Wilkinson, Eleanor. "What's Queer about Nonmonogamy Now?" In *Understanding Nonmonogamies*, edited by Meg Barker and Darren Langdridge, 243–54. New York: Routledge, 2009.

The Williams Institute. "Census Snapshot: 2010 Methodology, Adjustment Procedures for Same-Sex Couple Data." UCLA School of Law: The Williams Institute, 2010.

———. "LGBT Data & Demographics." UCLA School of Law: The Williams Institute, 2019. https://williamsinstitute.law.ucla.edu/visualization/lgbt-stats/?topic=LGBT#about-the-data.

Willoughby, Brian J., Scott S. Hall, and Saige Goff. "Marriage Matters but How Much? Marital Centrality among Young Adults." *Journal of Psychology* 149, no. 8 (2015): 796–817. https://doi.org/10.1080/00223980.2014.979128.

Winkler, Anne E. "Economic Decision-Making by Cohabitors: Findings Regarding Income Pooling." *Applied Economics* 29, no. 8 (1997): 1079–90. https://doi.org/10.1080/000368497326471.

Wu, Huijing. "Trends in Births to Single and Cohabiting Mothers, 1980–2014." Family Profile FP-17-04. Bowling Green, OH: National Center for Family and Marriage Research, 2017. https://www.bgsu.edu/ncfmr/resources/data/family-profiles/wu-trends-births-single-cohabiting-mothers-fp-17-04.html.

Yodanis, Carrie, and Sean Lauer. "Is Marriage Individualized? What Couples Actually Do." *Journal of Family Theory & Review* 6, no. 2 (2014): 184–97. https://doi.org/10.1111/jftr.12038.

Zelizer, Viviana A. "The Social Meaning of Money: 'Special Monies.'" *American Journal of Sociology* 95, no. 2 (1989): 342–77. https://doi.org/10.1086/229272.

Zucker, Lynne G. "The Role of Institutionalization in Cultural Persistence." *American Sociological Review* 42, no. 5 (1977): 726–43. https://doi.org/10.2307/2094862.

Index

ACT UP. *See* AIDS Coalition to Unleash Power (ACT UP)
age: differences/gaps between partners, 231n13; and marriage, 18–20, 34, 57, 66, 82, 94, 98–99, 116, 211, 218n11, 223n12, 226n2, 227n22, 229n15, 230n23
AIDS Coalition to Unleash Power (ACT UP), 38, 223n18
American Community Survey, 220n60, 221n74, 222n83, 240n9
American Journal of Sociology, 204

Baker v. State of Vermont, 221n68
"born this way" rhetoric, 236n25
Brown v. Board of Education, 221n68

California Supreme Court, 219n28
Cherlin, Andrew J., 6, 114, 143, 219n23, 220n53, 230n18, 230n23, 239n6
children and parenting: and family recognition, 224n26; legal rights for, 95–98, 228n9; and LGBTQ+ community, 98–99, 228nn9–11; in marriage, 6, 9, 14–15, 17, 20, 56, 75, 83–86, 88–89, 95–99, 106, 140, 146, 190, 201, 210, 220n60, 228–29n11, 228nn8–9, 240n9; outside of marriage, 4–5, 220n60, 222n85; and religion, 95, 228n10. *See also* family
civil unions, 27, 29, 33–46, 49, 221n68, 223nn10–11, 223nn13–14, 224n23, 224n25, 225nn27–28, 238n37. *See also* commitment ceremonies; domestic partnerships; weddings
class, 212; and gender, 103–4; and marriage, 238n40; and race, 209. *See also* education
cohabitation, 4–6, 17, 208, 217nn2–4, 222n87, 223n11, 229n12, 229n14, 230n19, 232n10; and finances, 139, 143–47
commitment ceremonies, 27, 30–47, 53–54, 193, 222nn3–4, 223n7, 223n13, 223n18, 224nnn23–24, 225n27, 226n13; communal, 38; and proposals/engagements, 114, 130–31. *See also* civil unions; domestic partnerships; weddings
Common Book of Pray, 236n27
conservatism, 84, 95, 167, 186, 235n13, 238n40
cultural norms. *See* social norms
cultural scripts, 10–13, 15, 18, 23, 36, 119–21, 127–29, 147–50, 193–201; for love, 11; for marital behavior, 106, 194–95, 199; for marital readiness, 104, 106; for marriage, 3–4, 10–12, 48–49, 78, 85, 107, 138, 147–48, 150, 153, 159–61, 165, 193–95, 198–99; for personal relationships, 230n1; for proposals and engagements, 45, 113, 116, 127, 129, 135, 194, 199; and rituals, 197; for romance, 197; and social expectations, 199; and social norms, 119, 199; and social recognition, 197; for weddings, 76–77
cultural sociology, 11, 33, 47, 129, 143

Defense of Marriage Act (DOMA), 16, 41–42, 192, 209, 233n26, 234n27
demographics, 5, 7, 213, 240nn9–11
divorce, 17, 30, 54, 90–91, 97, 105–6, 143, 145–46, 154, 221n74, 223n14; no-fault, 233n22
Dobbs v. Jackson Women's Health Organization, 202, 239n45
DOMA. *See* Defense of Marriage Act (DOMA)
domestic partnerships, 29, 33–45, 49, 223n13, 223nn9–11, 224n23, 225nn27–28. *See also* civil unions; commitment ceremonies
Durkheim, Emily, 227–28n27

education, and marriage, 4–5, 17–18, 211, 222n81, 222n83, 222n87. *See also* class
egalitarianism, 1, 13, 135, 200, 230n7
engagements. *See* proposals and engagements
essentialism, 236n25
ethnicity. *See* race

family: companionship, 218n17; institutional, 218n17; less heteronormative, 59; LGBQ/LGBTQ+ alternative to, 58, 62; and marriage, ideals of, 166; queer politics as challenging existing norms for, 57; and social recognition, 29, 42, 49, 77, 197, 224n24, 224n26; and social status, 33. *See also* children and parenting
family scholarship: on education and family experiences, 17; on finances in marriage, 141, 146; on marital planning, 102; on marriage, 3–5, 8; on marriage, and education, 18; on marriage, deinstitutionalization of, 7, 190; on marriage, social behavior in, 142; on no-fault divorce, 233n22. *See also* institutional scholarship
feminism, 1–2, 60, 62, 73–74; and egalitarianism and sexual freedom, 200; and nonmonogamy, 167, 235n11
finances, in marriage, 143–60, 157–59, 191, 234n31; family scholarship on, 141, 146;

and LGBQ people, 23, 136–62; and marriage equality, 143; and shared resources, 141–42; and taxes, 147, 233n25

gender: binary, 222n2; differences, 127–29, 135, 199; equality, 15; identity, 57; and marriage status, 61, 168–69; and nonmonogamy, 168–69; presentations (feminine and/or masculine), 127–28, 231n19; and proposals, 115, 127–29, 135; and social class, 103–4. *See also* sexual identity
Generations study, 229n15
Giddens, Anthony, 6, 176, 225–26n1
Goodridge decision, 202

hegemony, 58, 61, 235n9
heteronormativity, 3, 75–76, 81, 84, 94–95, 106–7, 194, 200, 230n7, 235n8, 236n25, 237n31, 238n36; and behavior models, 57; lesbian, 59; and marriage, 57, 59, 64, 217n1; and monogamy, 165–67, 170, 179–80, 184–86, 188; and proposals/engagements, 113, 115, 117–18, 120–21, 128–29, 131, 134–35; and relationships, 51, 63; standards, 58, 63
heterosexual marriage, 11, 13–15, 20, 22–23, 198, 200, 202, 215, 220n67, 224n20, 228n2, 229n12, 229n14, 230n7, 230n19, 231n13, 232n10, 233n16; and finances, 139, 141–44, 151, 160–61; and monogamy/nonmonogamy, 23, 163–68, 170, 178, 187, 235n13, 236n22, 236n24, 237n31; and normal, marriage as, 84, 96–97, 99, 102; and power of marriage, 29–30, 35; and proposals/engagements, 113–15, 117, 120, 123, 126–33, 135; and pulls of marriage, 56–58, 61, 63–64, 72
Holy Unions, 31, 36–38, 41–42, 222n5
homonormativity, 57, 75, 84, 226n7, 235n14
homophobia, 1, 182, 237–38n36
Hubbard, Jim, 227n20
Hull, Kathleen, 33, 49

individualization, 5–7, 144, 232n1
institutionalization, 6, 12–13, 22, 84–85, 114, 118, 144, 228n6, 232n1

INDEX

institutional scholarship, 3, 8–15, 145.
    See also family scholarship
institutional theory, 14, 200, 215;
    neo-, 9

Journal of Marriage and Family, 204,
    219n23

Kimport, Katrina, 8, 217n1, 219n28

Lamont, Ellen, 230n7, 236n24
Lareau, Annette, 213
Lawrence v. Texas, 82
legal marriage, 28–29, 33–44, 47–49,
    52, 144, 217n1, 219n28, 221n74, 239n2,
    239n45; and impact on relationships,
    50, 198, 207; and social legitimacy, 10–11;
    and social recognition, 29, 42, 44, 49,
    77, 197
legal rights: and marriage, 29, 39, 46, 68–
    69, 97, 186, 225n31, 239n45; for parents of
    children, 96–97; and social recognition,
    29, 41–44; as vulnerable, 186
LGBTQ+ community, 80–82, 200, 207,
    209–12; and children, 98–99, 228nn9–11;
    and egalitarian relationships, 230n7;
    and engagements/proposals, 129, 131–32,
    134–35; and equality activism, 236n25;
    and finances, 143; and gender equality,
    15; and internalized oppression, 64;
    and marriage, 10, 98–99, 217n1, 225n31;
    and monogamy/nonmonogamy, 163–65,
    167, 170, 182, 186, 188, 235n18, 236n24,
    237nn30–31, 238n36, 238n40; and
    pulls of marriage, 57–64; and sexual
    freedom, 15; and sexuality, 236n25; term,
    usage, 17
LGBTQ Family Building Survey, 228–
    29n11
love: and commitment, 5–6, 10–11, 28–32,
    37, 39, 48–49, 65–66, 71, 77, 93, 98, 107,
    111, 120–21, 148, 200, 217n1, 225nn31–32;
    cultural, 229n16; and marriage, 11, 29,
    100, 105, 107, 217n1; mythic, 11–12, 104–6,
    152–53, 229n16; prosaic, 11–12, 100,
    105–6, 229n16; and romance, 217n1.
    See also romance

marriage: and change, differing degrees
    of, 157–60; as changing and endur-
    ing, 3, 7, 12–15, 189, 207; character and
    strength of, 3, 7–8, 20; as companionate,
    5; critiques of, 57; cultural and social
    dimensions of, 28, 29, 33, 36–37, 49, 107,
    194–95; cultural-cognitive pillar of, 8,
    10, 161, 190, 193–95; deinstitutionaliza-
    tion of, 4–9, 13, 21, 166, 187, 190, 217n12,
    220n53; detraditionalization of, 6;
    disinterest in, 71; doing, 22–23, 102, 109,
    113, 144, 163–65, 184, 186–88, 198, 200; as
    enduring institution, 3, 12–15, 162, 189,
    207; fragility of, 152–53; future of, 201–2;
    gaining, 22, 25, 49; hierarchy to, 46;
    historic changes to, 3, 189; ideals of, 11,
    166; as individualized, 5–7, 144, 230n18;
    as institution, 1–15, 19–21, 22–23, 28–29,
    49, 51, 60, 65, 71, 75–79, 81–108, 114, 117–
    18, 135, 138, 140, 142–48, 152–53, 157, 159,
    161–62, 165–66, 170, 173, 187–93, 195–96,
    198–202, 207, 210, 220n67, 222n2, 226n12,
    228n27; instrumental view of, 65–70; as
    internalized, 9, 12–13, 20, 48–49, 64, 70,
    85, 94, 96, 107–8, 123, 138, 142, 144, 147–
    50, 153, 159, 184, 190, 193, 195–97, 199–201,
    222–23n6; legal barriers and incentives
    to, 145–47; and legitimacy, 10–11, 227n24;
    as normative, 8–9, 70–76, 82–108, 189–
    93; power of, 3, 6–8, 19–20, 22, 27–50, 81,
    87, 162, 192, 198, 224n24; pulls of, 21–22,
    51–81, 190–92, 194; rates and statistics,
    4, 65, 217n2, 240n9; reasons for, 64–78,
    92–99, 191–92, 225n32; as regulative, 8;
    and relationships, behaviors/feelings in,
    140, 142–60; and relationships, impact
    on, 22, 217n1; and relationships, resil-
    ience of, 140–41; remaking, 23, 198–201;
    rethinking, 1–23; and rings, 30, 36–37,
    40–41, 45, 80, 101, 193, 224n20; rituals
    and traditions of, 28–29, 193, 197; and
    security, feelings of, 137, 150–53; social,
    psychological, economic advantages of,
    5, 22–23, 197–98; and social meaning,
    227n24; and social obligations, 143; sta-
    tus, 9, 22–23, 29, 41–42, 45, 141, 147, 168–
    69, 184–85, 209, 211, 213, 222n87, 223n13,

marriage: and change (*cont.*)
225n28, 228n8, 232nn9–10, 234n34; strength of, 3, 7–8, 192–93; as tangible, 46–47. *See also* heterosexual marriage; legal marriage; marriage equality; same-sex marriage

marriage equality, 1, 11, 14–18, 28, 45, 47, 55–66, 82, 86, 89, 91, 207, 217n1, 220nn68–70, 226nn12–13, 239n3; and finances, in marriage, 143; historical timeline of, 221n69, 239n2; and monogamy, 182, 186, 188; and sexual identity, 167. *See also* same-sex marriage

masculinity, normative ideals of, and sexual attraction in gay male and bisexual communities, 235n8

Massachusetts Department of Public Health, 217n1

Massachusetts Supreme Judicial Court, 15–16, 224n19

methods and methodology. *See* research study, methods

Metropolitan Community Church, 207, 222n5

monogamish, 167–68, 235n18

monogamous, defined, 167–69

monogamy: abstract ideals about, 239n44; as choice for couples to make, 171; definitions, 167–68; and feeling comfortable in society, 182; and fidelity, 166, 236n27; and heteronormativity, 165–67, 170–71, 179–80, 184–86, 188; and marriage, 23, 163–88, 239n44; and marriage equality, 182, 186, 188; as normative and assumed, 234n3; norms, challenging, 170–80; norms, maintaining, 180–86; rates of, 170; and religion, 166; and same-sex relationships, 166, 175, 188; and sexual fluidity, 169, 175–80, 187–88. *See also* nonmonogamy

morality, and religion, 95

nonmonogamous, defined, 167–68

nonmonogamy, 163–88, 235n11, 236n25, 238n40; and boundary work, 238n36; and celebratory pride in sexuality, 167; and feminism, 167, 235n11; and gender, 168–69; and homophobia, 182, 237–38n36; as incompatible with ordinary/normal, 181; and internalized homophobia, 182; as liberating, cooperative, empowering, 167; and marital status, 168–69; in marriage, 23, 173–75; and open relationships, 182; and promiscuity, 167, 235n13; reflexive views of, 170–73; and same-sex couples, 235n8; and sexual fluidity, 175–80; social science evidence on quality of, 237n33. *See also* monogamy

norms. *See* social norms

Obergefell v. Hodges, 16, 202, 209–10, 217n1, 228n9, 239n45

Ocobock, Abigail, 220n67, 251

open relationships. *See* nonmonogamy

parenting. *See* children and parenting

Pavan v. Smith, 228n9

Pew Research Center, 221n69, 221n79, 225n31, 228n2, 230n19, 239n2

Pfeffer, Carla, 80–81

plastic sexuality, 176, 225n1

political action, 14, 223n18

popular culture, 11, 118, 132, 194

proposals and engagements, 111–35, 227n26; and commitment, demonstration of, 129–31; and commitment ceremonies, 114, 130–31; conventions of, 113; and cultural beliefs, 113, 129–30, 135; and equality, 131–34; and expectations, 115, 231n13; and gender, 115, 127–29, 135; and heteronormativity, 113, 115, 117–18, 120–21, 128–29, 131, 134–35; invited, 123–24; and LGBQ people, 22, 111–35; parties for, 30; planning for, 89; rings for, 111, 114, 123–26, 133–34; romance of, 88, 118–20, 133–34; scripts for, 113–15, 118, 120–27, 135; and social norms, 127; as symbol for relationships, 113, 123–24. *See also* engagements; proposals

queer: and challenging/disrupting existing structures and ideas, 57; and marriage, effects on, 61; politics, 20, 51, 57–58;

INDEX

term, usage for sexual and gender identities, 57; theory, 217n1. *See also* LGBTQ+ community
Queering Families (Pfeffer), 80–81

race: and class, 209; and ethnicity, 211–12
Rao, Aliya Hamid, 213
Rauch, Jonathan, 238n40
relationship duration, 19, 57, 94, 99, 137–39, 140–41, 147, 157, 160, 191–93, 210–13, 223n11, 226n2, 227n22, 231n12, 234n32, 234n34
religion: and children, 95, 228n10; and marriage, 5–6, 12–13, 49, 211–12, 223n7; and monogamy, 166; and morality, 95
research study, 15–19; methods, 207–16
Richman, Kimberly, 217n1
rituals and traditions: and cultural scripts, 197; marriage, 28–29, 193; and weddings, 31
Roe v. Wade, 202, 239n45
romance: cultural scripts for, 197; and love, 217n1; and marriage, 166, 194–95, 217n1; and memory-making, 118–20; of proposals and engagements, 88, 118–20, 133–34; and sentimentality, 79; women's desire for, 134. *See also* love
Romney, Mitt, 38, 224n19

Safe Schools Program for Gay and Lesbian Students, 82, 228n1
same-sex marriage: antigay backlash against, 221n71; banned, 221n71; benefits of, 220n68, 240n9; family scholarship about, 189; invalidated, 219n28; legalization of, 7, 22–23, 84, 161, 201, 221n74, 227n17, 240n9; public opinion on and social attitudes toward, 22, 217n1, 221n9; qualitative studies of, 226n3; sexualities scholarship about, 189. *See also* marriage equality; same-sex relationships
same-sex relationships, 3–4, 12, 15, 20–23, 72, 193, 207–8, 217n1, 220n67, 222n5, 229n12, 235n8, 237n33; and anxiety, 198; and changes, 106; and constitutional right to marry, 224n19; and finances, 156, 160; and legal marriage, 22–23, 50, 87, 106, 198, 221n68; and monogamy, 166, 175, 188, 236–37n28; and proposals/ engagements, 113, 115, 119–20, 123, 127, 134–35; remaking, 195–98. *See also* same-sex marriage

Savage, Dan, 235n18
Schilt, Kristen, 222n2, 236n25
Scott, Richard, 8, 145
scripting theory, and personal relationships, 230n1. *See also* cultural scripts
sexual fluidity, 169, 175–80, 187–88, 200, 236–37n28
sexual freedom, 15, 165, 188, 200, 225–26n1, 237nn30–31
sexual identity, 57, 86, 163–64, 167, 212, 215, 236n25, 236n28. *See also* gender, identity
sexualities scholarship and studies, 3, 80, 189, 217n1, 235n18
sexual orientations, 163, 236n28
social desirability bias, 237n30
social expectations, 70, 73, 80, 127, 142–44, 190–91, 197, 199, 212
social legitimacy, 10–11, 29, 42, 49, 193, 219n38, 224n22
social norms, 13, 134, 184, 188; and cultural scripts, 119, 199; for dyadic relationships, 76; as enduring, 142–45; for finances in marriage, 191; for marriage, 6–7, 22, 106, 161, 233n22; for marriage, and behavioral changes, 6, 9, 22, 142–45, 161, 191, 195; for marriage, and children, 95; for nonmonogamy, 166–67; for proposals and engagements, 119, 127, 199; and social expectations, 191
social recognition: and cultural scripts, 197; and family, 29, 42, 49, 77, 197, 224n24, 224n26; and legal marriage, 29, 42, 44, 49, 77, 197; and legal rights, 29, 41–44; and social legitimacy, 49; and weddings, 77
sociology: cultural, 11, 33, 47, 129, 143; family, 3, 6, 99, 190, 192, 212; institutional, 7, 10; of marriage, 6–7, 22
Spyer, Thea, 233n26
study. *See* research study

Swidler, Ann, 10–12, 47, 100, 105–6, 129, 143, 152–53, 229n16

Transformation of Intimacy, The (Giddens), 6, 176, 225–26n1
transgender people, 17, 207, 212, 222n2. *See also* LGBTQ+ community

U-Haul syndrome, of cohabitation, 229n12

Vermont Supreme Court, 220–21n68

weddings: as collective effervescence, 227–28n27; as cultural events, 80; cultural scripts for, 76–77; interpretations of, 236n26; obsession with, 30; as parties, 30, 80; rituals of, 31; as symbol, 76–77. *See also* civil unions; commitment ceremonies; Holy Unions
Williams Institute, 240nn9–10
Windsor, Edie, 233n26
Winter of Love (San Francisco, 2004), 217n1, 219n28